duties and delights

THE FRENCH LIST

duties and delights

THE LIFE OF A GO-BETWEEN

tzvetan todorov

INTERVIEWS WITH CATHERINE PORTEVIN

TRANSLATED BY GILA WALKER

LONDON NEW YORK CALCUTTA

Liberté · Égalité · Fraternité
RÉPUBLIQUE FRANÇAISE

Publication of this book is supported by the French Ministry
of Foreign Affairs as part of the Burgess Programme run by
the Cultural Department of the French Embassy in London.

Seagull Books

Editorial offices:

1st Floor, Angel Court, 81 St Clements Street
Oxford OX4 1AW, UK

1 Washington Square Village, Apt 1U
New York, NY 10012, USA

26 Circus Avenue, Calcutta 700 017, India

ISBN-13   978 1 9054 2 289 0

British Library Cataloguing-in-Publication Data
A catalogue record for this book is available
from the British Library

Typeset by Seagull Books, Calcutta, India
Printed and bound in the United Kingdom at Biddles Ltd, King's Lynn

Contents

vii › Foreword:
To Live According to Nuance

1 › A Peasant from the Danube

65 › From Poetry to Structures

105 › Criticism of Structuralism

143 › The Peasant in Paris

189 › Human Diversity

221 › The Humanist Bark

265 › Humanism: Practices and Works

293 › The Moral Meaning of History

339 › Memory and Justice

365 › The Contiguity of Opposites

409 › Epilogue:
The Life of a Go-Between

Foreword
To Live According to Nuance

I must have heard Tzvetan Todorov's name mentioned for the first time in a dark wood-panelled amphitheatre in the Sorbonne, when I was 18. The *Encyclopedic Dictionary of the Sciences of Language*, which our old professor called '*the* Todorov and Ducrot', rolling his Rs with his thick Burgundian accent, was required reading for students in linguistics. Everyone evidently imagined that Todorov boasted as venerable an age as our professor, if he was not already dead. What I enjoyed reading more was Todorov's *The Fantastic; a Structural Approach to a Literary Genre*, at a time when I would hang out in cafes with a few cinema-lovers discussing the meaning of Martin Scorsese's use of the dolly zoom in *Taxi Driver* or the ethics of Orson Welles' use of low-angle shots. In our own way, we were celebrating the end of the dichotomy between form and content; without really knowing it, we were steeped in semiology as though it had always existed.

tzvetan todorov

At about the same time, I came across Tzvetan Todorov's name in connection with *The Conquest of America*. One of my neighbours across the landing, fascinated by the Aztecs, had summarized it for me one evening. To my mind, there could be no connection between '*the* Todorov, an elderly linguist, and this Todorov, an original historian (which was how she presented him). It must be his son, I thought.

A few years later, I heard Tzvetan Todorov's voice on a radio show on France Culture. He was talking about moral life in the concentration camps (the subject of his book *Facing the Extreme*). He spoke with a slight accent, his voice was gentle and it sounded young. It must be his grandson, I said to myself, and he is philosophically inclined.

Then, while working on an article on racism, I devoured *On Human Diversity*, an examination of French thought on the subject from Montaigne to Lévi-Strauss, believing I was reading the philosophical grandson's brother.

The plot continued to thicken: from his texts on Benjamin Constant and on Rousseau to his exploration of humanist thinking in *The Imperfect Garden*, I kept track of Todorov's work from a distance.

One day in 1999, I met him for an interview and had to finally admit that the whole Todorov family I had imagined actually boiled down to this one fellow!

Of course, my discovery of Tzvetan Todorov's work did not take place in the naive way that I find it amusing to tell today, but the feeling was there, and it has stayed with me, namely, that this man had lived several lives in one. He has described himself as an '*homme dépaysé*',[1] an estranged man. And I found him estranging (*dépaysant*) at first, and surprising in his own gentle way.

_____

1 This is the title of Todorov's 1996 book in which he explores his experience of crossing from one culture to another. *Dépaysement*, in Todorov's use of the term, can best be described as a

At bottom, this then still vague impression was the driving force behind these interviews. When I began thinking about this project, I called it an impression of 'diversity', a diversity with which I myself was faced in my work. It is my job at *Télérama* to read wide-ranging essays in the human sciences, which means making my way through differing arrays of knowledge and opinions, and endeavouring as well as I can to relate them to one another and to their readers. We are all more sensitive at first to what resembles us: to me, Tzvetan Todorov's encyclopaedism and his concern with acting as a 'go-between'—all differences notwithstanding—guaranteed the possibility of a dialogue. He was well accustomed to searching for unity in diversity when it came to the work of other authors (he had done so with Jakobson, Rousseau, Bakhtin and Constant, to name a few); I did not doubt he could do likewise for himself and that he would be willing to take a dose of his own medicine, as he had already started doing in *L'Homme dépaysé*, published in 1996.

But if his output deserved to be clarified, discussed and re-examined, it was perhaps in terms not so much of its content than of the path it took. Tzvetan Todorov is not an obscure writer who requires an ardent exegesis: his writing is clear and he is not averse on occasion to the 'platitudes' of pedagogy. The path, on the other hand, made it possible to penetrate the mysteries of what guided the intellectual life of a specific individual and, beyond that, to comprehend the interrelationship between a man's thought and the world, between his thought and the history of his time.

---

feeling of estrangement and outsideness, a state that allows him to perceive what too much familiarity would have prevented him from seeing. See p. xxx for Todorov's discussion of the term. [Trans.]

tzvetan todorov

I would be making Tzvetan Todorov out to be older than he is if I said that he carries with him the memory of the twentieth century, and yet the man was precocious and the history of these last 60 years rich in events. Born in the Balkans in 1939, the year of the Nazi–Soviet Pact, raised in Communist Bulgaria, he was already lugging about several worlds when he arrived in France in 1963: a Slavic and Oriental culture, polyglot and universal, with a spirit of erudition that is often thought to characterize 'Eastern European countries' and which has much in common with European identity in the eighteenth-century but is also one of the paradoxical consequences of totalitarianism. He was carrying with him, more especially, his experience of a pent-up life, of repressed freedom of thought, of perverted political speech and of oppression in the name of the happiness of humanity.

All of this gave him a unique position on the French intellectual scene, of which he was truly a part. He found himself, in the footsteps of Roland Barthes and alongside Gérard Genette, at the centre of the then influential structuralist movement, while always standing apart. He never became a follower of Lévi-Strauss or Lacan or Althusser, and even less so of Sartre. He participated in the University of Vincennes adventure in 1968 while at the same time examining with no illusions the political aberrations of his friends.

He feels at home in eighteenth-century French thought, yet it is always as an 'outsider' (*homme dépaysé*) that he rereads this period and brings it back to life for us. More French by the heritage he assumes than many of our French intellectuals, he is also, deep down, the most European, and — few people know this — one of the most translated authors in the world.

Tzvetan Todorov tends to be rather reserved and rarely takes a public position about current events, and yet, by his background and his themes of predilection, he stands at the junction of many of our contemporary concerns. He knows how to describe the confusions and perversions of our modern democracies, favours the meeting of cultures to the clash of civilizations, and the value of the individual to the happiness of humankind; in short, he defends a critical humanism, free from the self-righteous bigotry of do-gooders.

The man is courteous and open, but there is a cautiousness and secrecy about him that make him harder to figure out than one might think. One thing is certain, though, and that is his search for accuracy and lucidity (he would say, more completely, 'for truth'); and this may sound dull to some people, but it seems to me that this search is of greater urgency today than the clear-cut spectacularity of dualism. 'Although we live in an era that is resistant to nuance,' Roland Barthes declared at the end of his life, 'I want to live according to nuance; now, there is a teacher of nuance, literature.' Tzvetan Todorov would not disclaim this ambition.

Lastly—I say 'lastly' but it may be what is most noteworthy about him—he is one of the very few intellectuals to emphasize the virtue of sensitivity: sensitivity to works of art (literary or visual), to human beings and to nature, a sensitivity that makes you love concrete, ordinary and profane life in a continuum with the life of the mind. In this sense, I regard *Éloge du quotidien*, in which he explores seventeenth-century Dutch painting, and *Éloge de l'individu*, in which he focuses on fifteenth-century Flemish art, as secretly his most revealing books.

Or to put it otherwise, they are the two slopes in the roof of the Todorov house that brings together and provides coherence to his different lives and his many interests: the Bulgarian and the Frenchman, the semiologist and the humanist, the lover of literature and the historian, the scholar and the moralist. For if the

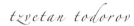

tzvetan todorov

roof is not the foundation of the house and does not hold it up, it completes it and it is precisely what makes a house a house.

Now, let us step inside.[2]

CATHERINE PORTEVIN

---

[2] These interviews were conducted between March and October 2001.

1. A Peasant from the Danube

The far end of Europe – A totalitarian country – My father – An education under Communism – 1956: a pivotal year – Finding your way in the grey area – Friends, books and trips – Leaving Bulgaria – Bulgaria, a closed chapter?

The far end of Europe

CATHERINE PORTEVIN: *Who were you when you came to Paris in 1963? You've spoken of yourself, of the young man you were then, as a 'peasant from the Danube'. The expression conveys the culture of Mitteleuropa and of the Balkans, to which Bulgaria, your native land, belongs, and, at the same time, a strong feeling of inferiority. Where did such a feeling come from when you were in fact a young, educated man from a cultivated family in Sofia, and not a peasant or the son of a peasant?*

TZVETAN TODOROV: The peasant from the Danube is Montesquieu's Persian in Paris, the ignoramus, someone who comes from far away. I did not think of myself as completely ignorant; but when you come from a small country, you always look at things with a certain amount of naivete. In my case, it was coupled with another factor: I not only came from a small provincial country, I came from a Communist country.

As far as the small provincial country goes, the Bulgarian people have, I think, a somewhat negative image of themselves, due in part to their past and, in particular, to the major setback they suffered at the hands of the Turks who defeated them upon their arrival in Asia Minor. Bulgaria's brutal inclusion in the Ottoman Empire led to 500 years of subservience that seriously undermined the population's pride. 'Materialism' and the capacity to adapt are, or are conventionally regarded as, national characteristics. Bulgarians are good at finding ways to put their personal interests first. All of which is not very glorious. Geography does not work in our favour either: Bulgaria is a small country situated at one end of Europe. We used to talk about 'going to Europe'—for us, it meant a journey to civilization!

And where did Europe start?

It started at Vienna. That was where everything worked, where household appliances and cars could run for several years whereas the ones we bought at home would break down after six months. Europeans had razor blades that actually shaved, socks that didn't tear, and they had real writers, scientists, painters and so on. Everything that came from the West benefited from an extraordinary and, to a large extent, ill-deserved prestige. We were convinced that everything there, from shirts to novels, was fantastic. I didn't doubt that Coca-Cola was a beverage worthy of the gods, the new name for ambrosia. I was very disappointed when, in 1961, I drank my first Coca-Cola in Poland—a very liberal country compared to Bulgaria. At home, as I was saying, it was the opposite: the shirts were badly cut, so were the pants—everything was poorly made. From this standpoint, Bulgarians suffer from an inferiority complex that can cause them to be aggressive when faced by others.

Is the Turkish era relayed in stories and epic tales?

It certainly is! We absorb, along with breast milk, stories and legends of Turkish cruelty, of powerless Bulgarian victims kept under slavery, 'under the yoke' . . . These are coded terms in Bulgarian: when we speak about 'slavery', we are referring to the Bulgarians under the Turks, not the blacks in America. In actual fact, historians agree that the 'yoke' in this case was rather light. There is no record, for instance, of the forced Islamization of the Bulgarian population. After conquering the territory, the Turks mainly confined themselves to levying taxes.

Under the Yoke *is the title of a novel by Ivan Vazov, which you must have read.*

Yes, of course. It's *the* national novel! An excellent novel, by the way, if somewhat overblown: truly eloquent, with great adventures, a cross between Dumas and Hugo. It describes the preparation of a Bulgarian uprising, which ultimately fails. Failure, once again! The theme is widespread in Bulgarian folklore too. We were victims! This collective representation scheme still has wide currency today. We draw a secret sense of satisfaction from depicting ourselves as former victims.

So this is what I meant by 'peasant from the Danube'. We had a strong sense of our provincialism.

Even an inhabitant of Sofia, the capital?

Yes, provided you would pick your head up from your everyday occupations. Obviously, the inhabitants of Sofia regarded themselves as subtler and more illustrious than other Bulgarians. Nonetheless, they were aware that they lived in one of the dark corners of Europe and spoke a language that very few people could understand. One of the consequences of this situation for me was that my parents made me study foreign languages very early, 'European' languages in particular. I took private lessons, primarily in English, then German, and finally, immediately before my departure, in French.

We regarded the outside world, including countries outside Europe, as necessarily better than ours. During the period when Algeria was 'socialist', and therefore an ally of the Communist countries, it was possible for Bulgarian doctors to go there and practice, and there was a real stampede! At the time, very few foreigners came to live for any length of time in Bulgaria; those who did were mostly from Third World countries, Syria in particular. Today, I wonder whether they too had the impression, when they came to Sofia, that they were 'going to Europe'! We even envied the non-Europeans, especially since these young students, exclusively male, seemed to be well off and hung out in the rare chic bars of the city. The height of our humiliation was that our most beautiful young women had eyes only for those Syrians who were just passing through, probably in the hopes of leaving Sofia one day (one night!). Our animosity towards those privileged rivals could easily take on racist overtones.

This inferiority complex, the way we overrated everything that came from the West, coupled with the ambient poverty, made Bulgaria resemble a Third World country — although I didn't realize it at the time. Today, this common affiliation influences my outlook on other 'developing' countries: whenever I go to one of them, the atmosphere of my childhood, the Oriental chaos, springs to mind. There's a strong sense of familiarity but I don't find it particularly touching.

Born in 1939, you grew up under the Communist regime, especially when you were a small child and during your early schooldays. How did you become aware that you were living in an entirely ideological world? Did it come to you in a moment of revelation or was it a gradual realization?

Bulgaria entered the Soviet Union's orbit in September 1944 when the Red Army divisions occupied the country. When did I understand the consequences? It is difficult to give you an exact date: one becomes imperceptibly conscious of such realities. Obviously, the hold of the ideological world started early. I began school in 1945. My life as a schoolboy therefore coincided with the beginning of the Communist regime—I was six years old. I have no recollection of any ideological indoctrination during the four years that correspond to primary school, although that's probably because my memory has retained no trace of it. Those were, in fact, the worst years of Communist Bulgaria, years of intense ideological struggle and repression. The memories I have of that period come to me indirectly by way of my family. My father, especially, found himself involved in some rather tragic events at that time.

What kind?

First I think I ought to briefly retrace the sequence of events. The Communists did not take total control of the government right away. In 1944, just after the Red Army's occupation of the country, the so-called 'Fatherland Front' was placed in control of the government. The Fatherland Front comprised all the 'anti-fascist forces', including the Communists. But the Communists had two key departments in their hands: the Department of Justice and the Department of the Interior. And with the Soviet Army behind them, they did in actual fact control the country.

Their first step, at the end of 1944 and at the beginning of 1945, was to undertake the elimination of all 'fascist elements'. The repression was quite brutal since, among other things, everyone who had been a member of any of the governments during the war period was executed, regardless of guilt: they were deemed guilty because they had been members of a guilty government. There were also killings without trials, the kind of savage purging that often occurs after a regime has been overthrown. These killings struck thousands of people who were simply in the 'public eye'—a pope (orthodox priest), a teacher, a journalist—and whose only mistake had been to have had a bit of power, if only the power of their prestige.

Then came a second wave of repression, in 1947, when the Communists openly took total control of the government and eliminated all legal opposition— their former allies in the Fatherland Front from the war period but also allies from the previous purge period. It was in these circumstances that Nikola Petkov was tried and hung.

tzvetan todorov

Nikola Petkov was also one of the members of the Fatherland Front who participated in rescuing the Bulgarian Jews during the war, as you recall in The Fragility of Goodness.

I found out about this much more recently, while studying documents from the period in preparation for the book. Indeed, Petkov, although he was a clandestine leader of the Fatherland Front, signed public petitions against the anti-Jewish measures. He didn't save the Jews, but he had the courage to take a public stand and protest against governmental decisions. It was an act of opposition in relation to the official position. He was doing the same thing in 1946 when he protested against restrictions on civil liberties. Only, in 1946, he was living under a real totalitarian regime. Bulgaria during the war wasn't a Nazi or, strictly speaking, a fascist regime; it was an authoritarian, conservative regime, dominated by King Boris III — similar, in this respect, to Spain under Franco or Portugal under Salazar — in which it was still possible to publicly express dissident opinions without being thrown into prison or killed. This is clearly evidenced by these documents concerning the rescuing of the Bulgarian Jews.

Do you remember Petkov's trial in 1947 and its impact?

My memories of that time (I was eight) have faded but it just so happens that recently — 50 years after the events — I provided the commentary for a sequence of Bulgarian newsreels showing the trial for Marc Ferro's programme on Arte, *Histoires parallèles*. So the episode is very clear in my mind today. Petkov's case also particularly touches me because of the pages that Romain Gary wrote on him in *La nuit sera calme*. Gary was the secretary in the French Embassy in Sofia at the time and he knew Petkov well. The sight of this man — of this true democrat with whom he had lunched a couple of months earlier — being hung inoculated Gary once and for all against the inclination to believe that Communism could represent the glorious future of the people.

Do you know what your father thought of Petkov's hanging? Do you remember any discussions at home about the event?

I was too young to understand adult conversations, and, what's more, I don't think my parents would have spoken in front of me, for fear of the consequences if I'd repeated what they said. Children at the time were familiar with the model of Pavlik Morozov. Schools were named after Pavlik Morozov, classes were calling themselves Pavlik Morozov, his story was held up as an example. Pavlik Morozov was the young hero of the Soviet Union, whose main merit was that he had denounced his parents. It happened during the collectivization. His parents had hidden grain and he thought it was very bad to do so because it is one's duty to work for the socialist homeland. So he denounced them and then was murdered by his evil parents or other members of his family. The lesson children were expected to retain was that in order to support the state and the Party, you must be willing to repudiate your own family. In my case, I must confess that I was a fervent 'pioneer' until the age of twelve, twelve-and-a-half. Pioneers were the equivalent of Boy Scouts, but the organization had a clear ideological thrust and this ideology extended to all aspects of life. For all that, I don't know if I would have been capable of doing my own little Pavlik Morozov act had I become aware of some dark treason committed by my parents.

My father, the only one of my parents who participated in public life, had become a member of the Communist Party and he probably did not have many doubts, at least not until 1947, about the truthfulness of official propaganda.

In the 1947 Bulgarian newsreels that I recently saw again, Nikola Petkov's execution was presented as the victory of the whole country over an enemy in the pay of Anglo-American imperialism. They reported thousands of telegrams sent by the population, all demanding an exemplary punishment for the traitor: there were workers from one factory signing a petition, peasants from a cooperative signing another, etc. I am positive that there was nothing in the least bit spontaneous about any of these signatures; it was all organized and supervised by the Party. Moreover, when people are not willing to ask themselves questions—and this is the case most of the time for the majority of the population—they readily accept what the state says as truth. At least when it concerns more or less distant matters that do not directly affect their daily lives.

My father

In 1947, as you were saying, your father didn't ask himself too many questions. But what about after that?

Very soon after came the third wave of repression. The movement was rapid compared to that in Russia, but we had started a lot later and we needed to make up for lost time. In 1948–49, we had the equivalent of the Moscow Trials: 1948–49 in Eastern Europe was like 1937 in the Soviet Union. It was in this third wave that my father found himself implicated.

How?

Let me backtrack a little. My father had studied literature and philology in Sofia, before leaving for Germany for three years (1924–27) to take his studies further. But, as he told me much later, instead of studying he spent much of his time militating in political circles run by Bulgarian Communist emigrants.

In Facing the Extreme, *you mention that he may have met Margarete Buber-Neumann there. She had the sad privilege of experiencing Stalin's camps before being handed over to Hitler, along with many German Communists, and being imprisoned in Ravensbrück for five years. After her liberation, Buber-Neumann valiantly fought against all forms of totalitarianism, and she wrote about Milena, Kafka's friend. You describe her with admiration in* Hope and Memory.

She was the exact same age as my parents and militated in the same circles as my father in Berlin. She recalls in her memoirs how she hid Dimitrov, the clandestine head of the Bulgarian Communists. But she was already much more engaged than my father, who was naively manipulated by a 'left-wing' organization that was really controlled by the Communist Party.

Years later, I arranged a meeting between my father and Manès Sperber, father of the anthropologist Dan Sperber, one of my best friends at the time. Manès, who was born in the former Austro-Hungarian Empire, had been a civil servant in the Komintern at the end of the twenties. They met in Paris and immediately started speaking to each other in German, and, of course, they found out that they had some friends in common. However, the differences between them quickly emerged in the course of the conversation. After an hour, Dan and I were no longer sure that bringing them together had been such a good idea: disagreements from 1927 were re-emerging. Both had become ardent anti-Communists but their anti-Communism had a one-upmanship to it that made it impossible for them to agree. I have often seen former Communists arguing like this; each one feels that the other has not sufficiently renounced his or her former convictions. They still bear some resentment towards each other.

Ultimately, my father managed, first in Germany and then through his work in Bulgaria, to become a genuine specialist on libraries. He even wrote a few books on the subject. He was an extremely knowledgeable man, with a passion for books and a great love for Chekhov, whose eight volumes of correspondence he had devoured. He was also an editor, a specialist in establishing texts by classic Bulgarian writers. Our house sagged under the weight of all his books. There were books in every room, in all genres and in several languages. When I was a child, I used to play in the middle of all those books; when I was older, I secretly sold some to second-hand bookstores for pocket money. Immediately after the new regime assumed power, my father was appointed Director of the National Library—a rather important position for which he was ideally suited since he was both competent and a man of the Left.

Was his competence actually the reason for his appointment?

At the time, yes, but after a while, competence was no longer enough: you had to be a good officer of the Party. This was already obvious in Lenin's famous statement: 'Communism is Soviet power plus the electrification of the entire country.' Lenin presented his statement in the form of an addition, but it wasn't that simple. What if one contradicted the other? Do you keep the good engineer because you need electricity or do you get rid of him because he's a bad Soviet? For my father, the problems began arising—although not flagrantly—around this issue. He said that he needed qualified people to work in the library and establish documentation, people who spoke foreign languages and who had, therefore, a higher education or who had lived abroad. In Bulgaria, in 1946, this meant people who had been privileged during the time of the old regime and who were therefore obviously not peasants or factory-workers. The question of higher-ranking employees was a key one for my father, and he did not exactly 'follow the Party line'! His superiors were just waiting for an occasion to get rid of him.

History provided it. The scapegoat of the third wave of repression, the counterpart in Bulgaria of Czechoslovakia's Slanski or Hungary's Rajk was Traicho Kostov. Kostov was the third most important man in the government. The first was Dimitrov, who had just died. A rumour spread that he had been poisoned on Stalin's orders; the same rumour had circulated about King Boris, purported to have been poisoned on Hitler's orders (legendary schemas are tough to break). The second was Kolarov, a Communist Party leader and an emigrant who had come back from Moscow. Then came Kostov, who had stayed in the country and become head of the Bulgarian Communist resistance during the war. When you examine Kostov's writings and acts, you can see that he too was a dogmatic Communist, hardly better than the others. His main 'failing' was that he was a man of conviction. And in a totalitarian system, at a given point in time, any conviction, no matter how pure, counts against you.

Because conviction is an expression of individuality?

Yes, and it enables you to build autonomy and that is potentially subversive. The individual must be entirely dependent on the higher power, that of the Party, or even directly on its leader. The slightest inclination to act on one's own must be broken. Kostov was somebody who followed his own reason and will. That doesn't mean he was a liberal—he was probably the one who organized the execution of Petkov, among others. What's more—and this was a mistake that proved fatal to him—it seems he opposed the policy of total submission to the Soviet Union, claiming to be motivated by the Communist ideal alone! So he was the one chosen to be the victim of the next trial. Kostov was not imprisoned right away. In June 1948, he was dismissed from his positions of First Secretary of the Party and Vice-Prime Minister and relegated to the less important position of Director of the

National Library—a post my father was invited to leave vacant. In June 1948, my father therefore lost his job and found himself at the head of a modest documentation centre, something considerably less prestigious. He kept in touch with Kostov for a while because he had to introduce him to his job. Kostov, who obviously had not spent a day in his life working for a library, did his best for several weeks as a good officer of the Party to learn about his new field.

He had to abandon the post the following fall; he was arrested, condemned and then, at the beginning of 1949, executed. *L'Humanité*'s correspondent in Sofia, Dominique Desanti, wrote a moving report on the trial. During the last session, when all of the accused were brought back into the courtroom, Kostov stood up and cried out: 'Everything that I was forced to sign is a lie, extracted under torture. I insist on saying this in front of the international press. I never committed the crimes I am accused of. The whole thing is a pure fabrication.' This left a strong impression on the journalist; I think that was when the first seed of doubt was planted in Dominique Desanti's mind. It would take quite some time for it to bloom, though.

These trials, that of Bagryanov and the other former ministers in 1945, of Petkov in 1947 and of Kostov in 1949, probably explain why I am allergic to political trials.

To all of them?

Nearly. There's always a possibility of abuse.

My father was implicated in this new wave of purges, not only by contiguity, but also more directly—the second most important defendant in the trial was Ivan Stefanov, one of his best friends. Ex-Minister of Finance, Stefanov was a committed Communist and, like my father, an acknowledged expert in his field; he had studied in Germany, in France, in Switzerland — in Europe! It seems to me that the elimination of former leftists who had been to 'Europe', who had received a higher education and acquired real proficiency in their line of work was a turning point in the history of Communist power in Bulgaria. Such people did not fit in any more. The state needed docile servants who owed everything to the Party, not to their own efforts, and these people had acquired too much autonomy. They thought they could judge for themselves, so they had to be eliminated. Stefanov's downfall put his whole circle of friends on the defensive. His family was really close to ours; his daughter was one of my brother's and my best friends.

So Stefanov was an important defendant in the 1949 trial and he was sentenced to life imprisonment. We saw him again when he got out of prison in 1956 and he told us what had happened, which pretty much corresponds to what Arthur London recounts in *The Confession*. Stefanov was not subjected to physical torture. He had been told that his confession was needed to prove Kostov's guilt, and that, for reasons of state, the evidence could not be revealed. So he recited his lesson without batting an eye. In exchange, they promised him that his sentence would be a mere formality and that he would be released the next day — which he was not, of course!

Interestingly enough, six months to a year after his release, Stefanov had joined the Party again.

How do you explain that? Is it the inability to let go of the past?

I think that for people like Stefanov and the Londons, the Party had become such a key part of their identity that they could not repudiate it. It was impossible for Stefanov to start his life anew. Here was a man who had truly suffered and yet was reconciled to those responsible for his suffering. He no longer held an official position—by then, he was in his sixties—but he was given some sort of job as an itinerant consultant and he could travel abroad again, which was one of the great privileges that everybody dreamed of in Bulgaria. My father, who had become a staunch anti-Communist by that time, kept away from him, and I stopped seeing Uncle Vanio, as we used to call him.

And nothing else happened to your father, even as an anti-Communist, aside from his professional 'demotion'?

A short time after, he was ousted from the Party. He tried to defend himself. He was summoned to meetings where he was expected to undertake a critique of himself and he would come home looking grim. The atmosphere was very oppressive. Yet he managed to hold on to his position as professor at the university where he taught his specialty (library and document organization), and he did so with no further trouble until his retirement. He was a popular professor, respected for his eloquence and extensive knowledge: it was clear that he didn't owe his position to his loyalty to the Party. He had become a public figure of sorts—of a type possible in the Bulgarian world—somewhere in what Primo Levi called the grey area: in certain respects, he was still a privileged member of society, benefiting from the regime; in others, he was a staunch opponent. Those who had been truly persecuted, who had spent time in prison, must have had no sympathy for a man who always moved with the prevailing current. But he must have been a thorn in the side of those who had only their careers in mind, since he had refrained from any serious compromise. At the same time, he always resented the fact that he had not been able to carry through his projects for improving the libraries. I learnt a lesson from that, a variation on Stoic wisdom: it is best not to confuse personal fulfilment and success in public projects.

tzvetan todorov

My father used to listen to the radio a lot—foreign stations, Radio Free Europe, RIAS or ordinary German stations. I can still see him with his ear pressed to the radio (the broadcasts in Bulgarian were heavily jammed, so he had to struggle to hear them). He would then give a commented summary of the news to his friends and family. These conversations took up a great part of his time. He was becoming more and more hostile to the regime, but he never had any public dissident activities. In those years, it was inconceivable. On the other hand, he regularly interceded on behalf of people who were being persecuted: he had kept up his contacts in high places.

He had no illusions whatsoever about the Communist regime—or about any other type of regime, for that matter. When the Berlin Wall fell in 1989, I was a bit surprised to see so little enthusiasm on his part. 'You know,' he explained to me, 'I've already heard many people promising that things will be better in the future.'

An education under Communism

That was your father. Let's come back to you. What is in the mind of the child, and then the young teenager, raised under, and partly by, Communism?

First I should tell you about the years when I was a believer, for it was truly a matter of 'faith' and the process of having faith and losing it is the same. I think I stopped believing in around 1953, the year Stalin died.

In 1952, I started secondary school. Between the ages of 10 and 13, when I was in middle school, I was very, perhaps ridiculously so, politically active. That was the only period in my life when I was a real militant activist. We all belonged to 'mass' organizations and I was the head of the young Pioneers in our school.

What exactly did that consist of?

I'm going to tell you about an incident from my childhood that still makes me blush with shame. I believe I've never spoken of it before. I was about 12 and was 'running' the Pioneers of my school, under the supervision of an 18-year-old girl who belonged to an older youth organization, a Komsomol of sorts. We had summoned a girl of my age to the organization's office (with whom I was probably secretly in love) and we admonished her for her inappropriate behaviour: she had flirted with three boys since the beginning of the school year. Such admonitions were not without consequence because, as the head of the organization, I could issue recommendations that would later weigh on the children's lives. We made a poor 12-year-old girl cry because she had smiled at two or three boys . . . and, to be honest, not enough at me!

And obviously she couldn't laugh in your face, as any schoolgirl in a democratic country would have done.

Most certainly not! She couldn't allow herself to show contempt. If she refused to engage in self-criticism, she would run the risk of being expelled from the organization. That meant that her admission to secondary school would be compromised — what would become of her then?

You might tell me that it is not like killing the Jews under the Nazi regime, and you'd be right. Bulgaria was by no means an extermination camp, and you cannot compare the incomparable. Totalitarianism — Nazi, Soviet or Cambodian — has moments of paroxysm when attempts are made to eliminate a part of the population: when the 'kulaks' or peasants are exterminated or the Jews and Gypsies are murdered or city-dwellers 're-educated' to death. But the rest of the time, you've simply got to live, and what is produced then is a deeply rooted gangrene, a general corruption of everything. What my anecdote illustrates is the elimination of the borderline between public and private, the strict moralism, the individual's vulnerability when facing a representative of the state–Party apparatus. It shows the corruption of the spirit of a child, of my spirit. It is an exorbitant power to put in the hands of a child! If I didn't turn out to be an apparatchik, it was most certainly due to my family environment: my fanaticism must have amused them (but also made them shudder).

So how did you lose your faith in secondary school?

The Russian school I attended was like a bilingual one; more than that, actually, because, in addition to the many hours of classes in Russian language and litera-ture, which we didn't complain about, all of the other disciplines — history, physics, chemistry and math — were taught in Russian too. This instruction was given to us by professors who came from the Soviet Union to spend a few years here. It must have been an El Dorado to them because life was much easier in the Eastern European countries — in the 'popular democracies' as they were called at the time — than in Russia. They had good salaries and were treated like aristocrats: imagine the French *coopérants,* or aid-workers, in Bamako — they were living the good life! Personally, I have rather good memories of those school days but that may be because things came easily to me; studies were never a problem for me.

Why did your parents choose that school?

Because it was the best. If you have the means, in Paris, for instance, you send your children to the Lycée international de Saint-Germain or to the École bilingue — to a school for the elite. The upshot was that my classmates included sons and daughters of high-ranking members of the state. On the other hand, my father had just been ousted from the Party and he was becoming more and more overtly opposed to the regime. Nobody asked me to play a leadership role; besides, the desire to do so had ceased. It was an inner change I don't quite know how to explain. That whole period of my life — being a leader and organizing —

lost its attraction for me. My ambitions never ventured in that direction again. One could say that I had turned my back—definitively—on political activity.

I situate this turning point somewhere around 1953 because that year was marked by Stalin's death. Recently, I opened a notebook that I used as a diary at the time and saw that on the day of Stalin's death, 5 March 1953, I had written: 'Stalin is dead; this surely spells war.' I must have been convinced of that. For me as a child, Stalin was what I would describe today as a Pharaonic figure: it was no coincidence that he was mummified after his death and placed in the mausoleum alongside Lenin (only to be removed a few years later). He was somewhere between man and God. He was wisdom incarnate and, moreover, he was our protector.

The warm face, the gentle smile beneath the white moustache, the benevolent gaze of the man in uniform staring at us from all the walls of the city. I can still see it today: the light grey colour, a little blue, a little red . . . It all spoke of peace, harmony, security. So with the great protector dead, I guess I thought that the worldwide conflict between the good (meaning us) and the bad (meaning them) was going to worsen and that there would be war in the next few months! In reality— but I didn't know it at the time—it was the end of so much suffering and the beginning of a 'thaw': the doors of the Gulag started to open. But for the child I was then, this date marked the onset of a sense of disenchantment. The leaders who replaced Stalin lacked that superhuman quality; we did not think of them as infallible.

This did not lead, however, to courageous acts of resistance. That very spring, a child in my class was accused of not having shown enough grief over Stalin's death. Attending this Russian-language school were children of Bulgarian Communists who had emigrated to Russia during the earlier anti-Communist repression and who were then in positions of power, but there was also a group of children of white Russian emigrants who had come to Bulgaria after the 1917 revolution. These children spoke Russian at home and were therefore naturally enrolled in the Russian school. A few years later, these families were repatriated to Russia in quite harsh circumstances. I think that this young boy must have suffered the heavy consequences of his half-hearted reaction to Stalin's death—his parents were probably already under surveillance. One day, soon after Stalin's death, his family vanished: they had been sent back to Russia, probably to somewhere in Siberia. I remember the incident, but I cannot claim that I stood up and protested at the time with 'Free Lebed!' banners and slogans.

Yet you remember his name!

I can still see him today: he had very blonde hair. I remember another incident when a student was excluded much later, at university, where I indulged in no political activity whatsoever, even though, like everybody else, I was a member of the 'mass' organization, the equivalent of the Komsomol. This time, I was deeply outraged, but I kept quiet because I did not want to be next on the list. I repeat, none of these acts were criminal in and of themselves: no one was pushing anyone into a gas chamber. But these are so many steps on a road that leads in that direction. You want to protect your own personal comfort and you are scared of the violence that you in turn may have to endure. So, each time, you yield a little more ground, you give up a little more of your personal autonomy. This fear is an integral part of the fundamental experience of the totalitarian subject. It creeps into everything and is responsible for the most contemptible attitudes: denunciations, base flattery, self-humiliation. But who could claim to be definitively immune to fear?

tzvetan todorov

In the Russian school, I met the children of all the big shots in the country. I thus became intimately familiar with the governing circles of Bulgaria. My best friend in school was Andrei. His father was an important man: he had immigrated to Russia during the twenties and I believe he worked for the NKVD, the Russian political police, during the Spanish Civil War. He had been something of an underground man in the International Brigades controlled by the Russians. He belonged to the innermost circles. He was, successively, Director of the radio, Minister of Culture and Ambassador to Moscow. His son, Andrei, was a very nice boy. We sat next to each other on the same bench in school.

1956: a pivotal year

In 1956, you were 17; it was the end of secondary school. It was also an intense year politically: the Khrushchev Report, the Soviet tanks in Budapest and so on. What effect did these events have on your thinking?

Indeed, it was an important year for me. That spring, in March 1956, we got wind of Khrushchev's speech to the Twentieth Party Congress of the Soviet Union. It came as a shock. For the first time in history, the crimes of Stalinism were officially enumerated and denounced. Until then, only the worst enemies of Communism had dared allude to these crimes and here, all of a sudden, was the head of the state, the number one man, who was doing so.

Obviously, the Report was kept secret and its very existence denied; it wasn't openly discussed in Bulgaria. But because Andrei's father was a deputy member of the Politburo, the speech immediately fell into his hands. That's how I came to know about it and I brought it for my father to read as well. Only certain members of the Party, most likely the members of the Central Committee, had direct access to the text; they must have been asked to summarize and comment on the part of the Report deemed appropriate for everyone. Incidentally, the French Communists were not supposed to know about it either. It was published not by *L'Humanité* but by *Le Monde* and *Le Figaro*, I think. In Bulgaria, of course, not a word was said about it in the press. It was as if it had never existed.

Andrei and I spent a lot of time discussing the Report.

What did he think of it?

The same thing as I did. We both thought these were atrocious crimes that had to be condemned so that they would never happen again.

But I'd like to tell you more about Andrei. I remember something that happened to him. He had invited me to come with him to the banks of the Black Sea, near Varna, to one of the royal palaces that had been turned into residences for the Politburo. Since Andrei's father was a deputy member at the time, his son was allowed to visit (such were the hierarchical subtleties worthy of the Ancien Régime). One day, in the summer of 1956, right after my graduation, I had the privilege of entering this holy of holies, the most inaccessible place of all, thanks to Andrei. I don't know what to compare it to in France: a cross between the Fort de Brégançon, a residence for the French head of state, and Aga Khan island, home to multi-millionaires. Political and financial hierarchies, which are separated in democracies, went together in Bulgaria: everything went through the political power and all powers were concentrated in the same hands. So I entered this sanctuary and was tickled to see that these people were like everyone else: paunchy vacationers in shorts at the seaside. I recognized with astonishment the Minister of the Interior, the Prime Minister and the Minister of Foreign Affairs among others.

A rather comical incident took place one day. Andrei and I were playing volleyball with these men, most of whom were my father's age. Frankly, they were quite bad at it! For my part, I made no attempt to catch a ball that the Prime Minister had missed. He shot me a look of disgust and must have asked Andrei later who that idiot had been who demonstrated so little respect in his presence. The next day Andrei said that perhaps it was better not to go back there.

What became of your friend Andrei?

After secondary school, his parents sent him to Moscow to an institute that may be deemed the equivalent of the ENA in France, a place where the higher echelons of the Party received an education. Back in Bulgaria, he had a dazzling career. An almost monarchical principle held sway in Bulgaria—this was, in fact, one of the significant traits of Communist regimes in general—and a caste of noblesse had been formed, a 'state' in the Ancien Régime sense of the term, transmitted through blood: the children of the privileged were automatically privileged. Marriages between offspring of members of this caste were encouraged. And power tended to be passed on as an inheritance. After all, the tyrant can only trust his own family. Zhivkov, the top man in Bulgaria, had two children himself, a son and a daughter. The son was reputed to be an irresponsible alcoholic and his father couldn't expect anything from him. But Zhivkov had high hopes for his daughter whom he believed would one day lead the country. She became the regime's number two, but she died long before her father did. Only in North Korea, where the son succeeded the father, did they manage to see through this form of power transmission and thereby reveal the monarchical aspect of Communist regimes.

So Andrei had a brilliant career to which he was destined by descent. His family was entirely shaped by the Communist experience. One of his grandfathers was among the founders of the Bulgarian Communist Party at the beginning of the century; his other grandfather had been killed under the previous regime, and his father was a high-placed Party official. Andrei therefore represented the third generation. He was trilingual since, before the Russian school where I met him, he had attended an English middle school. Moreover, he spoke French; in fact, he was born in Paris in 1938 when his parents were fleeing the repression at the end of the Spanish Civil War.

In all the exchanges we had, he always showed himself to be liberal-minded. He was a warm, intelligent boy. When he came back to Bulgaria (I was already in Paris at the time), he had started to move up in the hierarchy. After a while, he became Minister of International Trade. But he stayed on the fringes, presumably because he was too bright and too much at ease in everything. They used him as a valuable pawn but he never played a leading role.

And you never saw him again after you went to France and he to Moscow?

Yes, once very briefly in Paris. He headed a government delegation. We had a somewhat uneasy exchange at the time. And then I saw him again some time in 1988 or at the beginning of 1989.

Before the fall of the regime.

Exactly. My parents where quite old by then and my mother was sick. I was going back to Bulgaria regularly to see them. He came looking for me one day at their house in a very modest Volkswagen type of vehicle. We took a walk and chatted. He showed me his home—an ordinary apartment—and introduced me to his children who were already adults. I told him anti-Communist jokes (What's Communism? A winding path leading from capitalism to capitalism.) He gave a bit of a forced laugh.

Let me skip ahead. At the end of 1989, he was the one to organize the fall of Zhivkov. He became Prime Minister shortly after. He was something of the Egon Krenz of Bulgaria—you remember, the short-lived successor to Honecker in East Germany? However, in Bulgaria, the Communist reformers lasted somewhat longer than in other Eastern European countries. They eventually won the elections and stayed in power. Like Gorbachev, they too sought to reform Communism, to make it more viable by adding a dose of transparency and freedom of the press and by implementing more liberal economic policies in terms of private property and the free market.

A reformed Communism may have been their ideal but they did not want to relinquish power. Andrei Lukanov and others like him were responsible for the fantastic process of turning ex-Communists into the country's new capitalists. Everything that belonged to the state fell into their hands. These are the people who are the great Bulgarian capitalists of today.

Andrei left the government under pressure from the street and not as a result of elections, which had given him a majority. A build-up of strikes, demonstrations and international pressure put him in an untenable position. So he joined the Opposition, where he remained the leading figure with considerable control over the economic situation. At the same time, he must have been involved in all sorts of shady dealings, since he was the one to organize the conversion of apparatchiks into lawless capitalists. This probably explains his death: he was assassinated in front of the door to his building in 1996. The murder was never solved but it was clearly a professional job.

I will not write a biography of Andrei Lukanov but his was a very revealing life in many respects. Here was an intelligent, talented individual who became a

Communist leader. And it is because of people like him that I cannot condemn Communism in an impersonal way—I saw it at work among my family and friends. Andrei was the most apparent, clear-cut example, but there were others, with whom I was on less intimate terms, who came from the same milieu. Like Stefanov in my father's generation, Andrei belonged to the very core of Communist power. They were cultivated, charming, smooth-talking polyglots, competent in their line of work but they were, nonetheless, responsible for the disaster that struck their country.

Is it that intellectual superiority does not protect against the lure of power or blind adherence to an ideology?

In my opinion, the explanation is to be situated on a level beyond individuals. Like millions of others at the time, these were people who believed that Communism would bring about a better world. And so they overlooked the concrete results— what was happening in ordinary people's lives. They were willing to immolate people on the altar of humanity. That is why I hold so dearly to the opposite attitude: I am more concerned with individuals than with groups, and I am wary of big words like Peace, Justice or Equality. I'm always looking to see the price that will be paid for them and the realities they dissimulate. Or, to put it in more negative terms, this is what probably accounts for my insurmountable and excessive distrust of political activity and of all those who promote the collective good.

But at the time when you read the Khrushchev Report together with Andrei Lukanov, did he share your feelings of revolt against the crimes of the Communist regime and your hopes for change?

At the time, he was probably close to Khrushchev's positions. And I'm not sure that I really had an opinion of my own. Those few months in 1956 after the

Khrushchev Report constituted a short-lived intense moment in time when all hopes were allowed. We were under the impression that Communism was going to reform itself from the inside, by itself. I was in a relatively good position to observe this change: I could go play volleyball at the palace, I could read the secret speech . . . Then came the crackdown in Budapest in the autumn of 1956, and there could be no more illusions.

How did you react to the events?

With great intensity again. That was when my generation, which was just leaving school, understood that there would never be a deep-seated reform. Until then, we could imagine that the oppression was connected with Stalin and that, with his death, the page had been turned. It was in October 1956 that we finally understood that Communism would never develop into a democracy. We heard the news about the uprising in Budapest on Western radios; my father spent even more time than usual with his ear pressed to the radio. We listened, live, to the Russian tanks firing, and the Hungarian calls for help. There were vague hopes of an American intervention. Today I am thankful it didn't come: it would have triggered the Third World War!

But perhaps it would have spared millions of people from another 30 years under a totalitarian regime?

But at the cost of how many deaths and how much indelible suffering? I would rather by far that my parents live under totalitarianism than have them die under the bombs. To go in that direction would have meant choosing an abstraction—democracy and freedom—to the detriment of each person's life.

1956 was also the year you started university.

tzvetan todorov

I enrolled in Slavic and Bulgarian philology — the equivalent of *lettres modernes* in France. Most of the classes were rather boring. Literary studies were under total ideological control, and dominated by such notions as the 'spirit of the Party' and 'spirit of the people' which we were expected to situate in the works of the authors we studied. We found the 'Party spirit' only in the best Communist writers and the 'spirit of the people' in all the works that were allowed to be taught. All other writers were stigmatized as enemies of the people and consigned to the dustbin of history.

In addition to courses in language and the history of literature, we attended compulsory classes in Marxism–Leninism all throughout our schooling and regardless of our area of specialization. One year we studied the history of the Soviet Communist Party, another that of the Bulgarian Party; we also did political economy (of capitalism, which was bad, and of socialism, which was good). Finally we had the famous 'diamat' and 'histmat', dialectical materialism and historical materialism — philosophical digests in which pride of place was given to the works of the best philosopher, economist and linguist of all time: the great Stalin. Male students also had one day per week dedicated to military service — we learnt 'theory', which took the form of a series of empty formulae. This enabled us to leave university as reserve officers, totally ignorant, in reality, of the fundamentals of military art.

I spent five years in university.

It sounds like quite a regimented life!

At bottom, yes it was, but not in every respect. Life was not always dark and depressing; human beings are such that they look for and find reasons to laugh and rejoice in all circumstances. Being a Pioneer meant participating in a repressive ideological indoctrination, but it also meant hikes in the mountains during holidays, the outdoors and campfires—wonderful, unforgettable memories! The Hitlerjugend, in 1938, could probably have said the same thing. Years later, when I wasn't in school any more, I went to the country in a 'brigade' for several summers in a row. To offset the collapse of agricultural production, the government requisitioned students from the city and sent them to work in the fields for the summer. We did some earthwork and planted fruit trees. It was forced labour, so to speak (anyone who did not come risked being excluded from the Komsomol, then from university and eventually being forced to leave Sofia, which meant spending the rest of one's life doing earthwork). And yet I have good memories of those summers: leaving for the fields at six in the morning before the sun came up, the pleasure of physical exertion . . . there was something thrilling about it. There was also the camaraderie between boys and the flirting between boys and girls.

Finding your way in the grey area

During those years, you started looking for your way professionally. What were the possibilities for a literary person in totalitarian Bulgaria?

There was the possibility of doing research or of becoming a university professor, which was, after all, my father's line of work. But how could I make my way in such an environment? At the end of my fifth year, I had to write a Master's thesis. I carefully chose the approach I would take. My centre of interest was literature, but I was becoming a bit of a linguist out of necessity — it enabled me to escape the ideological hold. The closer the method to exact sciences, the more protected I was. Stylistic studies were preferable to literary studies, and grammatical studies were even better. When I managed to confine the texts to grammatical categories, I thought I had succeeded in outwitting 'them' (the powers that be, the ubiquitous controllers) and getting around the censorship.

My Master's thesis focused on a comparison between two versions of a short story written, 30–40 years apart, by a great Bulgarian writer. The second text was unquestionably more powerful. I concluded that this comparison would enable us to pierce the secret of literary beauty — nothing less! I've always had the desire to understand and explain everything! I thought, I was even convinced, that it was possible to elucidate the mystery of the art of writing. All I had to do was list all the modifications that this writer had brought to his text. For example, in the second version, he often opted for transitive rather than intransitive verbs, for concrete rather than abstract subjects and he stayed away from deverbatives, preferring conjugated verbs . . . The censors would find no fault with what I wrote! I was delighted!

I was also interested in the poetics of folklore: tales, riddles, proverbs, popular songs. Bulgarian popular songs are beautiful and the oral tradition is much richer there than it is in France where written literature developed early. In Bulgaria, nothing much was written during the 'five centuries of slavery'. As a result, all creativity was poured into folklore. I had studied these questions with a professor of ours named Dinekov, whom I liked very much. He was something of a model to me: a Party outsider, who did the strict minimum, nothing more. The poetics of folklore was another way for me to stick to the text's materiality: the formal constraints of the genre are strong, so they need to be studied. In addition, these songs could not be criticized for their lack of Party spirit (the spirit of the people was present by definition). It was this need to avoid ideology that was at the origin of my interest in the Russian formalists when I came to France.

You were happy to get around the censorship but it must have been boring for you to focus all your attention on pure technique!

You know, when you are immersed in this type of study, you find it engrossing! But on some level or another, it must not have been satisfying enough for me since, in the very last years before I left for France, I started wanting to publish and to become more directly involved in a literary and artistic life. It was probably more immediately flattering for my vanity than laboriously pursuing a university career. I was then, like so many others at that age, hungry for outside recognition. I did a little journalism. I met the one and only known dissident of the time, the poet Radoi Raline. During the war, at the age of 15, he had been a resistant, even a *maquisard* of sorts. As a result, he was above reproach and could allow himself to voice increasingly bitter criticisms of the regime. He wasn't really a poet; he wrote rhyming pieces, epigrams, funny stories . . . but he was one of the rare free men.

Raline worked on an evening newspaper with a vaguely cultural thrust—it was a cushy number. This was a characteristic situation: writers were not free to say what they wanted but they received a paycheck at the end of the month. Generally speaking, this was the case for everything that touched on culture: generously financed but strictly controlled. Such benevolence could take on a variety of forms. Painters, if they did not want to practise socialist realism, could still find work, for instance, drawing the letters of newspaper headlines (they were handdrawn instead of printed). And this source of livelihood was systematically reserved for painters. In this way, artists could secretly paint abstract works at home—since abstract art was not allowed—and still manage to earn a proper living. There were also retreats, grants and sinecures reserved for artists and writers. Several literary journals had sizeable editorial boards whose members were all full-time employees; publishers had a great many 'editors', many of whom were writers using the position as a cushy job. Of course, what was expected from them in return was ideological submission, enrolment in the service of the Party and spiritual prostitution. But artists could also get around the system, pretend and do their own thing.

I started to write some articles for that evening paper. I'm not sure that I'd be proud today of what I wrote. I was finding out what it meant to be part of the cultural life in a Communist country, learning how to manoeuvre and get around censorship. For example, I would praise 'those who fought for freedom' in the distant past — obviously, all the sentences had double meanings and I enjoyed that. Or, putting to use my comprehension of German, English and French, I'd read foreign newspapers and report on cultural events in the French, German or Anglo-American world in a way that I think was rather superficial. I wouldn't have dared praise them, but the mere act of writing about them was a reminder that another world existed.

That meant you had access to foreign newspapers, which must have opened new horizons for you, even if they were exclusively Communist papers.

To some extent, I did. I could read the 'progressive' Western press in the editorial office of the paper or at the Writers Union. I must have been able to read *Les Lettres françaises* rather than *Le Figaro littéraire* or *Arts* or *Les Nouvelles littéraires* (the French cultural weeklies of the day) and not only *L'Humanité*. There was enormous curiosity in my circles for everything that came from the outside; we knew so little about anything. But note the ambiguity here once again: real opponents to the regime — if there had been any at the time — would have found that I was compromising too much. They would surely have regarded all the activities of our small milieu as pathetic. But, alas, there were no dissidents in Bulgaria in the 1950s, not to my knowledge at least.

But today, now that history has retained the acts of dissidence, do you ever sense in the gaze of others a vague accusation for not having been one?

I do not feel a particular embarrassment today for not having been a more active opponent to Communism. How could you ask that of anyone? In a totalitarian country, where the government controls everything, one cannot live without making compromises. It simply does not exist. This is why I am wary of rash judgements about people in totalitarian countries. The choices one has are rarely clear-cut. You never ask yourself: should I choose good or evil? Should I betray my conscience or remain faithful to it? You imperceptibly adapt to a mode of being because the people who hold power, the ruling authorities, ask you to, because the media incite you to and because everybody else is doing so. You have to be able to step outside that world to realize that you are caught in a trap.

Vaclav Havel spoke incisively of this: the perversity of Communist regimes is that there is no 'them' on one side and 'us' on the other—'them' being the oppressors and 'us' being the victims of oppression anticipating the moment when we can liberate ourselves. Everybody participates, because it's our life and there is no other. It seems easy to imagine another attitude once dissidence became possible. But as long as there is none . . . And there is none, because the first to speak out is sent to prison or to the camps and the discordant voice disappears. Terror, if it is absolute, can be very effective.

During that first long period of totalitarianism, before the dissidents, before the 'thaw', it was impossible to imagine another life. The great majority of people chose—but once again, was there a choice?—to live here and now and, hence, to adapt. However, there were different degrees of adaptation which were decisive in our eyes. All cats were not uniformly grey in the totalitarian dark. When you went to 'mass' organization meetings (of your district, of your job, of your age group) without protesting, when you voted along with everybody, or participated in public demonstrations, you stayed on one side of the line. When you took your Party membership card, you went across to the other. Those were the people who had sold out, who had opted to forsake themselves, to submit a step more than absolutely necessary just to get ahead in their careers more quickly and to benefit from material advantages (in the 1950s, no one joined the Party out of inner conviction). We had utter contempt for such people. Everyone adapted to the situation, but the distinction between the 'strict minimum' and 'zeal' was something we felt very strongly about.

This inner complicity, this corruption of the soul is what seems to me, upon reflection, to be a particularly detestable feature of totalitarian regimes. At the time, what bothered us most were the shortages. It was an ongoing everyday affair. We would all go out in the morning with a shopping bag, not knowing what we would fill it with. Everything was so rare that you'd buy a product when you found it, not when you needed it. You'd go looking for onions, find nails and buy them. Hence the immense prestige of people coming (or returning) from Europe where you could find everything all the time. I remember our joy when someone would bring us if nothing else but a couple of rolls of toilet paper!

Friends, books and trips

How did you personally adapt to the situation? You explained how you got around censorship in the choice of your studies, but didn't you have the feeling of constantly falling back on avoidance strategies to get by?

To tell the truth, what mattered to me most was not the public sphere, university or journalism, but the private sphere, friendship and the life of the mind. I was living in a milieu of theatre people, poets and painters and I participated in their projects. They were young people of great talent. And it pleases me today to mention them by name, even if they don't mean anything to you. There were two outstanding directors, Willy Tsankov and Leon Daniel—I was especially friendly with the latter. There were theatre actors like Ivan Andonov, and poets such as Christo Fotev and Ivan Teofilov. Most of all there were the painters—Vessa Vassileva, Tochko Panayotov and my dear friend Nitcheto, Nikolai Nikov, who died since. And there were many others, including my best friend at the time, Sacho Bachkov, an unpredictable artistic character who dabbled in boxing and journalism. He was the son of a great Bulgarian illustrator who died a few years before I met him and he had inherited a black Mercedes from his father— it was an unheard-of distinction in Bulgaria!

It was a very lively time in the theatre world. These friends would stage classic plays with a contemporary resonance or take advantage of a momentary 'thaw' to show somewhat more subversive plays denouncing the ills of contemporary society. We were always playing with the limits of censorship; the borderline between what was tolerated and what was forbidden was always shifting. I am not talking only about politics in the narrow sense: many, remarkable formal inventions could also attract the ire of censors.

Did you talk about politics with your friends from time to time?

Only in relation to art, never directly. To question the decisions of the supreme power was unthinkable—we may as well have protested against rainy or sunny weather. It was almost considered distasteful if someone did so. The Communist regime had reached such a pitch of perfection that it seemed natural and, therefore, immutable. As a result, I was set against politics. And I was not alone. In fact, the overall effect of living under Communism was to turn us into staunch opponents not of Communism but of politics; it spawned generations of people who eliminated anything of political import from their horizons. In the most active way possible, we were intent on staying inactive.

On the other hand, talking of ways to deal with political constraints was totally accepted. For writers, the situation was difficult, because one is obliged to produce statements and theses when using language. But painters and actors, in spite of the canons of socialist realism, could also find themselves practising a form of passive dissidence, becoming exiles in their own country not so much by fighting the regime as by seeking the most honest way possible, in the circumstances of their time, to accomplish their vocation—namely, imbuing life with meaning and beauty.

After the fall of Communism, I read memoirs about that group of friends, published in Bulgaria. Each had the same sense of our group being a small island of freedom where true values were cherished, where we talked about human beings and God, about the meaning of life and of the absurd, about good and evil. Once we had raised an impenetrable barrier against the purely political world, we could go far with all the rest. And we did so in interminable conversations that lasted well into the night, and in drinking bouts that went on until the wee hours of the morning and that ended with us endlessly walking each other home. But this bubble could burst at the slightest contact with reality, and that's what eventually happened in the lives of my friends who stayed in Bulgaria. Often, only the warmth of human relationships was preserved—it was much greater than what I later found in France. But this is surely due to the Balkans—not Communism.

But isn't the experience you're describing common to all young people in their twenties: the intense, open discussions, the feeling of discovering the world together, without yet knowing where you're going? What additional intensity, in your opinion, came from living under a totalitarian regime?

There are always, in potential, as many gifted people in every society. Why do certain periods seem to be especially propitious to the blossoming of talent? Because the social context is supportive and not obstructive. In Bulgaria, as elsewhere in the 'socialist' world, a movement began emerging around 1960 that expressed itself less in artistic output than in the liveliness of its intellectual activity. The timid liberalization that came at the time of the Khrushchev 'thaw' awakened hopes. Gifted men and women eagerly set out to make up for lost time, to open up to the world, to create. They would soon discover that their hopes were in vain. But, in those years, they constituted a highly talented milieu. I have never since seen such a dense concentration of talent and intelligence. No doubt the very fact that repression in the political sphere was maintained drove the greatest minds to focus their energy on artistic creation, even more so when the art form stood on the fringes of ideology, as was the case for painting. There was a musical explosion as well, with extraordinary Bulgarian conductors and musicians! For those who wished to distinguish themselves without choosing a career in the secret service or in the Party (which was practically the same thing, by the way), totalitarian society left few possibilities: sports, arts, mathematics . . . In hindsight, we formed a rather cultivated milieu.

What books did you have access to?

We had translations of Western novels, some in Bulgarian, many more in Russian. We could all read Russian, which broadened our horizons quite a bit. We could always read the great Russian literature of the nineteenth century—Gogol, Tolstoy, Dostoevsky and Chekhov—all of which I found fascinating. There were also the Russian poets of the early twentieth century or a novel written by Kafka that had just been translated or Faulkner or Hemingway. We could find the great philosophical works translated into Bulgarian before the war. What was missing most of all, in fact, was Western news but were we really missing that much?

In Literature and Its Theorists, *you mention that you had read Koestler's* Darkness at Noon. *How was that possible?*

Actually, I read an English theatrical adaptation of Koestler's book by an author whose name I cannot recall. I knew a Communist English couple — a rare species indeed! — who were invited as professors to an English school in Sofia. I had become friends with them (all Western foreigners attracted us, even if they were Communists — we didn't have much of a choice), and they'd lend me books in English. One of them was an anthology of Pulitzer prize-winning plays between 1939 and 1959, and the play adapted from the Koestler novel was included in the volume. I was really impressed by it. I had never read a book that put Communism into question that radically. I had read the Khrushchev Report, of course. But literature like this, that questioned the Communist project itself, as Koestler did, was obviously not accessible to us. As for Orwell, with whom I felt close, I discovered him much later when I was in France.

Before coming to France, had you been able to travel abroad?

Twice, in 1959 and in 1961. The first time, I went with my mother to see my brother who was studying physics in Dubna, a scientific town near Moscow. We visited the small town where he lived as well as Moscow and Leningrad. It was a fascinating trip. I was 20 years old and I discovered Western painting on that occasion, through the superb collections of Dutch painters, the Impressionists, Matisse and others in Moscow and Leningrad. One of the very first things I ever wrote was a short essay on Gauguin, a painter I fell in love with.

In Moscow, I also met a few people in writers circles that were more active than in Bulgaria. I spent some time with Yevgeny Yevtushenko, who was at the height of his literary fame in the 'thaw' atmosphere of the day. The morning I met him, I remember he was going to read his poems in a stadium; there must have been 20,000 people there. Can you imagine 20,000 people — students, civil servants, factory-workers—coming to listen to poetry? I also met a woman who gave me texts in a form that was not yet called 'samizdat'; they included the poems by Pasternak that are found at the end of *Doctor Zhivago* (an unauthorized book) and unpublished poems by Akhmatova such as her 'Poem Without a Hero'.

Later, I went on a second trip, this time alone, to Poland, where I knew a Bulgarian who was studying cinema. It was in 1961. In Bulgaria, the ideological blackout was absolute, the political control, total: you really could not say a thing. But the Polish were already having what we considered astonishingly daring debates. We knew what was going on in Poland even though we couldn't read the language, because the Polish cultural service in Sofia had undertaken the task of disseminating a summary of events in Poland to Bulgarian intellectuals. They mimeographed a newsletter featuring translated texts of Polish dissidents, Leszek Kolakowski and others. The newsletter was sent free of charge to all members of the Writers Union, the Painters Union, the Journalist Union and so forth. These texts were a breath of freedom to us.

You may be wondering why I am referring to all these professional organizations. They have no real equivalent in France but, in Bulgaria, they were very important. Such organizations served ideological purposes but, at the same time, it was very useful to belong to them—they had holiday retreats in the country and club restaurants in Sofia where you could hear the latest gossip; they could lend you money at very low interest rates, and so on. These were typical institutions in our world! And they may very well account for my lack of enthusiasm for similar French literary and artistic organizations.

When you went to Poland, did you feel like you were 'going to Europe' even though the country was part of the same Communist world?

tzvetan todorov

The world I discovered in central Europe was somewhat different from the one I knew in the Balkans. I took the night train to Poland and stopped during the day in a different city each time: Belgrade, Budapest and (on the way back) Bucharest. Belgrade and Bucharest resembled Sofia and impressed me less than Budapest which was already a 'European' city. It gave you a hint of what Europe was like: the old city of Buda, the bridges over the Danube, the spacious cafes, the restaurants with their polite waiters, so very unlike the ones in our Bulgarian greasy spoons. On my only day there, I also went to the museum. I remember it had a Bruegel — another discovery for me.

Finally, I arrived in Poland. I knew enough Polish to read easy texts — the newspaper, even a novel by Brandys (whom I met 30 years later in Paris). Most of the time, I slept in a university campus in Warsaw. I was amazed at the beauty of Krakow. And then, from there, I went to Auschwitz. Later I spent a lot of time thinking about the concentration camps and I wonder why I felt the need to go there then. Because it really was a need — I thought that something essential for humanity had occurred there. I had to see for myself what was left of it. Obviously, the museum was set up to serve the propaganda and historical outlook that the Communists wanted to impose . . . But that was not what impressed me at the time — it was the mountains of glasses, hair and shoes.

Was the genocide perpetrated by the Nazis an important subject in Bulgaria?

No, it was a marginal subject, treated very discreetly! No comparison with France in the nineties, when it became the event of the century. The foundational event for us was Stalingrad, the incarnation of the Red Army's victory over the hideous Nazi beast. But there was no talk of Jews . . . not even in Auschwitz, for that matter. In the context of the museum that is now situated there, the former permanent barracks are dedicated to each of the nationalities deported to Auschwitz. There's a Russian pavilion, a French, a Belgian — and a Jewish pavilion, as one among others. Communist propaganda tried to avoid focusing on the Jewish identity of the dead who were considered 'victims of Nazism'. Our current outlook is so different that we have a hard time remembering the outlook before. Even at Nuremberg, the Jewish genocide occupied a marginal place. The main charge was 'crimes against peace', not crimes against humanity.

Leaving Bulgaria

Was it as a result of these trips that you began thinking of leaving Bulgaria?

The project of leaving Bulgaria did not figure in the picture I had of a life filled with studies, work and short trips. It came from an opportunity, and, because it was possible, it became desirable. Otherwise, it was too far away, too inaccessible and, most of all, too beautiful for consideration—to dream of going to Paris was like dreaming of going to paradise! I was not about to delude myself with illusions of that sort.

I owe the opportunity I had to my family. My father had a sister who, in 1945, was in Austria where she had lived during the war. She was a foreigner there and, at that point in time, such displaced persons were asked where they wanted to go. The choice for my aunt was to return to Bulgaria or go to a 'third country'. She wisely chose the latter. I remember they offered her the option of going to

Australia, Argentina or Canada. These were the three countries that were opening their doors to refugees after the Second World War because they were new, under-populated countries. For us, in Sofia, imagine how exotic it was! We all wondered what we would have done in her shoes. My aunt chose Canada. She was a pharmacist; she had to work for two years as a nurse in the Far North before settling in Toronto where she was able to practise her original profession and save a fair amount of money. Since she was single, she wrote to all her brothers and sisters who had stayed in Bulgaria offering to financially support each one of their children for a year in the foreign country of their choice.

That was a very generous offer!

What a generous and wonderful aunt she was! I am forever grateful to her. I see in her act a fine example of family solidarity which is transmitted from generation to generation. It also exemplifies the high esteem that this milieu of 'good' Bulgarian families had for education — in short, the 'values' of a particular society. Here's a tradition that makes sense! It was because my aunt — like my father and their brother — had been sent abroad (to 'Europe'!) by her father for a year that she wanted to offer the same possibility to the next generation. I am the only one who took advantage of the offer, even though we were six cousins. I was the youngest; the others were already wrapped up in their lives and their careers. I was just out of university so leaving for a year, well, yes, it suited me just fine!

Next, the choice of place was narrowed down. There was not a moment of hesitation: it was Paris. But you'd be mistaken if you thought I was attracted by structuralism, Roland Barthes or Jean-Paul Sartre. I knew nothing about any of that. For me, Paris evoked Impressionist paintings, a few movies and songs. I adored Édith Piaf, not Roland Barthes!

One of the rare French artists I had seen on stage was Yves Montand. He came to Bulgaria and I loved his show. He was an accomplished artist—I still think so. He took the art of music-hall singing to the pitch of perfection. He was just finishing a major tour in Eastern Europe and his concert was announced in Sofia. There must have been several concerts, otherwise all of the tickets would have been given out to members of the politburo and their friends. In this case, tickets were put up for sale. So, the evening before, at nine o'clock, we got in line at the ticket booths, ready to wait all night; we talked, took turns, ate sandwiches. The next day we bought tickets and there we were, that night, in Sofia's most prestigious auditorium. The curtain went up and this tall, handsome man, wearing a brown shirt and brown pants came running onto the stage and threw himself straight away into a typically French song. My memory of him is intact to this day. It was absolutely splendid. I still hum his songs from that period and, whenever I have the occasion on a radio show, I ask them to play *Les Grands Boulevards*. That was the quintessence of France to me. Why did I want to come to Paris? Because of the *Grands Boulevards*.

Of course, there was something disturbing about the fact that Yves Montand and Simone Signoret had taken a pronounced stand in favour of the Communist Party. It put a dampener on the picture. It was hard for us to understand how such wonderful people could have been won over Communism. They had actually chosen it, without being forced. How strange!

So your fascination for France had nothing to do with literature?

I knew little contemporary literature and no contemporary essayists or scholars at all. The desire for Paris was nurtured, on the other hand, by several mediators, foremost among them a friend, 10 years older than me, who was later killed in a plane crash. He was a lawyer in the provinces, nicknamed Karata, and he had one of the most brilliant minds I've ever known, filled with deep despair at the same time. Even though he had never left his native Bulgaria, he knew French culture and Parisian life remarkably well, including the physical layout of the city (he had a Métro map on the wall of his office). To him, Paris represented freedom and culture — the acme of the European spirit.

My father, on the other hand, who had gone to Germany in the same way, may not have been so pleased with my decision. But he didn't say anything. My father spoke German and had no connection whatsoever with France. Unlike Germany, France did not have a strong image for Bulgarians at the time. But I was attracted by neither politics nor economics but by culture, art and beauty. And France had all that.

Thereafter, we had to find someone in France who would send an affidavit certifying that I would have a place to stay so that I could ask for my visa. That was my father's job. He had met a French professor during a stay in Bulgaria. Finally, came the most serious obstacle: getting a passport. A passport was a privilege — in all totalitarian countries, not only in Bulgaria.

Didn't you have one to go to Moscow and Warsaw?

Going to a 'brother country' was easy. No one, on the other hand, went to France! But foolhardily I said to myself, 'Might as well give it a try.' I submitted a request and received no response for a long time so I resubmitted it and along came a refusal. There were other people who were much more set on leaving than I was. The artist Christo, for example, told me he crossed the border hiding on a train. He was much more motivated than I was; he hated Bulgaria so — including my circle, which he saw as overly compromising, smiley and submissive. He was much more rebellious by nature than I am. I was not the kind of person who would cross the border illegally. So I went to the Ministry of the Interior and asked for an appointment with the Minister.

It was as simple as that?

It wasn't very difficult. The possibility of meeting with a minister was one of the remnants of a generous project, as was the principle of equality between men and women that allowed women to work on roads or in the mines, or the gratuity of education and healthcare. The minister had reception hours for this purpose. You registered and waited. A few weeks later, I was called in. I entered a waiting room, sat down alongside other people, mostly very tense-looking women. Elderly women in Bulgaria, particularly from the lower classes, resembled veiled women, with big black headscarves and worn faces that gave them a distressed look. They were probably there to beg for the release of their brothers, husbands or sons from the many camps still thriving in Bulgaria. My turn came and I found myself facing a General, dressed in civilian clothes, who did not particularly impress me. (I don't know why, but people never intimidate me.) I explained my case. Our meeting only lasted three minutes because he immediately said to me: 'It's very simple. Permission to leave the country was denied because your request was made through private channels. It must be formulated by an institution, a university, for example.' And that was that. I left and three weeks later, I had my passport.

Interestingly, I was speaking to some people in Greece recently who were telling me that they do not see themselves as West Europeans because people in the West keep to rules and principles and do not take the 'personal factor' into consideration as they do. It is not a matter of corruption but of taking the particular individual into account. The abstract rule exists, to be sure, but, even when it is against you, you can always try to discuss the issue with representatives of the government and—who knows?—maybe the problem can be worked out. This possibility of personal interaction is what people from the Balkans find lacking at times in the rather cold world of Western regulations. I would even say that this impersonal manner in interpersonal contacts is the main criticism we make against 'Westerners'. And this is so even in relationships between individuals (never mind encounters with the administration!). To return to the minister I met with: he was probably also in charge of the camps but he did not see any inconvenience in my living abroad for a year. So I went to look for my former professors and the university assigned me a fictive 'specialized mission without expenses'.

You can see the extent to which the departure was a complex construction and not within everyone's reach. It grew out of the conjunction of a variety of factors: my aunt living abroad, the fact that my father knew some well-disposed people in ›Paris, that I myself had the incredible nerve to go straight to the top for permission, something that I would never have dared to do if I didn't come from a certain milieu—if, precisely, I had been a lowly peasant from the Danube.

Once you obtained your passport, didn't it ever occur to you, say, even when you got on the train, that you were leaving for good or at any rate for much longer than the intended year?

Not once. I had no intention whatsoever of becoming an exile. I cared too much about my friends, about human relationships in general. At the age of 24, I was part of a tightly knitted social fabric like I've never known since. I've spoken about the artistic and professional circles, but I was also involved, on a more intimate level, in very intense wonderful friendships. Then there was my love life, even if it was not, I admit, very satisfying. I was shy and the girls I fell in love with did not pay any attention to me, so I suffered in my own little corner. Anyway, it was all very engrossing. It was not easy for me to tear myself away from it all to go live in Paris by myself. I only made up my mind to go in the end because everyone envied me. I knew that it was fantastic to be able to go to Paris, but it was also painful. I loved my friends. That was life to me. The occasion to leave deprived me of my life.

No doubt, everyone feels this divide around that age, the impression that some day you will have to choose between 'life' and 'work'. In reality, it's an illusion. First of all, you don't have the choice; everyone is obliged to work one day or another. Moreover, work ultimately becomes 'life'. In the best of cases, a 'sublimation' occurs and the vital energy is redirected into a recognized, useful public activity. Nevertheless, it happens that this moment is perceived as a rupture. For me, it was particularly violent because the break coincided with a change of country. I was leaving the protective environment of my family and the comfort of my habits to enter the professional world. The change could hardly have been gradual. It was symbolized by this train: one person got on it in Sofia in the early afternoon, another got off two days later in Paris. This added a tragic dimension— I had to abandon what was most precious to me for the sake of some vague, ill-defined ideal. I took comfort in the fact that I was coming to Paris for only a year and would therefore have the advantages of both worlds! I held on to this conviction for quite some time.

I realize as I am speaking that the separation from my friends weighed more on me than the separation from my parents even though we got on pretty well. I had very few conflicts with my father about my behaviour. He was an authoritarian man on the outside, but tolerant with his children. Moreover, I shared with him an interest in the history of literature; we had even co-authored an article.

Regarding my mother—not only was I very attached to her, I also admired her, more than my father. Her life was filled with her love and caring for her family, for her children, her husband, a sister who was a painter and led a somewhat bohemian lifestyle and a few friends. I never saw her do a single selfish thing; her joys were through the others. I do not remember her raising her voice. To me, she embodied the ideal not so much of a wife or companion—the young girls with whom I fell in love did not resemble her—but of an affectionate, generous human being, devoid of ostentation or resentment. Yet the separation from my parents did not cause me much sorrow, despite our good relationship, or perhaps precisely because of it. I was sure of their love and could take it with me anywhere.

I left in April 1963 because I got my visa at that time and my father said to me: 'You have your passport, you have your visa, don't wait a single day. Staying until September is out of the question. Everything could change between now and then. Leave for Paris right away.'

Bulgaria, a closed chapter?

How long was it before you returned to Bulgaria?

I didn't go back until 1981, 18 years after my departure. I did not want to go back. I kept having this recurrent dream in which I went to Bulgaria and couldn't come back afterwards; it was my nightmare, literally and figuratively. I have since found out that many immigrants have the same nightmare. And it wasn't pure fantasy. There were Bulgarians who went back and were not allowed out again. They had become suspects, infected by the germ of Western decadence and grown contagious. I also thought of Georgi Markov, the famous Bulgarian dissident who had found refuge in London before being murdered by the Bulgarian secret police who used an umbrella to inject him with a highly toxic poison. Admittedly Markov was politically active and I was not. Let us keep in mind that, during this period, the cold war continued with renewed vigour and the so-called 'peaceful coexistence' was an empty phrase. This period lasted until the mid-eighties, roughly until Gorbachev.

Under Brezhnev and in Bulgaria under Zhivkov (who remained in power until the end), what was known as a 'period of stagnation' was, in fact, a time of malicious totalitarianism, with the State ready to steal, plunder, murder, imprison and scornfully disregard laws and borders.

Nonetheless, you went back to Bulgaria in 1981 before the fall of Zhivkov. In what circumstances?

Going there on a private trip was out of the question for me. I was invited to a conference that was held in Sofia so I went as part of the French delegation. This official framework was supposed to protect me. I wasn't going as a Bulgarian—I had my French passport and a Bulgarian visa. I had also taken the precaution of marrying the woman with whom I was living—in case she would have to arouse public attention to get me out of the Bulgarian prisons.

I could feel the rapid beating of my heart when we arrived at the airport in Sofia. We had to go through a security check, in a kind of booth. I handed my passport over to the officer dressed in a military uniform. He held onto it for a moment and then said: 'So, Tzvetan, you have been gone for a long time?' Not only had he used the familiar form of address and my first name, but the content of the question was unrelated to Customs. I humbly answered him, having immediately stepped back into my Bulgarian self: one does not contradict a member of the Militia. He continued, 'And what are you doing in France?' We were alone in the booth. All of a sudden, his telephone rang. He picked it up, said 'yes' three times, hung up and handed back my passport, stamped, without a word. Such shifts from rudeness to servility were quite characteristic of official relations in the totalitarian world. There must have been a camera monitoring the booth. My arrival had been announced for a long time; this officer had not been informed of it unlike his superior who was following everything on camera.

The 10 days passed (slowly). I was continually on my guard and did not feel at ease. I could not see the Bulgarians from the outside; I saw myself in them and got together with my old companions again. At the same time, my destiny had taken such a different turn that we did not belong to the same world any more. I gave my presentation at the conference (on the image of Bulgarians in France, later published in *The Morals of History*) and, when the time came for audience questions, a woman stood up and sharply attacked my talk with totally crazy arguments. What I had just said had to be demolished. Either she was sent to do so or she was overdoing it to attract attention to herself and earn a quicker promotion. The ideological combat was still in full swing.

The last day, I went to the airport with a heavy heart. My parents were there, in tears. I passed through the different barriers but I did not feel reassured until the plane was off the ground. Besides, I had made my return flight arrangements with Air France. I wanted to find myself in France as soon as I got onto the plane.

It's a reflex that many exiles or immigrants have. I'm thinking in particular of Algerians I know.

Yes, totalitarian countries are not the only countries to disregard the individual's rights and establish the rule of the arbitrary.

After that visit, I went back to Bulgaria, but not often and always for a very short time. Once or twice on the occasion of public events. In 1988, I went to receive a doctorate *honoris causa*. I had hesitated about accepting it. After all, it was an honorific distinction awarded by the university of a totalitarian country. However, those who had obtained it for me were fighting within the university for its liberalization and wanted to use this ceremony as a symbol and a weapon in their struggle. My father was very moved. I also went back for a conference on the French Revolution. I think it was in 1989, in any case some time before the fall of the regime. I encountered for the first time a new generation of Bulgarian students, much more brazen in their speech than we had even been. They were no longer strangled by fear all the time.

Added to these rare official occasions, were the strictly private family visits. Twice I brought my French family with me, once before my parents' death, once after. I wanted them to get to know this part of my existence a little. For a time, I returned regularly to visit my parents who were getting older and sicker and who could no longer come to Paris. My father died in my arms. The family with whom he was living and who were taking care of him warned me that he was in critical condition. I got onto a plane immediately. My father smiled at me and, as if he were reassured by my presence, surrendered to his death throes. He breathed his last breath two days later. I was alone with him at that moment. I closed his eyes, fixed his jaw so it wouldn't open. Then his body was washed and dressed. He was handsome. He was 92 years old and had just published a book of souvenirs.

Bulgaria is a chapter that, in my public life, is closed. Today, I feel a bit ashamed to say this but it's true. I don't feel much concern about Bulgaria's destiny. I'm much more interested in France's, obviously, and even of the United States'. At times, my detachment is held against me in Bulgaria; they predict that, sooner or later, I will feel the need to come back to my 'roots'. I don't think so. That's the way people are: they uproot themselves from their parents' family and attach themselves to their own children. My 'roots' are my children and they are French. And the idea that I owe something to Bulgaria for what it gave me is alien to me. I have debts only to people and these I try to honour.

I am not in Bulgaria but Bulgaria is still in me. It is certainly responsible for a good part of my choices, my affiliations, my temperament, etc.

Do you feel that you've chosen your destiny or that you were subjected to outside constraints?

Schopenhauer says somewhere that the individual can do what he wants but he doesn't choose to want what he wants. My being chooses my actions, but who chooses my being? Starting from what I am, yes, I can indeed exercise freedom. But I am not free to be what I am. Freedom of will exists, but it is exercised in relation to a pre-existing given, not in a vacuum.

What forms the human being remains to be seen. It is not a given definition once and for all.

Certainly. The being in itself changes because it is not made of a substance apart. Our life makes us what we are, and we make our life: both are true. Our nature is only a first custom, Pascal said. This is not true for the species, but it is for the person. Yet this raises another question: what explains the difference between two human beings that everything in the objective world brings closer? Why did Christo suffer more at the time from the lack of freedom than I did? And even closer still: what is the source of the difference in destiny between Christo and his brother Anani, a theatre actor, who stayed in Bulgaria? Georgi Balabanov, a Bulgarian director who also works in France, shot an interesting film about the two brothers some years ago (aired on French TV). It shows how their lives took very different turns but does not answer my question. Where does their difference come from?

What forged Christo's revolt and drove him with such force to leave, while his brother remained? Is this difference related to their childhood, to their professions, to the differences in age?

Did I myself freely choose to come to France, to practise this line of work rather than another? In one sense, I did, in another, I didn't. In any case, the search for an ultimate cause always comes up against a persistent mystery. This is where explanations reach their limit; beyond this, all one can do is observe the facts. This is why I do not believe in scientism and total determinism; I do not think that individual behaviour can be exhaustively explained by its causes. If we could, the human species would not be qualitatively different from any other, and I believe that it is.

Which does not mean that one should give up looking for the causes.

No. We can pinpoint the mystery and dissipate it somewhat. It is even our duty to take this search as far as possible, knowing all along that we will never fully attain our goal, keeping in mind this 'never', this limit that we will come up against sooner or later. And that is called human freedom. Freedom does not mean a lack of determination but, rather, the possibility of overcoming determinations.

Was there ever a point before you left Bulgaria when you felt that the compromises were becoming too hard to make?

My working life in Bulgaria didn't last long enough; I was too young when I left. That's why I have nothing really spectacular to confess. If I had stayed longer, there would have been that many more compromises. It was circumstances that enabled me to escape such a destiny.

Do you think you could have become an apparatchik?

tzvetan todorov

I think I would have been more like my brother. He had a brilliant career as a physicist, without entering the Party or being politically active. He became a member of the Academy of Science in Bulgaria. That was a tenable position, although admittedly easier to maintain in the fields of science, math or physics. In the humanities, the situation was trickier; it would have required something of a balancing act. But it was not impossible; after all, I think that Dinekov, the professor I mentioned who specialized in folklore, and even my father managed to do so. I'm not talking about refusing to compromise altogether. Holding to such a maximalist position would have quickly led you to the outer fringes of society, and made a vagabond or a delinquent of you.

What would I have become if I had stayed? Would I be the same person today or someone else? The question reminds me of Henry James' short story 'The Jolly Corner' in which a man returns to his country after spending 35 years abroad and wonders what his life might have been like had he not left. One night, he meets his double, a ghost . . .

Was doing the 'strict minimum' a tenable option over the long run? How did your old friends cope, for example? And, first of all, have you kept in touch with any of them?

Not much. One left for Sweden, another for Canada. We speak on the phone from time to time. I began relationships with a few people in Bulgaria after I left, in particular, the poet Blaga Dimitrova and the essayist Tontcho Jetchev, now dead. I arranged to have his essay 'The Myth of Ulysses' translated into French. He was a very endearing man, a man who perfectly illustrated the kind of human warmth that I sometimes miss here. But, generally speaking, the ties have weakened. When people don't see each other for years, their references are no longer the same and the common ground they once shared becomes too remote.

a closed chapter

My old friends—those who stayed—may not have changed much, but I have and the relationship cannot stay intact. I was thinking about this question again when I saw the movie about Christo and his brother Anani. Some members of the same group to which I belonged appear in it. They were still going to the same restaurants, still having the same conversations 30 years later! It was as if the past had replaced the future. At the beginning of the sixties, we were 20 or 25 years old and we could dream. For many of them, life had slipped by in this way, between hope and expectation, without anything ever happening. It's a bit like the character in another Henry James short story, 'The Beast in the Jungle', who spends his life waiting for his real life to start. I'm not saying that they are of lesser value as human beings. Maybe we are the ones who are wandering aimlessly, with our many activities, our public honours, our travels to every corner of the earth. But I cannot help thinking that, over there, a human potential was never fulfilled and that it is totalitarianism that is responsible for this huge waste.

People got mired in Bulgaria; they sank into alcohol. There was an awful lot of drinking going on. Alcohol is a common form of anaesthesia under totalitarianism. I wasn't far from going down that road myself. During my last years in Bulgaria, I was drunk nearly every night. The next day all I needed was a small glass to put me back into that same state of floating and feeling carefree, irresponsible, indifferent. Male comradeship encouraged this kind of life.

Is alcohol linked to Communism or is it a Slavic tropism, as the cliché would have it?

Alcoholics are to be found under every regime but there is form of drunkenness that seems to me to be more specifically related to Communism, to the need to flee the asphyxiation, the confinement and the impression that, sooner or later, you will always come up against a wall. The outside corruption, we later realized, is a form of pollution. Like in a Third World country but with industrialization to boot. Everywhere there was coal and steel polluting enormously. Nature was corrupted. In the same way, the nature of human beings ended up being corrupted. You had to resign yourself to live a pent-up life. Christo detested this. He could not even put up with his art professors, who were high-level instructors, because he felt the stifling atmosphere everywhere. To accept to live in such a pent-up atmosphere for a long time, one needs either a calm (not to say docile) temperament or a lot of luck . . .

In a certain sense, I chose the easy way out. I left Bulgaria.

2. From Poetry to Structures

A passion for literature – The elders – Roland Barthes, the grain of a voice – Science of literature – Narrative art – Revolutionizing education

A passion for literature

CATHERINE PORTEVIN: *In Bulgaria, you opted for formal analyses of literature to escape, as far as possible, the ideological pressure of the regime, but was this an activity that was deliberately separated from your love for literature or, on the contrary, did it enrich it? Did you conceive of this exercise as pure technique, with the real proximity to literature reserved to a separate sphere, like the piano tuner who also loves Bach might conceive of his work?*

TZVETAN TODOROV: Both were part of the same movement. The formal analysis was nothing but a convenient way of moving towards an understanding of what moved me in literary texts.

The immediate contact with literature has always been a true passion for me, as far back as I can remember. I devoured novels, plays, tales, poetry—I read much more poetry in Bulgaria than I have read since, particularly Russian poetry. I especially loved the early twentieth-century Russian poet Alexandr Blok who wrote about despair, mad love, lost love and bitter wisdom. It suited the soul of an 18- or 20-year-old teenager. I can still recite:

Noch'. Ulica. Fonar'. Apteka.

I wrote a text about him, about a hundred pages long, which has stayed in manuscript form. I wanted—already—to embrace life and work together, in a way not very different from how I proceed today when approaching the work of a writer such as Benjamin Constant or Vassily Grossman.

When I went to Leningrad, I made a pilgrimage to Blok's grave from where I took a little earth and carefully wrapped it in a piece of paper. I also went to see his house. The building was badly maintained and filthy; it was hard for me to imagine that such a sublime poet had lived there. I climbed a sinister-looking stairway to the fourth floor, paid my respects in front of the door to his apartment and left.

You see, I really love literature! The great works of literature seem to me to be above all else. I have never really changed my mind on the matter: as an activity of the mind, I set literature above philosophy and science. The thinking in literature can be as intense and as sharp, but it speaks to everyone and it spans the centuries. And not only does literature thereby contribute to our understanding of the world, but also adds beauty to it and thus makes it a better world. I really believe, although I have no way of proving it, that humankind is much happier with literature than it would be without.

But how can one turn this passion into a profession? I quickly realized that I was not made to be a poet or a novelist, even though I must have made some vague attempts at writing rhyming verses or stories when I was in high school. I had to find another path. Which? I didn't know. I groped in two directions. I tried my hand at literary essays, at writing short poetic texts, like prose poems. I also set out to understand how a literary work is made and how it works—an erudite undertaking that would fall within the framework of a scientific enterprise. This is the avenue I followed.

My choice was over-determined by the prevailing ideology that pressed me to flee debates of ideas and seek an approach that sidestepped them; and by the aspiration for rigorous knowledge to help penetrate the innermost being of literature. My passion for literature and my passion for understanding were joined in this choice.

So you arrived one morning in April 1963 in Paris with all these desires and questions. On whose doors did you knock?

I had obtained the equivalent of a Master's degree in Sofia. So I already had some knowledge of the history of European, Russian and Slavic literatures. All of this was useful but somewhat too factual — merely an accumulation of information. It was at that point that my years of real learning began. I think that's the way it goes for all students, at least in the humanities. University serves as a preliminary selection: you prove you are able to pass exams but you haven't actually learnt anything. True learning is a much more active process and involves working on your own. I consider university studies today, somewhat paradoxically, as both pointless in terms of the content that is absorbed and crucial in terms of the maturation they generate. The same goes for our youthful admirations which are both futile and necessary.

What I was looking for was a conceptual framework. When approaching a literary work, you are immediately dealing with words and sentences. This language substance is the object of a science: linguistics. I had already heard of it in Bulgaria. A series of Russian compendia published translations of texts by contemporary linguists, post Saussure. Among them were essays by the Danish linguist Hjelmslev that impressed us a lot at the time. Influenced by early Wittgenstein and by Carnap's logical positivism, his texts astounded us by their scientific rigour and logic. But this accumulation of knowledge remained piecemeal and unclear in my mind. The enthusiasm was there, but we did not know where to go with it.

I arrived in Paris in April, certain that I would be there for a year. So I was eager to take advantage of the situation and absorb as much as I could. Classes didn't start until the fall which meant that I had time between April and September to get myself oriented. But, as you know, the higher education system in France (the country of Descartes) is far from offering a clear, rational structure to the foreign student, not even perhaps to the French students. Between the École normale supérieure, the Sorbonne, the École pratique des hautes études and the Collège de France, I had a hard time finding my way.

What I would have called the subject I was interested in was the theory of literature or the study of literary forms or stylistics. I went to the Sorbonne — then the only university in Paris — and looked at the curriculum. There was no field called stylistics. The closest thing to it were courses concentrating on the study of Corneille or Marivaux or some other author's style. I was clearly not a Corneille or Marivaux specialist; I had never even studied French literature. I knew Slavic literature.

My professors at the University of Sofia had written letters for me to give to their Parisian colleagues that were supposed to make the first contacts easier for me. I asked to meet the dean of the literature department — his name was Aymar, I believe, a Latinist who received me with icy courtesy. Stammering and probably making more mistakes in French than I usually do, I told him I was interested in literature, in literary theory and in stylistics in general. He looked at me as if I had come from another planet and told me that there was no such thing, that literature must be approached from an historic and national perspective. The dogmatism was different than the one that held sway in Sofia, but it was just as vigorous. Since French literature is visibly not your field of work, try Slavic literature, the dean suggested; we have many good specialists in the field.

I then turned to a tenured lecturer in Russian literature, Sophie Laffite, who kindly received me. We talked a little about Blok's work, which she knew well. But I did not want to write about Blok; I had not come to France for that! I mentioned, somewhat reluctantly, the idea of doing a thesis on 'the short story as a genre', taking as examples Russian texts by Gogol, Chekhov, etc. 'Yes, why not?' she replied. But I didn't feel motivated at all. I had the impression that I was knocking on the wrong doors. I began thinking that I would not find what I was looking for at university, but I didn't care—I was in Paris!

I must have written about my difficulties to my father who directed me to his colleagues, the librarians. It wasn't a bad idea since they are, theoretically, well informed. I spoke to Mademoiselle Malclès, Deputy Director of the Bibliothèque Nationale. She was a single women, not very young, who received me in her tidy apartment. She listened to me attentively and I sensed that that she was actually going to help me. 'I'm going to look around,' she gently reassured me. And two weeks later she wrote: 'I finally found something. One of my friends has a son who specializes in psychology. I know this might seem remote from your interests, but he knows the Parisian world well and all the new things that are happening.' Do you realize what a complicated course this was? How many obstacles stood in the path of a foreigner or, for that matter, of anyone who was not in on what was going on? And how many people could have had access to an intermediary as competent and benevolent as this lovely Mademoiselle Malclès? I am also amazed by the role fortune played: without these coincidences, my professional and, thereafter my existential, engagement would have been different.

I went to Saint-Cloud to meet the man. As a freshly arrived Bulgarian immigrant, it was a terrifying journey. I remember my host well. In less than five minutes, he understood what I was looking for and told me, 'I know just the man for you. Gérard Genette. He is a senior lecturer at the Sorbonne and he has the same peculiar ideas as you.' Two days later, I met Genette in a dim corridor in what was then the Psychology Institute on rue Serpente where he was doing some practical work for I don't know which professor.

At the time, he had only published an article or two. He was a rather reserved man—we were unlike one another in this respect—but he was someone genuine. I never sensed the slightest pretence in him. We talked for about 20 minutes and we got on. I can still picture the way he looked then. He was 33, I was 24. Already slightly bald, he was wrapped in a green mac and drove an odd-looking car (at least to my Bulgarian eyes). He was assiduously reading books on twins because his wife was expecting a pair and they were somewhat worried about it. Like any self-respecting intellectual, he started with theory. We talked about one thing and another and then he suggested that I come, at the beginning of the school term, to Roland Barthes' seminary, in the sixth section of the École des hautes études, adding 'That's where "we" meet.' (We addressed each other at the time using the formal *vous* and did not switch to the informal *tu* until 1968!) It was the very first time I had heard Barthes' name mentioned. I really knew nothing about anything. Maybe I had heard of Sartre—and I'm not even sure about that.

So chance and the grapevine brought you to Barthes even though he had already published Mythologies, *which had attracted a lot of attention.*

Mythologies and *Writing Degree Zero*. But I had just arrived from Sofia and the least you could say is that the Paris intellectual milieu was hardly an open book to me.

During the first months of my stay in Paris, I also met a young Belgian researcher, Nicolas Ruwet, with whom I got on well. He had a great passion for music, which he had reluctantly given up as a profession to concentrate instead on linguistics. He was simultaneously shy to the point of awkwardness and very warm-hearted. He acted in ways that did not conform to the mould imposed on young students by the French university system. He had just finished translating into French Jakobson's collection of texts entitled *Essais de linguistique générale*; I think the book was not even out then. He introduced me into his circle of friends, students and novice researchers, none of whom were of French origin. There were a few Belgians, such as Pierre Smith, an Africanist, Lucien Sebag, a philosopher and anthropologist born in Tunisia and several others. The following year I went to live with them in a quaint hotel, the Louis XV, on rue de Seine. Thanks to Ruwet, I also discovered such great masters of cinema as Fritz Lang, Raoul Walsh, Otto Preminger and Joseph Losey. In strictly professional terms, I learnt about Lévi-Strauss, Jakobson and Lacan—gods to this small group. These companions, of my generation or a little older, are dead today: Ruwet and Smith died in 2001; Sebag, who left me his room and moved into another in the same hotel, shot himself in the head shortly after my arrival.

I had to wait until September to enrol in Barthes' class. At the same time, I found some other courses that interested me in varying degrees. André Martinet, a professor at the Sorbonne, mainly known for having engaged in a debate with

Jakobson, was giving a course on general linguistics as well as a seminar at the École pratique des hautes études on 'connotation' — secondary meanings. It had a connection with literature, so I went. I also attended Émile Benveniste's classes at the Collège de France.

I enrolled in a few other classes at the Institut Henri-Poincaré, where linguists were taught mathematical logic, set theories and the theory of probability. Shortly after, I published an article entitled 'Mathematical Procedures in Literary Studies' or something of the sort. I wouldn't dare read it again.

The title is admittedly puzzling! But where did your taste for science come from?

Not for science but for the scientific spirit. I was looking for rigour and precision, which I thought would be the way to enhance comprehension. Since language has a structure, I needed to know what it was and, to do so, I had to possess the right tools. I know this may seem ridiculous, but there was nothing preposterous about the impulse behind this enterprise. We live in a knowledge-worshipping world and I was affected by pressure from it. It is not that I reject knowledge today, but I will insist more on the fact that knowledge can take different roads: that of analytical science, to be sure, but also of the arts and even of social practices. In his letters to me, my brother, a professional mathematician, did not hide his condescendence; he must have thought that my mathematical inclinations were not very serious, which was probably true! For his part, he had a passion for poetry: mathematicians consider it only natural to come onto our ground. All the same, I think that my interest in the 'sciences' has left me with a certain discipline of the mind — at least, I hope it has.

But, ultimately, these courses did not take up much of my time. Having settled down in Paris and understood that university studies would not be of much interest to me, I decided to spend my days in the library. I got a card for the library at the Sorbonne. I would take bus number 84 and rush into the library first thing in the morning. At noon, I'd grab a quick bite at the nearby university restaurant before returning to the library and not coming out until closing time at 6 p.m. I was devouring books, compensating for the Bulgarian years of famine (especially the Western authors). I read everything that fell into my hands: literary studies, theories of literature, great essays. Starting with a few reference works I had read in Bulgaria—German authors such as Kayser, Spitzer and Auerbach—I read the works to which they referred, and so on. And then there were the journals. I read in French, English, German and Russian—quite a number of available works!

That was how I discovered Victor Erlich's Russian formalism, the first monograph on the subject, and it interested me more than the others. What the Russian formalists had done was really fascinating! They had demonstrated great inner freedom and true open-mindedness while choosing a precise angle of approach. Their unquestionable merit consisted in discovering new continents, so to speak, within literary studies and the literary work itself; not limiting themselves to the ideas conveyed by the work, the life of the author or character prototypes, but asking themselves how it is made. Eichenbaum had entitled one of his revolutionary articles 'How Gogol's Overcoat is Made', playing on the similarity between the tailor's craft and the critic's, the latter also capable of showing us how the 'overcoat' is made. Then Shklovski wrote 'How Don Quixote is Made'. They wanted to get inside the production workshop. I had the impression of a real discovery, and I was not alone in seeing a curtain rising and revealing a world that no one knew existed until then.

And yet the Russian formalists were not a completely new discovery for you; you mentioned that your father had their books in his library in Bulgaria.

Only a few. I lacked the overall picture. It is Erlich's book that brought home to me how very interesting their work was. The formalists were the starting point of my very first book, a compendium of their writings titled *Théorie de la littérature*.

I had talked about it with my friend Genette, who suggested the idea of publishing a selection of texts. It was in 1964, a short time after my arrival. Genette told me that he knew some people who might be interested and took me to the dimly lit offices of Éditions du Seuil on 27 rue Jacob. In one of them sat two men, facing each other and looking bored. Genette introduced me and I gave them my pitch. It was Marcelin Pleynet, Chief Editor of the journal *Tel Quel*, and Philippe Sollers, Director of the 'Tel Quel' collection. Both of them were nice, especially Sollers, a talkative man and a real charmer. He was enthusiastic about what I was bringing and so he published formalist texts in the journal that were 40 to 50 years old but still innovative. That was when I signed my first French publishing contract. It was pretty foolhardy on my part, when I think of it, since my French was still rather shaky. In fact, I had to enlist the help of a few charming female students with a faultless command of French, after persuading them of the nobility of the task!

Was Jakobson also a formalist?

Yes, but he stood somewhat apart because he was a linguist, whereas most of the formalists were not. Shklovski, Tomashevski, Eichenbaum, Tynianov and Propp all focused on literature, more specifically on prose. I was drawn to that aspect of things and learnt more from them than from Jakobson.

Shklovski came to Paris at some point during that period when I would get together from time to time with the *Tel Quel* group; it must have been in 1966. We had set up a meeting, which I went to with Jean-Pierre Faye, who was on the jour-

tzvetan todorov

nal's editorial committee at the time. I was to play the role of interpreter. Only, Shklovski was escorted by two watchdogs: on one side was his wife, who looked like a fearsome Russian baba; on the other, a man who introduced himself as the official translator and who was obviously from the KGB. Shklovski, a small bald man with a sharp mind, spoke to us of memories, 40 or 50 years old, that he had probably repeated hundreds of times, delighted to see that these Parisians were interested in stories from his youth. But the watchdogs did not let us have a minute alone with him.

The elders

You did not learn only by yourself in libraries, did you? What were the key encounters that influenced your development during this period?

Of all those whom I got to know at the time, three men stand out: Émile Benveniste, Roman Jakobson and Roland Barthes.

I attended Benveniste's classes on general linguistics for several years at the Collège de France and the École pratique des hautes études. He spoke so slowly, that you could write everything down without recourse to shorthand. He was remarkably clear and always interesting; we had the impression that we were penetrating the mysteries of language. His was a serene thinking grounded in immense erudition. There were only six or seven of us in his class at the time. After *Problems in General Linguistics* was published by Gallimard in 1966, he became something of a public success. This was due in part to the wave that bore structuralism; his book was published at the same time as Foucault's *The Order of*

Things and a few other titles in Pierre Nora's new 'Bibliothèque des sciences humaines' collection. As a result, this difficult volume became a bestseller and some 40,000 copies sold in a season: people were scrambling for copies. At dinner parties Benveniste was on everybody's lips and everyone swore by him. Of course, it was a typically Parisian phenomenon that did not correspond to any real interest. I don't think anyone actually read it. Yet, he had introduced a new outlook on facts of language, notably on everything he called 'enunciation', that is, the traces left inside a linguistic message by the context in which it was produced, by the person who speaks and by the time and place of speech. In this way, he embedded grammar in living experience. I had a real admiration for him, a man who seemed to live on another planet. He was small and very near-sighted. He gave the impression of not seeing anything around him; he would come in with his books and papers and step into another realm, that of Science and Knowledge.

A couple of years later, I got to know him personally. By then he'd had a heart attack which resulted in aphasia. He had no family aside from a sister, also single. I helped her find a place where he could be treated. I made my car and myself available to her, and we visited all kinds of rest homes that provided medical care around Paris until we found the right one. I went to see him regularly at the time. It was a moving experience: he couldn't speak but he understood everything. I'd tell him about my interests of the moment and suddenly he'd light up and point to something insistently: his *Problems in General Linguistics*. I'd go get it and he'd open it to a specific page and show me the exact place where he had written on the subject. I was truly attached to him as a person.

To me, Benveniste was the example of a pure mind. He was someone who did not live in this world, who was entirely devoted to knowledge. I admire people like that, who I do not resemble in the least. I am not patient enough to accumulate information year after year before extracting a few conclusions set in stone.

You couldn't have followed his example?

Oh no! I had too much of an appetite for life. I couldn't breathe in such thin air. I wanted to get a taste of everything. This was already the case in Bulgaria where I was passionate about theatre, journalism, literature, friends and so on.

The other true scholar was Roman Jakobson. I met him through Ruwet, his translator. I asked Jakobson to write the preface to my compendium of formalist texts and he agreed. I had actually already seen him from a distance in Bulgaria; he came to Sofia a year before I left. His books were not available there and neither my fellow students nor I had read any of them but we understood that he was something of a star, someone out of the ordinary. His talk at the university came as a real surprise, not to say a revelation, to me. By then he had started his work on poetry, analysing poems in all languages in his own way. He called it 'poetry of grammar, grammar of poetry'. He applied the method in French, for example, to Baudelaire's 'Cats' in an essay co-authored with Lévi-Strauss. He wanted to show that the linguistic material — the phonetic, grammatical and rhythmic content, even the rhetorical figures and themes — of every accomplished poetic text were rigorously structured. From the distinctive features of phonemes to the poem in its entirety, everything had to 'correspond'.

That evening, in a packed auditorium at the University of Sofia, he analysed a poem by our national poet Botev, a young genius of mythical stature who wrote only 16 poems before dying at the age of 28, killed in the struggle for freedom against the Turks. Jakobson chose one of the poems that every Bulgarian child knows by heart and about which, in theory, he could teach us nothing. In an hour, he revealed this poem to us in an unsuspected light by examining the interplay of personal pronouns, verb tenses and other strictly linguistic categories. None of this meant anything precise to me then but I remember being dazzled. It was an example of what I was looking for, a way of putting the rigour of a scientific approach to bear on the comprehension of works.

If you never read Jakobson, where did his reputation come from? Had you heard of him from your professors?

I don't think so. It was more by word of mouth. Only one of my professors focused on the linguistic facet of literature and, of course, he was the one I found most interesting. But he would not have dared praise such an important Western figure as Jakobson; his own interests set him sufficiently apart as it is. This professor, Yanakiev, specialized in Bulgarian versification and, incidentally, his work on the subject was one of the few books I took with me to Paris. It was a very solid, technical work that I thought would inevitably be useful to me. I haven't opened it since.

What did you like about Jakobson when you met him?

Jakobson was very different from Benveniste. He was an 'ardent lover' rather than an 'austere scholar'. He was not the sort of person to have his 'head in the clouds'. He liked drinking vodka and always had a bountiful supply of stories and anecdotes to tell. His curiosity was boundless. In his field, his insatiable appetite ranged from phonetics to epic poetry, from Russian to Japanese. He had an indefatigable passion that I admired. At heart, he was interested in everything with a bearing on human discourse. Everything related to language, art, creativity, everything. He was an omnivorous scholar. I was lucky to meet a man with such generosity of mind. When he came to Paris—which happened quite often—he would stay in a hotel or at the home of Sylvia Lacan, the psychoanalyst's ex-wife. No sooner had he arrived than he was already telling me about a new exhibition or an extraordinary show that he had just seen, or about an article that had just been published, and I realized that, no matter how much of a Parisian I had become by then, I still lagged far behind him! He had a great capacity for wonderment, which is the first step towards knowledge. What attracted me to him was the way that the rigour of the scholar–linguist came together with the most intangible of all things: poetry, art and beauty.

Did you always speak French to each other?

We usually did, although we'd exchange a couple of words in Russian from time to time. He could switch from one language to the other with great ease. English, French and Russian were his three preferred languages and it happens that these were also the three I knew the best, aside from Bulgarian.

Later, I became a sort of editor for him. I contributed to the French editions of several of his books, selecting and organizing the texts, writing prefaces and descriptive notices, correcting translations. I didn't want everything he had written to stay buried in journals and specialized publications. Even though I don't think that everything in the world revolves around the making of a book, I derive real pleasure from participating in the production of this object, be it through writing or supervising. When possible, I chose the picture on the cover and the typographical layout of the texts. It's rather like the joy of a craftsman in overseeing the making of an object from A to Z.

You seem to have kept a distance from the other 'masters' who were exerting a strong influence on structuralist circles at the time – namely, Claude Lévi-Strauss and Jacques Lacan. Why?

tzvetan todorov

We were impressed by Lévi-Strauss. He had just published *The Savage Mind*, and rumour had it that the last chapter of the book put a definitive end to the match between Sartre and him, to his advantage. I believed the rumour without questioning: knowing nothing about Sartre's philosophy, its refutation eluded me all the more. Lévi-Strauss' work was characterized by clarity of reasoning, a firm stand in favour of rational knowledge and a constant movement back and forth between meticulous analyses of details and daring generalizations. Aside from these qualities, which are still valid today, he manifested a scientific ambition that went over well at the time but that puzzles me a little more today. There is, for example, the famous formula in his article 'The Structural Study of Myth', published in *Structural Anthropology*, which I find rather unintelligible. Judge for yourself:

$$Fx(a): Fy = Fx(b): F_{a-1}(y)$$

[If I'm not mistaken the formula is $(Fx(a):Fy(b)::(Fx):Fa-1(y)$]

It was supposed to represent the irreducible structure of myth! I was in admiration—I was not put off by the abstraction—but, ultimately, Lévi-Strauss' work dealt with the structures of kinship and myths and not literature, which was my centre of interest. I was never in close contact with him. I was introduced to him, I remember, at a reception in his laboratory but, unlike his friend Jakobson, he was a reserved man: he blushed and disappeared and consequently I did too. So the interchange was reduced to next to nothing. Years later, I devoted a somewhat critical study to him, which later became a chapter in *On Human Diversity*. I noted certain declarations of radical relativism or peremptory condemnations of the 'subject' which I believed went beyond what he actually thought. I sent him the article before publication; he did not react.

As for Lacan, he was not a bit shy; he was more of a seducer and a manipulator. I also met him through Jakobson, but I did not have the same admiration for him as I had for Lévi-Strauss. I was a diligent reader of Freud and was fascinated by problems of language, from another perspective, but Lacan's convoluted, pretentious style made me want to laugh. His admirers reminded me of members of a sect, wholly devoted to their guru. Lacan sought to be striking and seductive, not persuasive through rational arguments; he wanted to alienate his listener's will, not make his listener freer. At any rate, that was the impression he gave me, which explains why I wasn't attracted to him. To me, expressing myself with as much clarity as possible is a matter of ethics, of respect for the person whom I am addressing. In this way, I put the person on the same level as me, allowing him or her to respond and hence to become a speaking subject in the same capacity as I am. As a reader, I want to be able to challenge the authors I read, to ask them questions. Is what they say true? Is it valid? I insist on allowing my readers to do the same. The cult of obscurity?—no thanks.

My only personal encounter with Lacan took place thus. After we were introduced, he lavished compliments on me; to hear him, you'd have thought that he had dreamt of nothing other than meeting me. 'You deserve to be part of my inner circle,' he told me, 'you are not one of those fervent admirers who attend my seminar and don't understand a word I say. Come to my place tonight, at seven o'clock and we will talk about it.' Prompted by curiosity, and flattered, I knocked at his door at the agreed hour. He was a different man. He looked at me with disdain, as if he did not understand by what right I had allowed myself to come and bother him. It was a whole strategy of seduction and then rejection, to cause dependence. I left and never saw him in private again.

Roland Barthes, the grain of a voice

How about Roland Barthes? You've already told us by what tortuous path you eventually arrived at his seminar. What was your first contact with him like?

I met him in October 1963, in his seminar, which dealt, if I'm not mistaken, with fashion. Barthes had felt compelled to write a rather boring sociological thesis on the subject, which he may not even have defended since he had just been appointed Director of Studies at the École des hautes études. There were some people attending his seminar, but not many, about 20, I think, nothing like the crowds in the seventies. So it was easy to approach him. What happened in class was not really interesting. What's more, Barthes didn't talk about literature; at that point in his life, he had moved away from it, presumably for career reasons, since he had entered the CNRS and then the École des hautes études as a sociologist. His course was entitled 'Sociology and Semiology of Forms and Representations.'[1] Little by little, a group of younger researchers gathered around him; it was Barthes' first 'small seminar'. There was Genette, Christian Metz, Claude Bremond, Violette Morin and a few others, including André Glucksmann, a friend of mine at the time. The two of us put together the fourth issue of the journal *Communications*, our very first public manifestation, and, later, other issues as well.

That was the period when the terms 'semiology' and 'structuralism' came into vogue. We saw ourselves as semiologists, not as 'structuralists' even though we had a passion for 'structures'. The word 'semiology' appeared in a few prophetic pages in Saussure's *Course in General Linguistics*, where he maintained that language is only a system of signs among others, like the Morse code or a highway code. In itself, that may not sound very exciting to study but with Barthes, and around Barthes, we understood this project differently. All human behaviours are charged with meaning, and semiology would enable us to examine what each one signified and the various manners of signification.

Would I be wrong in saying that semiology saw meaning everywhere but paradoxically did not address it, since all its attention was focused on the production of meaning and not on the meaning itself?

It all depends on the semiologist you choose as an example. In Barthes' case, there was a bit of everything! He was not an easy person to figure out. First of all, he changed a lot. He had the ability to let himself be deeply influenced by his models. He did not imitate them so much as appropriate their discourse, but with greater eloquence. This was true for Sartre, Brecht, Lévi-Strauss and Lacan. The same went for authors younger than himself: the master would follow the exam-

---

1 There is no trace of this course in his biography; on the other hand he was appointed in 1962 Director of Studies in 'Sociology of signs, symbols and representations'. [Trans.]

ple of his disciples. He had a highly malleable mind and, like an octopus, he would envelop and absorb you, drawing the best out of you. Then he'd tire, rather quickly, and move on to something else, to another infatuation. This could be quite disconcerting to the disciple who had inspired him!

For me, Barthes' identity was more in his style than in the content of his statements. Those who became familiar with him by reading him could not know this. Taken separately, each one of his texts could participate in a kind of intellectual terrorism, bombarding the reader with dogmas. But Barthes himself was as removed and ironic a man as can be. So much so that he, who, in immediate contact, taught us to be wary of all forms of dogmatism, practised in his own way a certain intellectual terror. He had a fondness for well-put phrases which, in hindsight, may seem excessive if not downright ridiculous.

And yet, Barthes was also an exceptional man whom I will never forget. Even if today I do not subscribe to the content of his theses, I still feel a true love towards him and a sense of great recognition. What remains dear to me, when I think of him, is his attitude, his gestures, his smile, the grain of his voice.

To come back to literary studies: how did you feel about the confrontation in 1965 between Barthes and Raymond Picard over Racine, which many people saw as a new quarrel of the Ancients and the Moderns?

Indeed, it was Barthes' *On Racine* that triggered Picard's attack. I was close to Barthes at the time but the issues in this polemic seemed somewhat cloudy to me.

In certain respects, Barthes claimed to be heir to Lévi-Strauss and to structuralism, but Lévi-Strauss did not really recognize himself in Barthes. He was even somewhat uncomfortable with the whole thing: here was Barthes claiming to draw on him for inspiration when it is not impossible that Lévi-Strauss felt closer to Picard! As an example of a structural study on an artwork, Lévi-Strauss would cite Panofsky's work, which was systematic, to be sure, but mainly grounded in scholarship and anchored in history. He saw Barthes' approach to Racine as something of a Rorschach test applied to himself. Rather than focusing on the text itself, the critic essentially designates and analyses the impression the text has made on him. Lévi-Strauss was quite far from such an approach: he was looking for structures, not impressions. In the end, Barthes defended a right to interpretation in *On Racine* without claiming to grasp the truth of the text or Racine's intention. His was a rather psychoanalytic reading of the text; this outraged Picard who saw it as an arbitrary anachronism.

Personally, I felt closer in this debate to Lévi-Strauss. I tended to side with 'science' and what Barthes was positing was subjectivity, and that is not structuralist at all.

In his History of Structuralism, *François Dosse speaks about an 'undulating, and shimmering structuralism' in reference to Barthes, but also to you and Genette – though whether he meant it as a compliment or not is hard to tell.*

Genette and I were a little more rigid than Barthes. Barthes was elusive. There is a beautiful photograph of him writing a pseudo-mathematical equation on the blackboard, an equation of the signifier/signified type, not as intimidating as Lévi-Strauss', nonetheless . . . He's holding a piece of chalk in his hand and smiling, as if to inject a dose of mockery into his own gesture. To me, this picture depicts Barthes well. Unfortunately, books don't always get smiles across. It's a shame because he was continuously joking about his own constructs when in friendly company, as if he were saying, 'Signifier/signified, connotation/denota-

tion — we're not going to really take such terms seriously, are we?' The learned terminology was for the public. The last words he spoke to me, a few weeks before his
death, were in this same spirit. He had just published *Camera Lucida*. In the middle
of complex reflections on photography, there were 20 pages on his mother's death,
poignant pages full of love, like that found in the work of certain reserved authors
(I'm thinking of what Marcel Conche wrote about his wife's death and the pages
by Pierre Pachet on the same subject). I bumped into Barthes one evening at
François Flahault's and told him that those were the pages that had deeply moved
me when reading his book. He looked at me and replied, 'But of course you know,
my dear Tzvetan, that the book exists solely for these pages. The rest . . .'

On the political level, Barthes demonstrated a relative lack of concern, not to
say an absence, of responsibility. I never heard him make revolutionary statements and I was grateful to him for that. He, at least, did not expect Communism
to bring about a glorious future! But he could have had what appears to me today
to be an overly aestheticizing attitude to the world. Take, for instance, his famous
article in *Le Monde*, 'Alors la Chine?' ['Well, and China?'], penned after his 1974
visit to Mao's China. What had struck him was the sound of Pi-lin-Pi-kong, the
government campaign against both the Communist leader who had fallen out of
grace, Lin Piao ('lin') and the traditional sage Confucius ('kon'). Barthes said: [it]
'rings like a joyful sleigh-bell'. And this he wrote at the height of the Cultural
Revolution in China, when thousands — if not millions — of people were dying and
the concentration camps were brimming over with prisoners. His travel companions, Sollers, Pleynet, Julia Kristeva and François Wahl, shared to varying degrees
the fascination for Mao that prevailed in Paris at the time. They imagined China
to be the future of humanity, but not Barthes. He found Pi-lin-Pi-kong aesthetically
interesting and treated it as a piece of music.

This attitude reflects what he described as the 'neutral,' a term he liked very much. A neutral discourse escapes the obligation to assert, judge or take a stand. This is, after all, one of the defining characteristics of writers who propose rather than impose in their writings, unlike politicians or 'intellectuals'. I would agree with him that the right of a writer not to make political choices ought to be defended. Criticizing the obligation for writers to take a political stand, Albert Camus said that if Racine had lived in the twentieth century, he would have had to apologize for writing *Bérénice* instead of fighting against the revocation of the Edict of Nantes. Hence, Barthes' desire to avoid 'engagement'. However, he did not present himself solely as a writer; he was — by virtue of his public position — an intellectual and an educator. The pure writer does not do as much as he did. Can you imagine Rilke writing for *Le Monde* or teaching at the Collège de France? Barthes' vocabulary was ambiguous as well: when he told us that language is fascist, could he and did he want to empty the word of all political content?

This aesthetic relationship to the world was somewhat aristocratic. Which brings to mind what Maurice Nadeau writes in his memoirs about the first time he met Roland Barthes. It was in 1946 or 1947 and Barthes had just come out of the sanatorium where he had met a former resistance fighter, who had in turn spoken to Nadeau about him. 'You'll see,' he had said, 'he's an intellectual from a good family, who loves Michelet and doesn't understand a thing about Stalin or Trotsky.'

Barthes wasn't a philosopher; he was even quite intimidated by great dogmatic and peremptory discourses. Ultimately he managed to find a way that was really his own late in life, in the last five years, and from then on he no longer produced assertive discourses or taught lessons. His *The Pleasure of the Text* was still quite imbued by the ideology of the day, but his last works, like the pages I mentioned from *Camera Lucida* about his mother and his *Roland Barthes*, resonate with a unique voice all his own, a singular voice that, instead of bombarding you with convictions, brings to life a human being.

He was a complex but truly extrardinary person. As soon as you met him, you could see his great intelligence. Without having to spell things out, he understood, and he would immediately shoot back with a brilliant comment. He was also extremely simple, anything but a mandarin and truly generous with all the young people around him. He never spoke to me like a teacher to his student; I regarded him more as a benevolent elder. At the same time, he was someone who was rather difficult to live with. His homosexuality played a part, I think, in his melancholy. Moments of cruising for young boys would alternate with moments of extreme dignity and an orderly life with his mother. In conversation, he often gave you the impression that he was bored. It was terrible because he was friendly with us, and we admired him very much, and suddenly you'd see him looking sullen. He'd become sullen easily!

I was close to him mainly until 1967. Barthes, Sollers, Jacques Derrida and I often ate together. I don't think that we had remarkable conversations; for my part, I must have been afraid of seeming unworthy of the company. I felt a little paralysed. It did not last long. I left for a school year to the United States and, when I came back, it wasn't quite the same. Barthes had started his seminar with a new group. Our mini-generation was over.

Science of literature

In structuralism, François Dosse pits the mother figure, Barthes, against the strict father figure, Lacan. You, it would seem, opted for the mother. And so you found yourself with a family of like-minded people, composed of teachers and companions, a family that was in the forefront of the avant-garde. You had everything it took to feel stimulated, not to say elated by the grandeur of your ambitions.

They were so grand that I constructed a discourse at the time that I think was rather pretentious. I dismissed all the others for their vague impressionism, maintaining that what we were going to do was science!

This science of literature, or poetics, as I liked to call it, was going to define the constituent categories of literary discourse. Poetics is an analysis of the virtualities of literature, the categories of discourse which literary works are made of: it therefore becomes the laboratory in which one forges the instrument used to analyse one aspect of the text, the specifically verbal aspect. You can find a whole series of verbal, phonic and rhythmic properties implemented in a poem; levels of meaning are deployed that ancient rhetorics knew how to identify. This is true of the narrative genre as well, even though they are not as readily noticeable as in a poem—the reader is always faced with a complex organization of temporalities, viewpoints and narrative modalities. The very sequence of peripeteias obeys schemas that we find from one text to another. To better understand a work, it behoves us to become aware of this subtle architectonics. Such was the hypothesis that guided me at the time.

The role of poetics in literary studies can be compared, in certain respects, with that of philology, created in the nineteenth century, which teaches us all that is necessary to understand texts that are remote from us in time or in space. Philology afforded us a better grasp of the evolution of vocabulary, syntax and the historical context. Philology and poetics provide the reader with tools.

That is how you define poetics today, but at the time you had more 'totalizing' ambitions for it, if only by positing it as 'scientific'.

Neither Genette nor I conceived of poetics as supplanting the analysis of literary texts, as ousting all other approaches. We simply felt that there was a gap that needed to be filled: rhetorics had been forgotten, versification neglected, narrative techniques ignored. At school, we studied the circumstances around the writing of the work and the history of literature but never the text itself. Poetics did not have hegemonic pretensions, yet at that juncture in time there was good reason for us to give it priority. I quickly saw, however, that those who felt that we were intoxicated by the power of a commentary-producing machine greeted our interest in categories of literary discourse with reticence, not to say downright hostility. They criticized us for ignoring the specificity of the individual work, not realizing that we were actually proposing instruments that made it possible to describe this specificity. I have to admit, though, that some of what I wrote in those days must have seemed unpleasantly arrogant—a sign that my 'years of apprenticeship' were not over.

In your Introduction to Poetics, *one of the chapters reads like a veritable agenda, like a manifesto for this science of literature. It includes a particularly scathing note on education, which, 'for obvious ideological reasons', focuses on literature to the detriment of all other discourses. There is a very militant feel to it but exactly who was militating for what?*

It was clearly not political activism; I would even say that it was anti-political in a way. The framework of my 'combat' was narrow. The question was: how do I speak about literature? I felt that I was helping to introduce a perspective that had been missing in the French debate—even though it was not utterly original; after all it was that of Aristotle's *Poetics*, no more, no less. This 'combat' for poetics was fuelled by my knowledge of the Russian formalists. I might add that this small book, *Introduction to Poetics* (originally published in 1968 as a chapter in the collective volume *Qu'est-ce que le structuralisme*?), is my most widely distributed book to this day. It has been translated into about 20 languages and still sells well, probably because of its didactic, almost textbook character.

Yet you said that Genette and you did not see yourselves as structuralists.

It was a catchall term that could designate everything and anything. I strongly felt this imprecision at a 1966 conference at the Johns Hopkins University in Baltimore, which was probably perceived from the outside as structuralist. René Girard, who taught there, saw himself as a structuralist in his own way because his *Deceit, Desire and the Novel: Self and Other in Literary Structure* examined the structures of the novel, even though this had nothing to do with the content of other structuralist works of the time, such as Jakobson's. Girard invited a dozen of the 'talked about' Parisians and I happened to be among them. In reality, these people had next to nothing in common and, from today's standpoint, our gathering was rather comical. There was Barthes, Ruwet and myself (for 'Literature and Linguistics'); Lacan, who gave a performance (that attracted much attention) in an English rendered incomprehensible because of his thick French accent; philosophers such as Derrida who had just published a few sensational articles; Jean Hippolyte, a philosophy historian from another generation, translator of Hegel's *Phenomenology of Mind* and Lacan's friend; Lucien Goldmann, a Marxist sociologist of literature; Jean-Pierre Vernant, historian of Greek mentality, etc.

So you found out that you were all structuralists in the plane?

We hardly knew each other. Barthes and Ruwet aside, I was a friend of Derrida's who was rather recalcitrant to the American world at the time. After the conference, he and I visited New York. He already knew the city and I was dazzled by it. It would be hard to imagine a city more different from Sofia! The spirit of the city and its cosmopolitanism were a real discovery.

To return to our conference: this eclectic gathering was supposed to represent structuralism, the New Critique, the New Wave and who knows what else. Since then, I have always regarded the designation 'structuralism' as a ragbag. Foucault and Althusser were said to be great philosophers of structuralism, yet I could not see what I had in common with either of them; I didn't know them and I wasn't interested in them. The person I was close to was Genette—we shared the same material, almost technical, approach to literature. We had nothing to say about the death of the subject or about power, and Lacan's texts were not much help to either of us. What Genette achieved with 'Narrative Discourse: An Essay in Method' in *Figures III* represents, in my opinion, the culmination of part of the work we were doing during those years. It was published in 1972, a year after my own *The Fantastic, A Structural Approach to a Literary Genre* – another book that has been translated a lot, perhaps even read. In it, I gave a formal definition of the fantastic genre as characterized not so much by the appearance of the supernatural as by the hesitation of the character and the reader about whether they are confronted with a natural or a supernatural event. I also studied the narrative themes corresponding to this definition: 'I' themes and 'you' themes and so on.

Narrative art

True to your characteristic desire to understand, you needed to know 'How Gogol's Overcoat is Made'. Was discovering the secrets of the making of these works your way of loving them?

Narrative construction was indeed one of my main interests at the time, and it was the subject of much of my writing. Let me give you an example of the questions that interested me. I had noticed, while reading all sorts of narratives, that they were often structured around the tension between two orders. One of them concerns the temporal and causal sequence of events: this is the 'doing' aspect. The other is related to the growing comprehension we have of the same event or character: this is the 'being' aspect. In a whodunit, these two aspects take the form of two independent plot lines: on one side, there is the detective's investigation that proceeds over time; on the other, we keep coming back to the same point, to the same event, namely the initial murder, each time coming closer and closer to the truth. This tension can assume very different forms. In *The Quest for the Holy Grail*, the Knights of the Round Table are looking throughout their adventures for an object, the Grail; but there is also a different quest going on, a spiritual one, focused on the Grail's nature itself. I was interested in the different forms of interactions between the two; they enabled me to observe the logic of narrative development better.

I published several studies of this type, in literary rather than university journals, such as *Tel Quel* and *Critique*. I also studied the proliferation of narratives in *The Arabian Nights* and their different forms in *The Odyssey*. And with Barthes as my advisor, I prepared a graduate thesis, which I defended in 1966, on Laclos' *Dangerous Liaisons*. I studied the procedures of the epistolary novel (what does the presentation of the story through an exchange of letters bring to the novel) and, at the same time, the logic of the actions in which the characters are engaged: Valmont, Madame de Merteuil, Cécile, Dancény and the others. The twists and turns of the story all seemed to me to illustrate a few simple patterns.

During the same period, you also took an interest in 'indirect meanings' which was already a way to question meaning and not only form?

The conditions of meaning production could be more accurate. We are playing with indirect meanings all the time: we say one thing to get something else across, without the direct meaning disappearing. But how exactly do we proceed? I devoted a short book to the question, *Symbolism and Interpretation*, which provided an overall picture of the vast field of secondary meanings, whatever name we give them: allegory, symbol, suggestion, allusion, metaphor or irony. For example, I analysed the mechanism that triggers the interpretation, the search for an indirect meaning. There must be certain clues that alert us to the need to go beyond the apparent sense; contradiction, discontinuity and improbability often play this role. Elsewhere, I examined the nature of the segment that is interpreted: is it a word or a clause? And what form does the relationship between direct and indirect meaning take? Basically, in all of this, it was a matter of understanding the very process of understanding.

More generally I was interested in showing how literary forms emerge from language: I termed this relationship 'endogenesis', birth from within. The character and the action are an expansion of the word and the verb. Rhetorical figures become principles of narrative organization. Diderot said: 'The contrast of character is, in the composition of a drama, what antithesis is in discourse.'

Always this need to reveal structures, to find rules of functioning and classification.

You don't know how true that is, since the other type of work I took up during these first years of apprenticeship involved producing a synthesis of research in a field. My mind must do this kind of thing on its own while I'm busy doing something else, since such syntheses seem to come to me spontaneously, without much effort. I managed, in some way, to extract the central facts from my different readings in Russian, German, English, even in French. This was already the orientation of my contribution to *Communications* (8), then in my *Introduction to Poetics*, and, finally, in 1972, in the *Encyclopedic Dictionary of the Sciences of Language*, written with Oswald Ducrot who took care of the linguistics part.

Revolutionizing education

You seem to have pursued your education outside the confines of the university. Was the teaching of literature there of no interest to you?

I must admit I did not have a very high opinion of it. Firstly, I didn't think much of the content. I complained, as the formalists had already done, that we never talked about the texts themselves but only about the circumstances surrounding them: the author's biography, prototypes of the characters, loads of factual information that did not seem to make the meaning any clearer. And when we did talk about the text itself, it was only to paraphrase it with the addition of a few superlatives, such as 'deep', 'penetrating' or 'admirable'.

Secondly, on an institutional level, I found the model of an academic career that was offered rather oppressive. At the time, anyone who wanted to teach in university had to write a *thèse d'état* which took about 10 years, if not more. First, you needed to find an author to write about—only dead authors were authorized and most of them were already taken by other Ph.D. students! The thesis had to be a synthesis of knowledge, covering everything that could possibly be known about the author. All attention was focused on the scope of scholarship, none on conceptualization. This system forced you to work on one subject only for a very long time; in the best of cases, you became a professor when you were 45, first in the provinces and then, for the most hard-headed, at the Sorbonne.

The hierarchical pyramid was immutable. The Sorbonne was its centre and summit, since its professors reigned supreme over everything: they were in charge of the *agrégation* juries;[2] they had a decisive role in the appointment of professors; they controlled the publishing of book collections; much more. It was this mandarin pyramid that was partly dismantled in 1968. The candidates, especially the more ambitious, necessarily converged onto this centre or summit; coming under the protection of one of the Sorbonne's mandarins guaranteed the smooth development of their careers. This meant that the professors had to follow the progress of numerous students, which only added to an already heavy load of administrative tasks. It was difficult for them to work on new subjects; their work was often confined to handling already established situations. It is no accident that the best French historian of literature throughout that period was not a professor at the Sorbonne—I'm thinking of Paul Bénichou, of course, who was teaching in the United States and, that too, only part time so that he could devote himself to his research.

This system did not preclude the presence of some brilliant individuals. But even intellectually gifted professors ended up delivering a monotonous discourse due to the overwhelming charge of administrative and ceremonial duties. None of this appealed to me in the least. I was never interested in academic power; all I wanted was to progress on the path of knowledge, to understand literature better.

---

2 The highest competitive examination for teachers in France. [Trans.]

With the offhandedness of someone from the outside who did not go to the École normale (phew!) and who had not gone through the *agrégation* exam (phew! phew!), I had the feeling of being free. Some people must have thought me rather insolent; others, on the contrary, must have appreciated me for the same reason. I remember in particular a 10-day symposium in Cerisy on the teaching of literature that I organized in 1969 with Serge Doubrovsky where I must have looked rather odd, dressed as a hippie.

How about you? When you were a student at the Sorbonne, 15 years later, did you find the same spirit, more or less, that I've been describing?

Not exactly: stylistics, general linguistics, the 'literary theory' you were looking for was taught. I began my studies in 1979–80, the year of Sartre and Barthes' deaths. I enrolled in literature at the Sorbonne (Paris IV) in September 1981. I was more interested in linguistics than in literature, where the courses seemed to me to be quite boring. I studied Saussure, Trubetskoy, Jakobson, Chomsky's generative grammar, even Todorov and Genette! But I don't think Paris IV was the university where 'things' were really happening in those days. For my part, I also spent some time at Censier where I used to accompany a friend of mine and sit in on a couple of cinema courses. That's where I learnt what semiology was.

As for you, what were your ideas on the teaching of literature at that time? You mentioned the Cerisy conference in 1969: that was the same year as the creation of Vincennes, in which you participated. What kind of innovations were you advocating?

Vincennes opened its doors to students in January 1969. In the summer and fall of 1968, I was on the preparatory committee for the creation of the university, particularly its literature department. We tried to imagine what an education in literature could be like where one did not have to worry about the traditions dominating the profession. Thanks to a series of delegations of power (the minister Edgar Faure appointed Las Vergnas as Dean and so on, down to us), we found ourselves in the rather exceptional position of starting from scratch. We could invent anything! It was an exhilarating feeling. I was all for this type of revolution even though I suspected that prior traditions would ultimately reassert themselves to a certain extent.

We therefore built an entirely different programme. Centuries of tradition burst asunder; the names of authors no longer sufficed to define the subject of classes. Concepts, on the other hand, made a spectacular entrance. We studied literary genres: poetry, novel, theatre, but also the short story, the narrative, autobiography, diary, etc. We tackled literary currents as well — Symbolism, Romanticism, Naturalism. The different approaches became visible, like literature and psychoanalysis, literature and linguistics, literature and sociology, literature and philosophy, and multidisciplinary approaches were welcome. We devised an abstract grid with different types of approaches to the subject of literature. Subdivisions based on centuries seemed artificial to us; we were not against history but we didn't want to see everything through its lens. Instead of limiting ourselves to French literature, we preferred talking about 'French and general literature'. We decided against the adjective 'comparative' because it implied studying the national literature first and then undertaking a comparison, whereas we wanted to study literature — that's all, literature as such. When I think about this programme today, I can still feel the headiness of it. It's not hard to see the emerging danger of discourses on works supplanting the works themselves. In our defence, I would say that we were reacting to an extreme situation — the exclusive rule of empiricism. A state of balance between the two could only be established some time later.

When I say 'we', I'm thinking especially of Genette and I, but we weren't the only enthusiasts involved in this adventure. The atmosphere at the French department of Vincennes seemed good to me. Not everyone shared our ideas, of course;

besides, we were both outsiders in the department—Genette was working at the École des hautes études and I was at the CNRS—but they were given a warm welcome. Friendly relationships were developed with people who were following different paths—I'm thinking, in particular, of Jean-Pierre Richard, a very insightful critic and human being, and of Jean Verrier and Michel Deguy. There were also some very interesting students attending classes during those first years, people with unusual backgrounds and careers—nothing like a class of *normaliens*[3]—and, as a result, more stimulating.

Vincennes constituted a unique adventure in a creation *ex nihilo*, with no need to burden itself with precedents. In the aftermath of its creation, the journal *Poétique* was born, a forum for the expression of this new attitude towards literature. A funny tidbit: originally, the journal was subsidized by the Sorbonne! We had spoken with one of the Vice-Deans, Jean-Baptiste Duroselle, an historian, who found it amusing to stir up a little trouble amongst his literary colleagues. The journal was published by Éditions du Seuil, which provided us with a lot of support. It was directed by Genette and me, and for a while by Hélène Cixous but she did not really get involved in day-to-day affairs and shortly thereafter left the two of us alone.

Genette and I got on well with one another. We were more complementary than alike. I appreciated his intellectual rigour and his priceless sense of humour. He must have benefited from my boundless curiosity and my ease with human contacts. I was always commissioning articles and he was turning them away. I'd fling the doors wide open and approach everyone; he would select rigorously and close the doors again. During our 10 years of managing the journal together (in the seventies), we published many translations of authors from foreign countries

---

3 Students of the École normale supérieure. [Trans.]

as well as articles on subjects in fields other than poetics. We put out a series of special issues on a wide variety of subjects, such as 'Rhetoric and Philosophy,' 'Powers of Language,' 'The Realistic Discourse,' 'Popular Literature Genres,' 'Irony,' 'The Teaching of Literature' and 'The Theory of Reception in Germany'. At the time, we directed a collection of books at Seuil. There too, the working relationship with Genette was very pleasant and efficient.

I might add that *Poétique* was not merely a series of publications; it was also a network of professional relationships which quickly turned into friendships. Putting out a journal together with other people is, in this regard, a perfect pretext. Such friendships extended beyond the borders of France. I'm thinking, for example, of Peter Szondi, professor at the University of Berlin, a highly refined man whose fragility I had not perceived (he killed himself in Berlin in 1971); he had a remarkable knowledge of classical and modern literature, equally at ease in philosophy as in literary commentary. He was, above all, an open, warm-hearted and spiritual man. He listened to me with kindness during our walks in Berlin and in Paris, and would make brief, discreet remarks that allowed me elevate my sights a little.

There was also Paul Zumthor, a great medievalist and an equally engaging man. He laughed like a child and his generosity knew no limits. He wrote scholarly works but also novels and poems. He was always ready to take off on a new adventure of discovery. His tireless curiosity had led him, for example, to the very depths of Asia, Africa and America to study oral poetry; he spoke with contagious enthusiasm about anonymous singers as if they were international stars. He did not feel at ease in the French academic system either. Born in Switzerland, he taught mostly in the Netherlands and in Québec.

In these terms as well, the *Poétique* adventure was rewarding for me.

3. Criticism of Structuralism

Too much structure, not enough meaning! — The future of human sciences — Literary truth — Criticism at the service of meaning — Poetics, an embarrassing heritage? — Teaching French in school

Too much structure, not enough meaning!

CATHERINE PORTEVIN: *The ambition of semiology, leaning on linguistics, was to become an omnibus and unique discipline. How do you justify and judge this ambition today?*

TZVETAN TODOROV: It was an excessive ambition. There was a reason for it: everything signifies in the human world, that is perhaps its distinctive trait. And this has always been what interests me. I want to describe and comprehend the human condition under its different forms, to observe the human signature. All throughout their lives, human beings interpret the world and communicate with their fellow creatures. I have made my profession out of these constituent characteristics of the human being. I interpret the words and gestures of others; I act in my turn by means of language and I share my judgements with readers. Meaning is everywhere. However, to think that it should form a unique discipline with meaning as its subject is a giant step that I would hesitate to take today. International conferences on semiology still meet today, but one of the rare remaining pioneers of the

sixties to still bear the torch is my old friend Umberto Eco. (I can still see us danc-
ing all night long at the Paradiso club in Rimini. I don't think we ever had a conversation about semiology.)

I went to the first international congress in Milan in 1974 and I realized I was
not where I belonged. It quickly became clear to me that I would not gain much
from listening to a researcher holding forth on the highway code or kinship relations as a system of signs. If semiology tries to set itself up as a superhuman science, subsuming all others, then it makes no sense to me any more. I'm in favour
of making studies more interdisciplinary but that kind of unification seems barren
to me. If, on the other hand, the point is to enhance the awareness of researchers
to the dimension of meaning and interpretation that is present in all human activities, then the idea of semiology can play a positive role.

*Your place in the structuralist movement is definitely not easy to grasp. For example, you
were not a 'Jakobsonian' – you seem to have been more influenced by the man than by his
work.*

That's true. As I told you, I liked the man for his generosity of mind but I did not
admire everything in his work. I felt a little hesitant even then about his analyses
of poems based on his famous 'poetry of grammar' hypothesis. And I never felt
that same thrill as when I heard him analyse Botev's poem in Sofia. He had really
opened my eyes then; he had given me greater insight into the poem's meaning
which should, of course, always be the effect produced by literary commentaries.
But I found the analyses I read afterwards less convincing. They gave me the
impression of a vast display of resources producing rather slim results. Too much
structure, not enough meaning. All the machinery he set up did not reach the
poetical core. I'd read his analyses but his examination of the arrangement of

phonemes, rhythms, metaphors and grammatical categories in, say, Baudelaire's 'Cats' and 'Spleen' or in Du Bellay never furthered my grasp of their meaning. So what's the point? The demonstration illustrated nothing other than the demonstration itself; the motor was running idle. The means were in danger of becoming the end.

Much later, I came to understand another aspect of Jakobson's work: its place in the cultural and political context of its time. We must remember that Jakobson's ideas, formulated in his youth but to which he remained faithful (despite shifts in vocabulary) throughout his life, were those of the futurists, the poetic avant-garde of his day who also saw a continuity of ideas between their artistic revolution and the political revolution raging around them. It was no accident that the great Russian futurist Mayakovsky became the Soviet regime's bard; neither was it an accident, I might add, that the Italian futurist Marinetti was an admirer of Mussolini, instigator of the other totalitarianism. Jakobson himself spoke in his first texts in 1919 about the 'unity of fronts' between the Soviet deputies and the futurist poets. Later, he deplored the Soviet system's abuse of power but remained, at heart, quite close to the projects of his youth. Witness his total lack of reservation concerning the political engagements of Mayakovsky (admittedly, an old friend) and his closeness with the Aragon–Triolet couple (the lady, also an old friend). This can be partly explained by his theory of language and art — Jakobson conceived of language as an object; he left no room for subjects or values.

Are you suggesting that a totalizing ambition can become a totalitarian ideology or go hand in hand with it?

Let me be clear about this: Russian formalism, and subsequently structuralism, are not variants of totalitarianism. Totalitarianism is identifiable firstly by its monism, its refusal of distinctions. Formalism, on the other hand, sought to position itself outside the confines of ideology — which is already a distinction — and it established a multiplicity of forms and levels within the literary work itself. It defended the autonomy of literary art, whereas totalitarian thinking refuses all autonomy. Formalism is absolutely not an ideological dogmatism. Thus, it is not by accident that the formalists were persecuted by the Communist regime. When I mention the affinity between them, I'm speaking in terms of a global conceptual framework, certainly not in terms of the specific content of the doctrines. The relationship, if there is one, is to be situated on a more abstract level. The formalists defend a 'reifying' view of language and, in a certain way, of man, and the exclusion of the subject as well as of values; hence, at the same time, of morals and politics.

At what point did you put some distance between yourself and what we could call the 'structuralist ideology'?

It happened in several stages. There was a whole period during which I too was participating in this ideology without realizing it. After the 1972 publication of the *Encyclopedic Dictionary of the Sciences of Language*, which wrapped up a period for me, I was looking to broaden my horizons. On the one hand, I started to take an interest in non-literary texts. I worked with a psychiatrist on the written and spoken language of psychotics, I also studied genres of popular literature, such as riddles, witticisms and magic formulae. I observed how techniques used in literary works were also at work in other verbal productions. It was interesting but it was nothing more than a superficial extension of what I had been doing before.

On the other hand, I wanted to learn about the history of my area of study, reflections conducted in the past on signs, symbols and signification in art — a huge field. This led to *Theories of the Symbol* and a variety of other texts, such as a long introduction to Goethe's aesthetic writings. This was an historical work but of an unusual type since, instead of tracing the continuity of one tradition, I set out to study the most representative moments of several traditions. Ever since, I have stuck to this initial, and actually paradoxical, choice of a discontinuous history, focusing on the moments that seem to me to be the most significant and revealing.

How did this work on the history of your field, set forth in Theories of the Symbol, *drive you away from structuralism?*

When I broadened my horizons in this way, I lost the scientific convictions that were mine at an earlier stage. This historical perspective ended up strongly relativizing my prior 'science'.

The vast field that we designate by such terms as 'signification', 'representation', 'interpretation' or 'communication' has been approached throughout history from different angles, using highly varied terminologies, but the object itself has always remained the same. Logicians were not to be confused with grammarians, theologians with art thinkers, rhetoricians with specialists in hermeneutics. And let's not even talk of the philosophers who were another breed entirely. Each one stayed confined within his own discipline and vocabulary, even though the object was the same. I wanted to get these isolated discourses to communicate with each other. This seems to be one of my obsessions, perhaps related to moving from one country to the other. I am always looking to eliminate barriers, to cross borders and discover bridges between seemingly independent areas.

For this purpose, I immersed myself first in ancient thought from Aristotle to Saint Augustine (the latter's work was a real eye-opener); then in the history of ancient and recent rhetorics (I discovered this field that had disappeared in the nineteenth century, gradually replaced by literary history and textual analysis). I read aesthetic texts on imitation and beauty. This is how I became familiar with the thinking of German Romanticism which transformed our way of understanding art. It abandoned the perspective of imitation to situate art itself at the summit of human activities and regarded the work as an end in itself, thus opening the way to studying it as form and structure. A hundred years later, formalism and structuralism were the culmination of this choice.

The great principles that Jakobson sets forth in *Questions de Poétique* are a summary of the aesthetics first formulated by the German Romantics at the beginning of the nineteenth century, before being synthesized by Coleridge (who returned to England impregnated with the thinking of the Schlegel brothers and Schelling) and finally reshaped by Edgar Allan Poe. Poe transmitted this conception to Baudelaire, and it is not a coincidence that Baudelaire was Jakobson's great tutelary figure, alongside the Romantic poets and the Russian futurists. The Romantic aesthetic is posited, like Jakobson's, on the idea that, in poetry, language becomes an end unto itself, what Jakobson calls the 'poetic function'. Yet, just as disregarding this dimension of poetry would be regrettable, so reducing poetry to this is absurd. Bold minds are constantly being threatened by abusive generalizations.

I came to realize in this way the extent to which the structuralist approach—which until then I had perceived as the attainment of truth and not as one possible choice amongst others—was actually historically determined. That is why I can say today that *Theories of the Symbol* is a book that changed me.

Changed you or brought you to the breaking point?

Changed me. The years between 1972 and, let's say, 1979, were a period of unconscious mutation for me. It led me to a new approach in which language became a way to the world and meaning prevailed over form. Before then, my works focused on the powers of language and on literary forms, on the art of narrative and the varieties of symbol. After that, I found myself talking about ethics and politics, situating myself in an historical and anthropological perspective. But it was a gradual change, not a new start in the opposite direction. Today, people sometimes ask me how a former structuralist and semiologist can hold such different positions. My impression is of a change in direction, not a movement backwards. Maybe I can explain it by saying that our works of the period sometimes participated in a broad outlook, sometimes in a narrow one.

Meaning?

The narrow outlook, to me, consisted in pretending that in discourse there is nothing but discourse, that there is no significant relationship with the world. Whereas the broad outlook involves recognizing the presence of both the discourse (which a certain form of 'idealism' does not do) and the world. The narrow outlook says: there is no author, it is the language itself that is speaking, 'it' speaks. The broad outlook says: discourse imposes constraints on what will be said but, behind it, there is a subject expressing him or herself, a subject endowed with thought and will. This second version is still mine today.

In the sixties, I had the sense of starting from a deficiency. To my literary colleagues, as to philosophers or sociologists, discourse did not exist in its own right; it was considered a mere vehicle, totally passive and inert. In much the same way, the Platonic tradition refuses to see that discourse is a thing and not only a way to reach things, that it has its own laws, which are partly responsible for what is found in each utterance. In a comprehensible swing of the pendulum, structuralism reversed the tendency by entirely ignoring the world and the subject. At the end of *Mythologies,* Barthes went so far as to maintain that all social forms belong to a system of signs, and that, in reality, we are never dealing directly with the world but only with discourse. I did not really share this outlook, but on occasion I must have bowed to certain paradoxes, carried away by the rapture that radicalism brings. It is a real pleasure to make 'bold' statements: 'You think words designate things? Well, you're wrong! Words designate other words!' Declarations such as these gave us a heady feeling of intoxication.

That being said, the fact that language, discourse and the work's materiality itself were reintegrated into the realm of knowledge still seems to me to be a positive achievement. In a similar vein, my taste for examining systems, for precision in vocabulary or for making the implicit explicit are all legacies of my 'structuralist' period. It simply took me some time before I was able to distinguish between a certain rigour of thought and the objectivity of knowledge.

If you prefer, I remain interested in the structural analysis of texts, provided that it does not supplant every other approach; I am more wary of structuralist philosophy. 'Structural' is not equivalent to 'structuralist'.

The future of human sciences

You could have left it at that, becoming a practitioner who doesn't meddle with theory. Instead, you undertook a critique of structuralism which can be read in the chapter on Lévi-Strauss in On Human Diversity. *In it you raise theoretical objections, in particular to the exclusion of the subject. How did the nuances you just discussed turn into real grounds for a break with the structuralist movement?*

I saw a few intrinsic weaknesses in this movement and I was trying to overcome them.

The first concerns meaning. I've just discussed this in relation to Jakobson; I have not changed much since on this point. During this period, I was analysing texts by Henry James or Dostoyevsky, interrelating all levels of organization: plot, rhetorical figures and ideas. I was striving to attain a balance that was different from Jakobson's. In my work, form was subordinated to meaning. My goal was to interpret the thinking that unfolded in *Notes from Underground*.

The second has to do with values. Not the values of artworks—I still do not believe they can be measured—but the values that permeate human life and that we cannot *not* take into consideration. Inevitably, the critic's commentary participates in the world of values. It behoves human and social sciences to keep in mind that they are also moral and political sciences. Here, structuralism is of no help to us at all. But let's keep things straight: values are omnipresent in the object of enquiry, not in the enquiry itself. They are part of the ultimate goal; they form a horizon that should not be lost from sight. They are not a rule of investigation. To begin with, enquiry aspires to truth, first to the factual truth of adequation and then to the global truth of disclosure. Along the way, research must be free from moral supervision, free from worrying about profitability. You cannot seek truth properly when you know from the start that it must conform to what is right.

Finally, as you noted, structuralism ignores the subject with its freedom and therefore its responsibility. It is very interesting to have disclosed the constraints that come from language or from the art form itself, exercised alongside social and mental determinations, but that does not eliminate the individual's freedom— neither, as a result, does it eliminate the interest we can have for this individual. The structuralist temptation to study the work, and only the work, was bound to fail: the work is always overflowing on all sides. In practice, we are obliged to isolate segments or perspectives but it is dangerous to reify this practical necessity into a theoretical postulate.

The engagement of the subject in the object, of human beings in their works, which structuralism wanted to put aside, finds an odd illustration in some texts written at the time. I would like to come back to Lévi-Strauss for a moment. I do not think that the four volumes of *Mythologies*, the culmination of Lévi-Strauss' structural analysis of myth, will be read much in the future; if they are, it will be more as a collection of myths than as a science of myth (with the exception of the 'Finale' to the last volume, written in a different frame of mind). What people will continue to read, on the other hand, is *Sad Tropics*, a great book. It's a funny lesson! To its author, *Sad Tropics* was a digression, the book he wrote when he put his scientific work aside. Yet what a profound, wise and sad book it is, rich in knowledge and ideas! Is this not what the human sciences can do at their best? That is how knowledge progresses—if it does not engage its author utterly, it is nothing more than scholasticism. The one who knows must be put into question by his or her work. Let's take another example of a book that overturned our way of perceiving the world: Hannah Arendt wrote *Eichmann in Jerusalem* as a news article. But she became so totally engaged in it that she put into question, oh so painfully, her whole identity. That is what enabled her to transform our way of understanding Evil.

I'm always struck, when I'm on thesis juries, to see that the most interesting part of the work is often the introduction, where the author speaks in the first person and explains what prompted him or her to choose the subject. It's much more interesting than the body of the dissertation which is usually an exercise 'in the style of . . . '

Isn't this a literary view of the field, wherein the narrative is what constitutes human sciences?

I'm often baffled by this huge thing that is known as the 'human sciences' and which absorbs so much energy and funding, which is taught in universities and which spreads to research centres, symposia, missions and so on and which seems to feed on itself . . .

And you say that the human sciences involves telling stories! You're just being provocative!

That is not exactly what I'm saying. It is true that the narrative element is particularly effective (just think of Freud's famous case histories), although it is not indispensable. But, yes, I do think that the manner of writing is not a matter of indifference. This 'manner' includes the genre (narrative or not), the style, but also the place reserved for the author. From this point of view, human sciences are confronted with a formidable rival: literature. I wonder whether, on a precise topic, works in the human sciences have more to teach us than a novel by Balzac or one of Montaigne's essays. Personally, I find that they do not necessarily further our knowledge of the human condition any more than literature and they are so much less pleasant to read! I'm afraid that these endless streams of paper—theses, reports, communications— are doomed to immediate oblivion. The result is utterly different when the individual manages to be personally involved, to invest the knowledge of the world with his or her own particular experience. To be sure, such things cannot be forced and it is difficult to ask for funding for this.

Do you mean to say that knowledge and learning do not exist if they are not embodied? Aren't you defending a somewhat elitist stance by positing the superiority of literature in approaching the world?

No, that would be going too far. First of all, knowledge of nature exists, mainly in a way that is independent from the speaking subject. Knowledge of the human world is obviously not limited to literature. The best works in the human sciences share with literary works the characteristics I've just talked about but, in addition, their use of abstract language and the affirmative mode lends itself to rational discussion and the transmission of ideas. I am not out to replace scholars with novelists; I'm only calling attention to the fact that novelists may have a thing or two to teach us.

I am not an obscurantist. I want knowledge to progress, but I fear that we may not be cultivating the most appropriate form today for deepening and transmitting it. Eliminating subjectivity, value judgements and questions of meaning is a mistake. They need instead to be preserved and encouraged. But there is not a chance that my hopes will be answered. The CNRS, to take this emblematic example, is in the grips of a computer frenzy that reduces the work of human science researchers to summaries, key words and numbers — to a completely disembodied knowledge which is, between you and me, devoid of interest. This approach is based on the illusion that we can totally depersonalize research in this area.

This, for me, is a typical example of what I call 'scientistic' thinking, which tends to subordinate the end to the means. The computer is a wonderful instrument — who would deny it? But if it is the computer's capacities that direct the course of research, then we are facing an absurd situation. Our CNRS administrators would like to make sure that everything we do can be quantified and reduced to key words. They would have rejected *Sad Tropics* for not complying with their norms and asked its author to leave the organization! They refuse to understand that, in our field, the subject thinks and writes and that such activity cannot be reduced to numbers (not even to 'the number of publications in journals with editorial boards'). They look at us suspiciously if we do not ask for sizeable funds. What kind of research can one do without machines? If this continues for many years to come, the 'technicist' frenzy will end up stifling institutional research in human sciences. It is a pre-programmed form of self-destruction, the outcome of the rule of instrumental thinking.

Literary truth

Let us return to your thinking in the seventies. We often tend to explain intellectual devel-
opments a posteriori, as if they resulted from pure reasoning. That is what you have just
done! But, in concrete terms, what prompts changes in thinking? You have explained the
intellectual reasons behind your break with structuralism but by what means – readings,
encounters or events – was it consummated?

You're right. The reasoning comes after the fact. But the causes of inner changes
are difficult to identify because they escape our consciousness.

During those years, I had a few intellectual encounters in circles that were
sometimes distant from mine and that I can now say were crucial in changing me.
For example, in 1972, I spent a long evening in private with Isaiah Berlin, the great
historian of ideas, in his magnificent house in Oxford. I can still remember the

paintings that were hanging on his walls. He told me about his encounters with Akhmatova and Pasternak in Russia after the Second World War. He was an extraordinary conversationalist—I drank his words . . . and he kept on serving me vodka while he remained sober. I could not keep myself from admiring him. He did not try to influence me in the least; he was just himself, that is to say a fascinating person. His interests were far from poetics and semiotics, yet what he said about politics, history and human beings moved me deeply. I felt that I should no longer keep that part of me locked up. In retrospect, I think it was a good thing. It's good that another individual can get inside you and shatter your grids of interpretation of the world, so that you are compelled to forge new ones. If we are not able to be receptive to what's new and unexpected, and transform ourselves in relation to it, it means our minds have become petrified. The encounter with individuals throws pre-established categories into disarray. Human beings must prevail!

Ten years later, I had an encounter of the same nature with Paul Bénichou; my admiration for him drove me to rethink my work. We became friends, in spite of our age difference (Bénichou belonged to my father's generation). What was most striking about him at first was the scope of his knowledge: he had mastered three centuries of French literature history in depth, from the seventeenth to the nineteenth and, unlike other scholars, he knew how to integrate this knowledge in his fastidious thinking as a critical, modern humanist. He immersed himself in the past like nobody I know and, in his analyses, he questioned the authors of those days as if they were his contemporaries. His point of departure was always our common humanity. He also taught me, through the barely formulated advice he would give me, to leave behind the easy delights of polemics. His ideal was peace and he embodied it in his own life. He died recently, in May 2001, at the age of 93. I was really very moved to speak at his funeral.

In 1984, you published an interview with Paul Bénichou (reprinted later in Literature and Its Theorists), *which must not have been much to the liking of your friends at the review* Poétique?

Maybe not. Genette and I stepped down as directors of *Poétique* in 1979 because we felt that 10 years were enough and that it was time to make way for others. A few years later, I proposed this interview with Bénichou to the journal; it was refused. In it, we evoked the complementary nature of the various approaches to literature which posed no problem to me, personally. To get to the meaning of a work, you must analyse it from the inside but also situate it in a context which, in Bénichou's case, meant within the history of ideas. But this tolerance for history and for ideas apparently ran counter to *Poétique*'s editorial line which demanded that poetics supplant other approaches to works, not come in addition to them.

We can clearly see the line along which the break occurred – because there was definitely a break here – and that was on the question of truth and the question of values. In 1984, in Literature and Its Theorists (*which brings together texts published before*), *you have clearly left the confines of poetics, since you assert that 'literature is not only made of structures, but also of ideas and history' and that 'literature* [. . .] *is a discourse* [. . .] *that seeks truth and morality.'*

And it was a text on the idea of 'poetic truth' that was a catalyst in the final break with *Poétique* a few years after the Bénichou incident. I had submitted an essay on the subject to the journal, and it too was refused. In my study of Lessing's, T. S. Eliot's and Baudelaire's thoughts, I brought up precisely this relation that every text maintains with the outside world. It seemed indispensable to me to reassign a central place to this question now that we had compensated for the former lack of 'theory' and interest in literary technique. After this second refusal, I left the editorial board. It was a truly fundamental disagreement and I had to act on it. I also must say that the whole debate interested me less and less. The books and articles that were being mailed to me did not speak to me any more. It seemed to me that all they did was focus on the construction of the text, without raising their eyes and looking at the world. I realized that there was a dividing line between us. If I wanted to put my attention to bear on the truth or the values brought by literary texts, my place was no longer in the framework that I had contributed to establishing, that of poetics. I do not regret having done so.

My position had changed. But in what way? Our opinions are forged through contact with the world; if the latter changes, keeping them intact is absurd. Literary study, in fact the whole French intellectual context, is not the same in 2000 as it was in 1965. That's not all, of course—I must have changed as well. A different relationship had developed between my identity and my ideas, between my life and my profession.

You haven't answered the crux of my question. Is it legitimate to talk of truth when it comes to literature? At a time when people are dubious about the idea of looking for truth in human sciences, even in science itself, you are looking for it in literary texts! What do you mean by 'truth' and what made you choose this singular path?

Let's be clear about this. I do not claim to possess the truth, just the right to look for it. I maintain that this is a legitimate quest. Even at the height of my structuralist period, I never stopped thinking that it was possible to approach the truth and that trying to do so was a worthwhile task.

The word 'truth', you know as well as I do, has several senses—all of which are challenged today by a certain form of scepticism, relativism or perspectivism. The first sense is that of adequation, the relationship of exactitude between the discourse and what it designates. This is factual truth: the Russians won the battle of Stalingrad, not the Germans; Jews were killed in the gas chambers in Auschwitz. Contemporary sceptics contest even this type of truth. But so do totalitarian regimes, which is probably why they outrage me so. Under the Communist regime, truth was treated with contempt—scientific results (oh, those bourgeois biologists!) and historical facts were dismissed out of hand. It went so far as to erase from photographs the faces of Bolshevik dignitaries who had fallen from grace.

This characteristic of totalitarian regimes has been treated eloquently by Orwell in *1984* and by Raymond Aron in his beautiful preface to Max Weber's *Politics as a Vocation*. Whatever your doubts about the notion of truth might be, Aron explains, you cannot help asking yourself whether or not the Moscow trials were rigged, whether or not Trotsky was an agent of American imperialism. For someone like me who has spent a good part of my life in a world that denies the difference between truth and lies, this kind of 'epistemological doubt' is unacceptable. Here, the borderline between 'fact' and 'interpretation' is very clear.

One can grant you that this 'truth of adequation' exists and nevertheless contest a more general idea of truth: the truth, precisely, of an interpretation or of a doctrine. As for literature, what truth does it aspire to establish?

We clearly need another notion of truth for cases when we say, for example, that an history book successfully recreates the atmosphere of a period or that a philosopher's thoughts enhance our understanding of the human condition. I call this a truth of disclosure: a particular discourse or interpretation may not content itself with the exactitude of facts, but delve deeper to uncover the hidden meaning, to produce a picture that enables us to have a better grasp of certain events. It is clear that, from this point of view, no interpretation can be declared definitively true or the sole true interpretation; a new, even better one can always appear. But it is also clear that certain interpretations and certain thoughts seem to come closer to the truth, to delve more deeply than others.

This type of truth of disclosure is also within the reach of poets and novelists; it is even what we appreciate most in their writings, particularly with authors of past centuries. Ordinary readers read them not only to find factual information, to enjoy the local colour or to admire the narrative technique, but also to gain a better understanding of the human condition and, therefore, of their own lives. Read Flaubert's letters, the word 'truth' is never off his lips: 'I try to be as truthful as possible,' he keeps saying. Milan Kundera had an apt way of putting it: he said that the novel tries to reveal a hitherto unknown bit of existence—a possibility of the human being that we ignored before the novel revealed it to us. The novel is not merely this, of course; literature cannot be reduced to philosophy or science for it is also a source of entertainment, a mirror to current affairs, a play of the imaginary. But great literature is measured by its truth.

There was something good about the old term 'imitation' in that it recalled this link to the world. But it was also inappropriate in so far as literature does not copy the world—neither does painting, for that matter—and the term did not clearly evince this fact. The artist and writer do not depict the world directly, only their experience of the world. This is why, if the experience is mediocre and insignificant, the work will be too. Masterful technical skill will not be of much help. The force of experience, which is what counts here, is not to be conflated with the truth of adequation. A painter does not have to be 'realistic' to give us the impression that he or she has reached into the truth of the world: Cézanne's apples are no less true than Chardin's. The same goes for writers: the demand for truth does not prejudge the style of the work at all. Fantastic stories or marvellous tales describe events that have never occurred and will never occur but this does not prevent them from revealing something about the human condition and the way of the world.

How can this truth be measured? This time, you cannot go somewhere to check it out and documents serve no purpose. The only way it can be measured is indirectly, by observing the echo of a text. If it is persistent, then it is a sure sign that we are approaching the truth. If people have been reading Plato for 2,500 years, it is because he tells us something true about human beings. The proof that Baudelaire speaks the truth in his poems is that so many readers see themselves in them and learn them by heart. The measure of this truth is depth, not exactitude.

You are manifestly not an adept of the school of textual criticism known as 'deconstruction'.

Practitioners of deconstruction not only say that they've abandoned the idea of looking for truth (and I'm not even sure that they stay true to this agenda) but also challenge the idea of coherence in the thought of a writer or philosopher. On the other hand, they are sensitive to the blind spots, the hidden contradictions, the impossibility of systematizing thought.

Searching for contradictions, discrepancies and tensions may be a good starting point for interpreting someone's thinking, but one should not leave it at that. It is altogether too easy, not to say naive, to imagine that one can clearly see what the author ignored. How can this be true when dealing with powerful thinkers such as Plato, Descartes or Rousseau?

In the structuralist years, the École normale published a journal called *Cahiers pour l'analyse* – a digest of the methodological radicalism of the day. It devoted a special issue to 'L'Impensé de Rousseau' ('The Unthought Dimension in

Rousseau'), as if this was what was most important and most interesting in Rousseau's work. As for me, I compiled a small collection of studies on Rousseau and entitled it *Pensée de Rousseau* (*The Thinking of Rousseau*). It included articles by Victor Goldschmidt, Leo Strauss and others, who had taught me that you had to take the apparent inconsistencies as your starting point to discover the deep-seated coherence. It is rather presumptuous to believe that we can easily catch out somebody of Rousseau's calibre; it would be better to patiently try to understand why he says things that seem, at first sight, to contradict each other. This is, moreover, much harder to do.

The constant danger that threatens interpreters of authors from the past is a type of ethnocentrism of the present. We are all tempted to see in them the precursors of our own thinking today — when we are not arrogantly noting the 'unthought' dimension of their thinking, the inconsistencies and blind spots. But we learn nothing from giving in to this temptation; all we do is confirm our own convictions and reinforce our pride in our ability to embrace the other's thought and judge it. The real interest of these authors, as of distant cultures, resides precisely in the aspect of their thought that is irreducible to our own thinking, in the challenge that they address to us and the changes they provoke in us. Not because we imitate them but because we want to communicate with them.

Criticism at the service of meaning

Can we conclude from your evolution that, when one starts taking an interest in the world and in ideas, one loses interest in form and literary theory?

One is no longer interested in it for its own sake. In any case, it is no longer a source of passionate interest. And one needs to be motivated by passion and intense curiosity.

Having spent 10 years polishing the instrument, I had to use it. Or I would have been like a carpenter who makes a hammer and never strikes a single nail. But it is the nail that holds the house together, not the hammer! Such was the nature of the 'change in direction' that I took at that time and that seemed perfectly logical to me: it consisted in taking into consideration the work that we ourselves had accomplished. Since the instrument was ready, or improved at any rate, the moment had come to use it. Poetics as an instrument, yes; as the ultimate goal of research, no. Actually, what surprised me was the fact that others did not notice the change or did not want to take it into account. Hence, that I was not followed more than I was. I left *Poétique* and it continued to work the same areas it had for so long. My departure had no effect at all.

Trying to determine literary specificity strikes me today as a trivial activity. Like others, I was inspired by Jakobson's famous statement: 'What interests us is not literature but literariness' (in Russian, *literaturnost*: I think I must have been the one to come up with the French term for this, *littérarité*, since this is how I translated Jakobson's neologism in my anthology of the Russian formalists). Today, I see literary specificity as a question of history, not of language (the boundaries vary with time) and, in any case, I find it more interesting to concentrate on what is *also* literature rather than on what is *only* literature. I want to know literature, not literariness. What do I care about knowing the specificity of 'what we will call painting'? What is fascinating is the picture, not the name we gave it at one point or another.

From the literary studies of those days, what still has relevance for you?

If I take a retrospective look at the output of those years, leaving aside my own work and Genette's, about which I cannot be objective, my preference goes to two types of work.

Firstly, the commentaries on texts. Certain texts require elucidation and critical commentary, because we have forgotten the original context or because the author's thought is complex and difficult to understand or because the author deliberately sought obscurity. Whether it be for one of these reasons or a variety of others, commentaries are useful if not downright indispensable. They help us gain a better understanding. Take for example Bénichou's commentaries on Mallarmé: what a wonderful help they are for the reader! Outside France, Joseph

Frank's great work on Dostoyevsky comes to mind (a volume of which has been translated into French). It exemplifies my ideal of a literary study. It is an amazing work grounded in a huge body of knowledge on nineteenth-century Russian society, philosophy, political debates and Dostoyevsky's own biography. All of this constitutes a context of incomparable wealth within which the purely literary analysis of the novels unfolds. The result is that I understand *Crime and Punishment* better today than I did before reading Frank. In a more philosophical vein, I like to cite Victor Goldschmidt's commentary on Rousseau's Second Discourse (*On the Origin and Basis of Inequality Among Men*), which is an invaluable tool of study.

The other type of work is the literary analysis focused on a study of human behaviour, a cultural period or a paradigm of thought. Take the example of René Girard. He is a brilliant textual commentator, but his analyses always participate in a larger perspective — that of the human condition, sometimes within a precise historical framework. Take also some of Bénichou's books, such as *Morales du grand siècle* (*Morals of the Great Century*) or *Le sacre de l'écrivain* (*The Consecration of the Writer*), which are remarkable, in-depth interpretations of changes in mentality in the seventeenth and nineteenth centuries. Then, to take another example outside France, there is Ian Watt's work on modern literary myths — *Faust, Don Juan, Don Quixote* and *Robinson Crusoe* — a beautiful analysis of the contrast between the ages of the Renaissance and Romanticism. All these authors take literary works as a starting point but do not limit themselves to them — they use them as a way to go elsewhere.

Ultimately, the literary criticism you like, while having absorbed certain methods introduced by poetics, maintains a rather classical approach to literature?

tzvetan todorov

To paraphrase one of my friends, I would say that it doesn't matter if the method is classic or modern as long as it helps me understand better. What strikes me, in both of the practices I've just described, is that the critical study is always auxiliary in character. Either it is at the service of literature and humbly contents itself to shed light on the meaning of the work. Or it puts literature itself at the service of understanding more about human beings, their societies and their history. When, on the other hand, literary studies are intent on fulfilling more than this auxiliary role, they tend to become somewhat shallow; the discourse ends up revolving around itself. To sum up: the changes in which I participated in the sixties and seventies were necessary, but they also produced sterilizing effects that must be counterbalanced today.

Poetics, an embarrassing heritage?

After the change in direction we were just discussing, you dealt less with literature in your work. Then, some years ago, you became a member of the Conseil national des programmes (CNP), an advisory body headed by Luc Ferry, within the Ministry of Education, whose task was to provide an orientation to the national curriculum and supervise its content from the beginning of primary school to the end of secondary school. You sat on the board as a specialist in literature. What is the relationship between the work you were doing in the sixties and your activity in the CNP?

It's true: my participation in the CNP starting in 1994 brought me back to literary studies. The CNP had no decisional power; it made recommendations on the orientation of programmes. The group brought together renowned academics and teachers, physicists and historians, biologists and literary specialists. The atmosphere was light-hearted, with people freely expressing their opinions. I learnt a lot from it.

The very fact of sticking to a programme can be problematic. Our best school memories, as I'm sure you know from experience, are attached less to the knowledge that has been transmitted to us than to the professors who managed to invest themselves in what they were teaching. Students can tell the difference between teachers who confine themselves to droning out their courses and those who get their passion across. Keeping this in mind should give us a little perspective on our debates about what should be taught. When Daniel Pennac tells us that sometimes all he needed to do was read texts aloud in class for the lesson to bear fruit, there is every reason to believe him!

This can also be a very reactionary position. Like claiming that the ability to recite and to imitate the teacher's beautiful reading is a guarantee that the text has been understood, and that that is enough.

Learning by heart is the most mechanical educational approach that exists, and yet it has its virtues. My daughter attended fourth grade in a small school in the country where she had an old-fashioned teacher who must have been close to retirement age. He taught as his teachers had taught him in the thirties and forties. Well, thanks to his reading out loud and the learning by heart, he infected his pupils with the virus of love for poetry from which my daughter still benefits today.

In other words, all we need is good motivated teachers and we'll have good teaching. It's a bit limited as a solution for the CNP!

I agree. We cannot content ourselves with saying that teaching essentially depends on the understanding that exists between people and on the passion that they invest in it. The contents that are transmitted favour the student's autonomy more than the affective relationship, and it is autonomy that is our goal. Moreover, we can obviously ask all teachers to teach the same subjects, but we cannot ask them to be driven by the same passion. To facilitate the work of teachers and pupils alike, we must therefore agree on the contents and methods of instruction.

The fact is that the teaching of literature in school is problematic because there is even less of a consensus in this field than in others regarding what should be taught. More precisely, the higher the level of schooling, the more disagreements there are as to what the students should learn. Everyone basically agrees that pupils in primary school should learn reading, writing, the rudiments of grammar and of analysing and composing simple texts. But after that?

Generations of students, of which I am part, were educated using the Lagarde and Michard *or other similar textbooks. In addition to a method grounded essentially in the history of literature, the two main characteristics of this approach were: (1) to attach importance to French literature only, a literature constitutive of the national identity and hence in line with a patrimonial vision of literature; (2) to organize the progression of learning on the basis of the march of the centuries: the sixteenth and seventeenth in tenth grade, the eighteenth and nineteenth in eleventh, the twentieth in twelfth. This purely historical and national approach is a thing of the past. And that this is so, we owe, in part, to you. Do you disavow this today?*

The famous *Lagarde and Michard* textbook, with its short summaries, dates, biographical notes and text analysis questions, can indeed symbolize the old educational programme. It was not worthless but it wasn't great either. The content of our programmes and textbooks are different today, but I wonder whether it is really better or whether we have opted again for what is easy to teach. It sometimes reminds me of the story of the guy who is looking for his key not where he lost it but under the street lamp because that's where the light is. We are always tempted to teach what lends itself to teaching, not what would be useful to the pupils.

What do you think of the current content of literary instruction in middle school?

This new teaching — and I'm coming back here to your preceding question — was indeed influenced by our studies in the structuralist period, by what I might call our small 'revolution'. I discovered that we are now teaching middle-school pupils a kind of abridged version of our studies in the sixties, and that their programme resembles the one we had proposed in Vincennes in 1968! I suspected as much from my children's studies in school and from the sometimes mediocre marks they would get when they asked for my help, and this was confirmed by the overall view I acquired when I joined the CNP.

And are you proud of this influence?

Today, I am opposed to what seems to me to be a misguided drift—a fact that draws sarcastic comments from my colleagues along the lines of 'Here comes the battle of Todorov II versus Todorov I!'

So you reject everything that you initiated?

No, of course not. What we did was liberating. Taboos fell away and new approaches to texts became possible. But, for all that, the marks left by our work on secondary school education are far from satisfying.

In what respect?

What we have in school today is a purely mechanical approach to texts that atrophies literature and, by the same token, the teaching of literature. Instead of studying the works, children study rhetorical figures, the variety of viewpoints that can be adopted in a narrative and the different poetic forms. Such notions are only interesting as tools to get to the meaning. What matters most is to be deeply moved by literature, and hence by thought, beauty and so on.

Literature is thought. It speaks the truth about man and the world; it transmits values. It does so not only through the monologue of the main characters speaking on behalf of the author or through direct comments by the author. A thought slips into the way a narrative is developed, the way that images are put together. When it comes to this, structural analysis gave us the means to recognize this play on forms and interpret its meaning. But the means must not obscure the ends. To know how to distinguish internal focalization from external focalization or metaphor from metonymy is not a goal in itself. If my daughter had been taught only to differentiate between metaphor and metonymy, she would have been put off by poetry for good!

The same way many children were put off by music because they were required in conservatories to take four years of theory before they could touch an instrument!

In other words (and with some exaggeration), in the past, instead of studying literature, we studied the circumstances in which the works were created and, to sweeten the pill, a few superlatives about their quality were added. Now, instead of teaching literature, we teach the concepts meant to serve for their analysis. We have put the method in the place of the object of study. This is the crux of the misunderstanding: turning the instrument into the goal. It is not the instrument itself that is to be blamed, or the work we did in those days, but how it is used. It would make sense to study the instrument—if at all—in university. The methodological thinking can be useful, although, even in this case, it should not invade everything (the pressing issues of the Vincennes period are a thing of the past). But in secondary school? The methods?—well, we take what we have at hand but they are makeshift expedients. To study them instead of the texts is a serious mistake, to my mind. Yet, there is a natural tendency to do so in the study of literature as elsewhere.

Even so, methods are precious to the life of ideas and to the comprehension of worldviews. The question is, rather, when are they useful to study and at what level in education?

At any rate, I am certain that there is no point in teaching them to children, to the detriment of the discipline itself.

Teaching French in school

In the spring of 1999, a controversy erupted in the pages of newspapers, in particular in Le Monde, *about the teaching of literature in school, with alarming titles like 'Literature is Being Assassinated'. Does your criticism concur with those expressed at the time?*

Not in the least. I even participated in the debate in an op-ed article published in *Le Monde*, and took a stand against the majority of critics. When dealing with a complex subject like the teaching of literature, more than two positions or 'sides' are possible, even if demagogues and public opinion would rather see things in terms of black and white, or, in this case, in terms of conservative and modernist.

I found the campaign denigrating present-day literary instruction distasteful, firstly because it cast onto the Ministry of Education the shadow of a conspiracy: someone very bad was depriving our children of free access to literary works! What was astonishing was that this accusation came from two opposing sources. On one side, there were university professors who advocated an elitist education

—the kind of people we would have once called mandarins—speaking through their mouthpiece, the *Société des agrégés*. And on the other side, there were teachers from the field, mostly from secondary schools, trying to hold onto the last remnants of a dying radicalism. Conservatives and anti-establishment protesters alike joined in an unconditional condemnation of *libéralisme sauvage*,[1] or unbridled liberalism (have you noticed how liberalism these days is always described as unbridled?). They imputed to the Ministry an underhanded attempt to turn schools into robot-producing machines. One cannot help but recognize the fact that, with the help in particular of certain media, this unlikely mix of people with opposing interests became a formidably effective lobby.

You are denouncing the ways these opinions were expressed. But, when it comes to content, wouldn't you be inclined to agree with those who defend the idea of grounding the study of French in literary texts?

I have several fundamental disagreements with them too. The first concerns the very principles of education. What is its purpose? Our dear *républicains*, as these neo-conservatives are called, have a ready answer: to impart knowledge. But that's not an answer. First of all, what kind of knowledge? The knowledge they inherited 20 or 30 years ago? But why should it be immutable? Do these *républicains* think they're so perfect that they want everybody to resemble them? French education does not necessarily stand up well in comparison with that of other countries. In any case, knowledge is not an end unto itself. School must prepare people for life and it is for this purpose that it teaches knowledge and skills. We cannot, on principle, refuse to see the school system adapt to the needs of the soci-

---

1 In France, the term liberals is basically applied to adherents to laissez-faire economic policies, in contradistinction to social democrats, for example. A liberalisme sauvage would be an ultra-liberalism in which free-market capitalism runs wild. [Trans.]

ety that sustains it. I might add that recognizing this need does not necessarily mean selling your soul to global capitalism.

Another point on which I do not agree at all concerns the threat that is supposedly hanging over literature as a result of opening up the programmes to non-literary texts. The neo-conservatives who signed the petitions in *Le Monde* against the way French is being taught in secondary schools today, cried out, 'How horrible! Students are being given texts to read that are not all literary!' Then they brandished a horrifying list of examples — a comic book, a newspaper article and even, it seems, instructions for the use of a microwave oven — only to triumphantly conclude: we, the signatories, think that Racine is more useful to French students than oven instructions! When you see people reaching this pitch of demagoguery, there is reason to wonder about the true motivations of the petitioners.

But you who believe in the virtues (in the strong sense of the term) of literature, you obviously also think that Racine is more useful than oven instructions.

Of course. Presented in this way, one can hardly not agree. That's what demagoguery is all about!

Literature, literature! Literature, in different periods, was not always conceived according to the same criteria. The very notion of literature is relatively recent — it did not exist as such before the nineteenth century — and its frontiers are continually shifting. Constant's diary was not considered 'literature' until 50 years ago, and yet I see in it today some of the most striking pages he ever wrote. Why must I isolate genres in this way? *Adolphe* is literature, so it's in, but *Cécile* is autobiographical, so it's out, and so are *Religion*, which is science, and *Principles of Politics*, which is politics. Yet, throughout all these texts, a single thought unfolds and the construction devices are equally interesting in them all.

To study a newspaper article from time to time, why not? Not everything that appears in the press is idiotic — you, of all people, will not contradict me on this.

Maybe the debate is charged with all the more symbolic import in so far as literary studies are, in reality, of less importance.

That's true. The percentage of students that take the literary baccalaureate option dropped from 33 per cent to 10 per cent in a couple of years. Proof of the decline in literary education, which will continue if we don't do anything about it.

What would you consider an ideal education?

First of all, we mustn't lose sight of the obvious fact that teaching French is not solely a matter of teaching literature. School has another mission too: it must teach students to understand and express themselves, orally as well as in writing. The life situations awaiting students after school are varied, and they have to be at least a little prepared to face them. The forms of discourse that they must learn to master are also varied. They are not limited to the famous dissertation — one form of exercise among many others — that we tend to blow up out of all proportion. And the French teacher is the one who is in the best position to provide this kind of instruction. Otherwise, students will end up taking 'communication' courses outside of the framework of the common school. Why should this knowledge and these skills be banished from our school system? Must we really remove anything that can be useful in life from the school curriculum?

This then is an important part of the teaching of French that must be recognized. Alongside it comes literature. I also think that literature has a lot to teach everyone. It introduces us to a world of meaning and values better than any other form of discourse, better than moralistic admonitions, better than the press, better than philosophy itself. Reading Gavroche's story can change a pupil's life. Many ways of seeing the world are internalized thanks to literary texts, thanks to the inventions of writers. Everyone's inner world is enriched by literature. The question is how to make sure that students profit from it as much as possible. And when it comes to this, the recipes of the conservatives do not seem better to me than modernist–technicist solutions. It is absurd to be for (or against) reform on principle; it is not a matter of doing or not doing as before, but of doing well.

Of course. But, concretely speaking, what about the programmes?

First of all, as I've already said, the focus should be on the texts rather than the methods. Which texts? The notion of an immutable literary canon has been contested. This is one of the consequences of May 1968 and the demand that teachers be free to choose the texts they want to teach. We do not study a set corpus any more. Yet, it seems to me that we should come back to a somewhat more circumscribed body of works: it is the price we must pay to make sure that everyone in a society like ours possesses a common culture. This will not prevent individuals who have the desire and ability from becoming more cultivated and stepping over the boundaries of the 'canon' in all different directions. The fact remains that it does not really matter if students leave high school without knowing the difference between internal and external focalization, but it matters if they haven't heard of *The Flowers of Evil*.

Let me add that these great literary works should not be selected from French literature alone. It is not as documents about the French nation or as exercises in linguistic virtuosity that they interest us but as signs of humanity. Today, populations move around more than ever and we live in Europe, not only in France. The fact that these works will have to be read in translation does not shock me in the least: that is how we read them as adults, why should we deprive our children of them? Everyone should be familiar with Greek tragedy and Arab tales, English drama and Spanish novels, Gogol and Dostoyevsky, Tolstoy and Chekhov. Ignoring them is like destroying the Buddhist statues in Afghanistan — it's impoverishing the human heritage. That being said, there is no reason why, say, a good half of the curriculum could not still be consecrated to the study of texts from the national corpus of literature.

Literature is addressed to us all, no matter where we come from, but it also belongs to a specific time. As heirs to European culture, we must be familiar with its key moments; we cannot act as if the history of the country did not exist. In this respect, literature has a lot to teach us. Thanks to literature, we can understand the opposition between the closed world of the Ancients and the open and moving world of the Moderns, the emergence of the individual in the Renaissance, seventeenth-century morals, the revolution of the Enlightenment, the crisis of Romanticism and the situation of contemporary human beings faced with the massification of society. Of course, our understanding owes thanks to literature but also to other media that are not studied enough in school: the visual arts, in particular, painting, sculpture, film, television, etc.

The main difficulty is to agree on what we should know. But it can be overcome if we proceed as we have done for economic or political history. In the latter case, we have worked on the assumption that, to master codes of conduct in our world and avoid discrimination later, it is important to have a common foundation of knowledge, and hence to know something about Greek democracy, the Roman Empire, the birth of monotheism and so on. Why couldn't we find a similar common foundation for the history of culture, literature and art?

Once the corpus of texts and the teaching goals are defined, we come back to the same problem you raised at the beginning of the discussion: how should we study literary texts? If you say, as you have suggested, that all methods are good, aren't you basically saying that the only good method is a good teacher?

The freedom that teachers would lose (a little) in the answer to the 'what', they would gain back entirely in the answer to the 'how'. The curriculum must indicate, in my opinion, only the general orientation: we study the works to gain a better understanding of their meaning and, through it, of human existence. As for how to proceed, that would be up to the teachers themselves. There is nothing wrong with that.

That is what would be, in my opinion, if not an ideal teaching of French — let's not fool ourselves — at least a better, more fulfilling one in every respect. But you see, to establish even this much would require overturning so many traditions and overcoming so much resistance. I don't think it is about to happen very soon! And so I content myself with adding my own voice to the general discord.

The voice of a literary man?

The voice of a man with a passion for literature, who is convinced that it can help us immensely in understanding the world.

4. The Peasant in Paris

An anti-political in France in the sixties – The ambivalence of May 1968 – May 1968 at the university – 'Your life is there' – Foreign, assimilated, estranged – The meeting of cultures – Fully entering the world

An anti-political in France in the 1960s

CATHERINE PORTEVIN: *You arrived in Paris in 1963 when the cold war was still raging. Inside and outside France, the Communist Party and, even more so, the Communist ideology in the form of Marxism–Leninism, were very influential, particularly in student circles. What was your perspective on the political engagements of your new friends?*

TZVETAN TODOROV: It wasn't until the fall of 1963 when the school term began that I really got to know French students and young researchers. And it is true that they often identified with the Communist dream, even when they were not involved in any organized activities. Some, though, were active in the Communist Student Union (the UEC). Here were these nice people, open and generous with me as a foreigner, who were committed to a political project whose detrimental effects I knew well and for which I had little sympathy. I came from a country that had turned their dream into reality, and getting out of it was an experience of liberation for me!

The enthusiasm of these young French people for Communism seemed ill-considered, to say the least. First of all, because they aspired to a regime that abolishes individual liberties, elevates lying and hypocrisy to rules of conduct and provokes economic disaster. But also because these people, who professed revolutionary ideas and campaigned for the dictatorship of the proletariat, lived, for the most part, petty-bourgeois lives, the lives of bohemians and the bourgeois, what we call *bobos* today. And they didn't seem to realize that this pleasant lifestyle of theirs would have been suspended, if not repressed, if the regime to which they aspired had really taken hold in France. It did not seem to cross the minds of my friends at the time to bring saying and doing, ideas and acts, values and life in line with each other, whereas it was becoming more and more crucial to me. This then is the attitude that I started to demand from others . . . and, more slowly, from myself.

It is just the kind of thing that one demands from others to begin with! And you reproached them for their lack of coherence?

Oh no! Political conversations bored me to the highest degree and the least you could say is that I wasn't looking for controversial arguments at that time. All the less for I had long given up trying to change the people I met and make them resemble my ideal. Instead, I would put aside what I did not like about them. I must confess as well that there was a big difference between these candid, open people and the apparatchiks in Bulgaria. In France, outside executive or intellectual circles, belonging to the Communist Party did not further your career.

What did they expect from you as someone from an Eastern European country?

They would probably have liked to see me confirm their political dreams; their sympathy was addressed first to a representative of the 'socialist' world. But I threw back at them—albeit with moderation—a negative picture of what existed there. I would tell anecdotes that made a mockery of this world. How they maintained their sympathy for me, in spite of what I was saying, was a mystery that I did not try to solve.

I might hasten to add that this description does not apply to all the people I was seeing at that time. One of my best friends was the painter Martin Barré, who was perfectly indifferent to the question of Communism and never dreamt for a moment of transforming society. He was not bourgeois in the least and he could be called bohemian only in the sense that he was constantly penniless. He had been part of the lyrical abstraction movement after the war but had radically changed his style thereafter; it was a highly reckless move with regard to the buyers who did not follow him. So Martin made a living from carpentry, painting interiors and other handiwork. He was the one who taught me how to use my hands but also to appreciate the art of painting better. He himself had classical tastes — he was a great admirer of Velazquez — although his own painting was conceptual, and, incidentally, it brought him success again in the last years of his life. Martin corresponded to the image I had before I came to France of the Parisian artist: sophisticated and broke.

Your other friends were not unduly bothered by your anti-Communism, and neither were you by their Stalinism?

The fact is that, at the time, I was not anti-Communist, I was anti-political. I was more than apolitical, I fiercely rejected politics! When Communism came up in conversations, I did what I could to change the subject. The naive, irresponsible attitude of the French would provoke a snicker of derision in conversations with friends from Eastern Europe, with Poles, Romanians or Hungarians. I spent very little time with Bulgarians in Paris, no doubt because of my initial desire to assimilate. Besides, I didn't know many. The only other Bulgarian in my milieu was Julia Kristeva, who arrived from Sofia about a year after me. We had a courteous relationship but nothing more; we were not really friends. To come back to politics, I felt that I had lost enough time living with Communism against my will—the first 24 years of my life. I was determined, now that I was free of it, not to give it a single minute of my attention.

Wasn't this something of the same frame of mind that you were in during your Bulgarian years? How does one get rid of habits acquired through more than 20 years of education under totalitarianism, such as the aptitude for double-thought, the sense of caution, dissimulation or secrecy, and the ability to create small spaces of inner liberty to make up for the absence of big ones in public?

You don't change from one day to the next—consciousness always lags behind life, as my professors in Marxism in Bulgaria would have said. The clearest effect that totalitarianism had on me was the following: for many years I was persuaded that all politicians were double-dealing demagogues, and that anything said in public was necessarily a lie. Same thing for newspapers. I have since become an avid reader of the daily press but, for the first 10 years of my life in France, maybe more, I did not read the papers. I felt that I would be wasting my time taking an interest in the world when I had no power over it, and I had the impression that people took positions to mask their interests rather than to express a personal conviction, no less an eternal truth. Without realizing it, I was in fact perpetuating the rules of conduct that I had observed around me in Bulgaria. It is totalitarianism that condemns us to this frustrating back and forth between the empty rhetoric of public discourses and the cynical avidity of private desires.

Do we ever totally free ourselves from our past? My Bulgarian years surely continue to influence my reactions today. In a review of a recent book, a critic reproached me for my 'conscientious non-conformism'. I do not believe that I am a systematic non-conformist but it is true that I do not hold myself back at all from saying what I think, in all circumstances. I have the feeling that if I did otherwise I'd be betraying the convictions I acquired during my life in Bulgaria—at the time, what we were being asked for was conscientious conformism. Another mark left on me by my Bulgarian years was the persistence of fear. In the street, if I had to talk to somebody about Bulgarian politics, I would turn around first to see if anybody was listening. I grew out of that but I suspect that my tendency to avoid conflict is also a legacy of those years when disagreements of opinion could lead to consequences with the police.

Still, you must have been seething inside to hear the speeches of your French student friends?

The Communist, para-Communist, radical or revolutionary discourses that we heard quite a bit at the time disgusted me, but I did not *have to* listen to them—a huge difference in comparison with Bulgaria! I must say that the Communists, taken individually, could have a profile that I found interesting. For example, Pierre Daix, Editor-in-Chief of Aragon's weekly *Les Lettres françaises*, showed a keen interest in the Russian formalists and consequently in my translations. Now the formalists had been the target of repression in the Soviet Union, even if none of the key authors had been assassinated.

At the time, I was not aware of the dreadful dispute between Daix and David Rousset in 1949–50. Rousset had launched an appeal to former prisoners who had been interned in German concentration camps to take a stand against other camps that were still in operation, especially against the Soviet camps. Daix, a former prisoner of Mauthausen, accused Rousset of lying and called him an imperialist agent. Rousset sued *Lettres françaises* for libel, and won.

Daix ran a journal that was still Stalinist from certain standpoints, but that, at the same time, concentrated many of its pages on culture and literature—and this I appreciated. Since then, he has declared that he already had his doubts in those days. At least not in public. He reminded me of a few of the cultivated 'liberal' Communists I had known in Bulgaria several years earlier, who wanted to prove by their personal open-mindedness that Communism could be reformed from within. So Daix extended a warm reception to my collection of Russian formalist texts. He organized a round table at the journal and published a transcription of the discussions. His network of personal relations encouraged him to do so— Aragon and Elsa Triolet were friends of Jakobson.

But beyond the individual people who had direct ties to the Communist Party, the entire intellectual and political debate in France was shaped by and structured around Marxism. The Soviet Union's victory over Nazi Germany in 1945 boosted the Communist ideal by giving the victor a certificate of respectability. The existence of the anti-fascist coalition legitimated the inclusion of Communist countries and democratic countries within a common entity, an entity comprising radicals and moderates. Now, it is common knowledge that intellectuals have always preferred the boldness of radicalism to the caution of moderation. Preparing for revolution gave meaning to lives that had none and represented hope for all the people throughout the world. But, to me, *les trente glorieuses*, the 30 golden years of French economic growth from 1945 to 1975 have always seemed to be 30 disastrous years for political thought. Ideologically, these were years of stagnation, years of an intellectual blackout, when every discourse was judged by the yardstick of the Marxist–Leninist *doxa*. This shallow ideology dominated the intellectual world, exercising supremacy over all other voices by marginalizing them. Yet there was no dearth of such voices: there was Aron who preached in the wilderness, Camus who was censured by Sartre, and Gary who was not taken seriously. Gary was relegated to the category of commercial author when he was not only a remarkable novelist, far superior to Sartre, but also a thinker whose political and human wisdom surpassed that of most of his contemporaries.

Speaking of Sartre—he was the dominant figure in the intellectual life of those years yet he seems to be absent from the landscape of your books and your conversations.

Sartre often seemed to me to embody a posture for which I had very little respect. Obviously, I am not reducing him to that—he wrote some brilliant pages that have nothing to do with his political posturing. As you know, without being a member of the Communist Party, he articulated a discourse that was equally dogmatic and that exerted a truly paralysing grip on thought and even on research. The human sciences flourished only after shaking off this Marxist hold, and Lévi-Strauss had to oppose Sartre at the end of *The Savage Mind* to legitimate his own enterprise.

Later, I was not surprised to see Sartre selling issues of *La cause du peuple* in the streets and getting involved in Maoism. I found it, to be perfectly frank, pathetic or grotesque, depending on my mood. Here was an ageing man adopting adolescent postures. Worse, he did not even realize that there may not be anything commendable about imitating teenagers! Certain infatuations and crazes can be excusable, even appealing, when you are 20; at his age, with his experience, they were mainly proof of an immense (and blameworthy) political immaturity.

The ambivalence of May 1968

After that came May 1968 and then you could not ignore politics any more.

Yes and no. In 1967 and 1968, I wasn't in France. I had been offered a teaching position in the French literature department at Yale University in the United States, which I accepted with enthusiasm, postponing my entry to the CNRS for a year. It was an invigorating experience for me, I would even say joyful. For the first time I received what appeared to me to be a fabulous salary, even though it was at the very bottom of the pay scale. I bought my first car, although I didn't have my licence yet. It was a taste of freedom! And I liked the classes. Ultimately, I've taught more in the United States than in France. I appreciated the American students who were open-minded and full of good will.

As for political life, the debate I witnessed there seemed more concrete and, therefore, more justified than the revolutionary ravings of my Parisian friends. In France, young leftists let themselves be taken in by a dream, embodied first by the

Soviet Union and later, by Cuba and China. The Right mainly defended the privileges of the upper classes. The United States, on the other hand, was just emerging from the great political debate on civil rights and the recognition of African-American rights in the South. Racial problems were an all-too-palpable reality. The political and intellectual turmoil in reaction corresponded to real needs—it was not a distant battle, experienced vicariously. At Yale, in particular, under the influence of the charismatic local chaplain, Bill Coffin, the engagement in the struggle for African-American civil rights was strong. A number of my colleagues actively participated in the movement. Racial problems were not rare in New Haven, where Yale is located. The Black Panthers group had been active there and there had been a trial. There was a sizeable African-American community and we sometimes went to black districts at night to dance or listen to music. I developed a passion for jazz, which had been prohibited in Bulgaria. All of this was new to me; I was discovering a whole new world.

Another subject of controversy had emerged since the time of the Civil Rights Movement. By the time I arrived in the United States, the Vietnam War was in full swing and so was internal opposition to the war. It was often the same militants who, after having fought for civil rights, fought against the war. On campus, the great majority of students were anti-militarists, based on arguments that you can easily imagine. However, there was also a sizeable group of 'Victory in Vietnam' advocates who were in favour of the United States engagement in Vietnam. A few professors who came from Eastern Europe, as I did, spoke in meetings—rather courageously, I must say, since they faced hostile audiences—to denounce the Communist invasion sweeping through South Vietnam. They explained to these well-intentioned students that it took courage to resist evil, that it was a matter of duty to defend democracy everywhere in the world.

Again, I did not take part in these debates but I watched them with great interest. I find that we have not given enough thought since then to the issues at stake in the Vietnam War, in political not psychological terms. Much attention has been given to telling, filming and delving into the experience of the American soldiers there and the suffering of victims but there has been very little debate about what we think today about the legitimacy of the intervention. Should we or should we not have reacted to what was clearly an invasion from the North to the South? Should we have defended our allies or let the Communist aggression continue? Those who denounced the use of napalm bombs were right, of course; American policies were brutal and excessive. At the same time, pacifist movements, by serving the cause of North Vietnam, also contributed to establishing the dictatorship in Vietnam that still rules today. In the end, Ho Chi Minh did more damage than the South Vietnamese leaders. These same issues are coming up today in the debate over the 'right to interfere'. Is it legitimate to massacre in the name of justice?

So you were far away from France in May 1968. And you didn't see what was going on?

Strictly speaking, no, I didn't, since I came back to Paris on 31 May. At the beginning of the month, I learnt through the American press that students in Paris were occupying the Sorbonne, that they were setting up barricades in the Latin Quarter. A revolutionary temperament may not be my salient character trait but the idea of seeing for myself what was happening excited me. Thinking that historical events do not occur every day, I decided to return as quickly as possible, as soon as classes were over.

It was not that simple: not only was Air France on strike but the airports in Paris were blocked and all the flights had been cancelled. Then TWA obtained the right to operate flights and I took the first plane out. We landed at the Brétigny-

tzvetan todorov

sur-Orge military airport where we were driven in a covered truck to Montparnasse and left at an intersection. There were throngs of people all over the streets, very few cars since there was no gas, and the Métro was not working. It was rather picturesque.

After a few days, I had found my bearings again, along with my friends, and a place to live. I settled in and took up my position at the CNRS. 'May' continued through June, although with less momentum. I attended a few demonstrations — it was hard to avoid them all — and I still remember the acrid smell of teargas.

What impressions did May 1968 leave on you and, in hindsight, what role did these events have in France?

Even at the time, I saw two dissimilar components at work which is why I think its historical significance is twofold. Roughly, I would say that May 1968 was an end in political terms and a beginning in social terms. In *La pensée 68* (*French Philosophy of the Sixties: An Essay on Antihumanism*), Luc Ferry and Alain Renaut discuss the paradoxical conjunction of a programmatic anti-individualism and an extraordinary individualist thrust — a bizarre, sometimes preposterous combination of liberal desires and fidelity to dogma: Cohn-Bendit was emblematic in this respect. But for me, at that point, the two facets seemed clearly distinct from one another.

On the one hand, on the social level, a liberation movement was under way. French society had undergone deep-seated changes while preserving old forms that had become more and more anachronistic. The economic boom, the generalization of education, the sexual liberation with the Pill were so many factors that rendered the hierarchical, confined society of the Third Republic increasingly untenable. May 1968 constituted a breach in the established order and a fresh breath of spring swept through the streets: people addressed one another using the familiar *tu* form, looked each other in the eye, helped one another. In universities, where everything had started, students stopped attending lectures and challenged the power of the mandarins. New social relations were being created. That is why May 1968 was often a joyful time to live through!

On the other hand, on the political level, May 1968 was a movement of submission, not liberation. The political ideals of the Maoists, the Trotskyites and the orthodox Communists, the only ones you could hear amongst the students, left me deeply sceptical for I was familiar with the realities that these words concealed. Piotr Rawicz, an author of Polish Jewish origin, who has since died, wrote a rather sarcastic book about the events; I wasn't far from sharing his impressions.

The violence, at least verbal, that these young people demonstrated was extreme. In theory they were firmly determined to exterminate the 'bourgeois scum'. Fortunately, words alone do not kill. In his *Memoirs*, Raymond Aron recalled that the radical Hegelian and rather secretive philosopher, Alexandre Kojève, who was also a high official in the French government and a subtle advocate of tyranny, had asked him while the events were going on, 'How many deaths?' 'None,' Aron replied. 'Then nothing happened in May 1968 in France.' This lofty position seems excessive to me. Something did happen—a social upheaval. But at the political level, it's true that nothing much occurred. The reason for this is probably that, among the leaders, there was no one like Lenin capable of seizing power with a small well-organized group. Lenin was as much in the minority in Russia in 1917 as the Maoists in France in 1968!

I might add that, fortunately, the time had passed as far as the advent of the Communist revolution was concerned. From a political viewpoint, it was anything but the inauguration of a new era. The movement was even quite regressive, like the last rays of light of the dying day. It was a whole system of ideological rigidity that reached its peak in 1968, before slowly collapsing. Politically, 1968 was an arrière-garde and not an avant-garde movement, a final burst of energy that barely postponed the disintegration of the Communist ideal (which was truly shattered a few years later, in the middle of the seventies), to prepare, in its own way, the present-day reign of liberal thinking.

May 1968 at the university

What were the effects of May 1968 in the academic world in which you lived?

Upon my return from the United States, I went back to the École des hautes études, to the welcoming, liberal and calm atmosphere to which I was accustomed only to find, much to my surprise, extreme unrest there too. I say that I was surprised because, to my mind, it was senseless to extend the demands that the May 1968 movement was making at the university level to the École des hautes études. I understood the desire to break the mandarin stranglehold on the Sorbonne, which was indeed all-powerful, onerous and oppressive. But it was precisely the École des hautes études that offered an alternative solution, a place where this oppressiveness did not exist, where relationships between professors and students were easygoing and even friendly; we were all people who were committed to individual or common projects. In short, the whole university system should have been a little more like the École des hautes études!

tzvetan todorov

But, no! The protest movement was in full swing there too. It took the form of a solemn demagogical gathering, conducted by people who had no scientific or professional merit but who had taken the lead in the hopes of gleaning some lasting privileges in the midst of the surrounding uproar. At the mass general assemblies (the AGs as we called them) that were being organized day in–day out, the professors were summoned to present their self-criticism. And there was poor Barthes—who was hardly a mandarin, although he was not a revolutionary either—extremely ill-at-ease, not so much because of these speeches—after all, he was used to speeches—but due to this outburst, this violent eruption of vulgarity, an unbridled vulgarity that invaded everything. He had to make believe that he was very seriously listening to these idiotic speeches and nod in agreement when these dull people told us that, in the name of the revolution, Barthes, Greimas and I don't recall who else had to promise in public to establish more 'democratic' practices. But how could one still talk of democracy when it consecrated the reign of ignorance over ability and the triumph of manipulation—of might over right?

It was however suggested that the spirit of Barthes' Mythologies *had in part paved the way for the May protest movement. How could he be considered an enemy of the cause?*

But that was not the issue at all! The speaker in the meetings at the École des hautes études would have been utterly incapable of producing a critique of Barthes' writings or even of the content of his courses. What they were criticizing was the status of the professor; they were challenging the very existence of the teacher in the name of the egalitarian principles of democracy. That is the demagoguery! Democracy sets up an overall legal framework in which all citizens have equal rights, but it in no way obliges us to eliminate all hierarchical relations in society—that would be impossible, of course. Children cannot take care of their parents—the relationship is hierarchical. The very existence of school is based on inequality: some people know, others do not. We can discuss the modalities of this inequality, but to want to abolish it is pure intellectual drivel.

During the summer of 1968, some of my friends, Genette in particular, asked me to participate in the creation of a new university. We have already spoken about Vincennes in terms of the content of literary teaching. But that was only a very small facet of the adventure. The other side of the picture, which was much more important on a public level, was the political unrest. The aim of Edgar Faure, then the new Minister of Education, was, if I am not mistaken, to create a university in Vincennes in line with the desires of the protest movement. The university would serve both as a laboratory for new educational practices and as a pole of attraction for troublemakers, in the hopes that they would leave the other universities in peace and carry on as they liked together in Vincennes.

The strategy worked quite well. The creation of Vincennes contributed to quelling the unrest elsewhere. Precisely because it was a very free new institution, it drew the leaders of a variety of political movements that had surfaced in May. The conflict shifted as a result: it was no longer between the bourgeois society and the revolution but between Communists and leftists. In Vincennes, the Communist Party took hold of the institutional reins and provided the majority of administrators and professors. Alongside the Party (or maybe inside — such fine distinctions are beyond me), you could find Althusser's disciples, with well-formulated, well-structured discourses. I can still hear Étienne Balibar, Jacques Rancière and a few others, leading countless AGs with great panache. Despite their skill, their discourse seemed delirious to me on a political level. Intellectually, the rhetoric functioned perfectly but, at bottom, it was nothing but propaganda in support of totalitarian society — as if it hadn't done enough damage already!

On the other side were the Maoists. They mainly campaigned for the destruction of the bourgeois machine that was the university. They were there to keep the machine from running, unlike the Communist comrades who wanted to make it run their way. The Mao group was led by André Glucksmann and Judith Miller, also by Alain Badiou.

tzvetan todorov

What part did you take in the political unrest?

None directly, but I did not hold myself back from saying what I thought when things went too far. I was particularly struck by one incident. Very small groups of extreme right-wingers, exasperated by the existence of the extreme leftists in Vincennes, tried to infiltrate the campus for purposes of surveillance and provocation. One day, one of the leaders of these small groups, François Duprat, came to Vincennes. He was no angel — a few years later he died in circumstances that were never totally clarified when his car, filled with explosives, blew up. He was identified, 'unmasked' during an assembly, and punished: his clothes were taken off, he was covered with ketchup and mustard and kicked out of the university to the triumphant boos of the actors in this ritual, with Glucksmann and Miller in the lead. I was beside myself with rage to see that, in the name of good principles, or principles that were thought to be good, a human being could be humiliated to this point. It was, for me, the clear demonstration that the end does not justify the means. And moreover, in this case, that nothing justified the end. I was all the more upset in that I knew the people who were involved well. In the throes of a collective madness of sorts, they were capable of doing as people had done in Soviet Russia — except that they hadn't the wherewithal — of massacring in the name of good (or in this precise case, of just humiliating). But the act of humiliating someone demeans those who are doing it; their triumph offends our idea of what human identity is. I had been close to André Glucksmann before, in 1966 and 1967, when he was writing his thesis with Aron and was attending Barthes' seminar. That day, I voiced my indignation to him. 'He's a fascist,' he calmly objected. 'I think that you're the ones who are fascists,' I replied. It was a lynching — admittedly a symbolic one, but a lynching nonetheless. The fact that Duprat was an extreme right-wing militant did not change the nature of the act for me.

I thought it was necessary 'to act' in response to this incident — there was a lot of 'acting' going on at the time! I wrote a tract condemning this type of humiliation, which ran counter to my idea of ethics. Several of my colleagues in the French department signed it, among them Michel Butor. We mimeographed it, like good little activists, then distributed it in the university. It was immediately attacked by a counter-tract that lambasted the 'wide-eyed humanism' of Butor (as he was much better known than I was, he was the target of the attacks), saying that his thinking 'had been more inspired during the days of the Nouveau Roman'. For the first time, I asked myself whether the Nouveau Roman had indeed been anti-humanist. Later, I asked myself the same question about structuralism.

In any case, it was the first time you were labelled — albeit indirectly — a 'wide-eyed humanist' but it was not to be the last.

At that time, I was not looking for a family of thought and I did not feel concerned by the 'humanist' label. But I felt a real sense of relief a few years later, when the ideal of human rights replaced the Communist beacon. This change was not so much provoked as marked by the release in France of Solzhenitsyn's *The Gulag Archipelago*, a book that, in its turn, led to the awakening of the 'new philosophers' (including my former friend Glucksmann who was as dynamic as ever). It would be interesting for a man like him to write the story of his metamorphoses from Aron to Mao and from Maoism to a kind of moralizing interventionism. A lot of former Communists have done so, recounting their initial passion and how the scales fell more or less slowly from their eyes; fewer leftists have done the same. Some of my friends today will talk about their early Maoist years, often in very funny terms, but only in private.

'Your life is there'

What about you? What was it that made you rethink your anti-political stance? May 1968 or the publication of Solzhenitsyn's book?

Neither. If anything, May 1968 did just the opposite: it confirmed my disgust for political engagements. Again, I'm not talking about the changes in lifestyle, which delighted me and from which I profited. At university, human relations had lost their ceremonious stiffness and become more easy-going and friendly. In the private sphere too, you could feel more frankness around you; the old conformism had collapsed and the new conformism was not yet in place. The widespread use of contraception made sexual relations easier. But I found the political projects that were being discussed either frightening (these future leaders would not have hesitated to open camps to reform the enemies of the 'people') or purely demagogical — both were masks behind which personal ambitions were concealed. The proliferation of hollow discourses is one of the distinctive marks of totalitarian regimes.

The publication of Solzhenitsyn's book did not have a liberating effect on you?

I saw the echo the book had and I was happy to observe its impact. I watched an impressive television programme with Solzhenitsyn and admired in him his superiority—not of intellect but of depth and humanness. In comparison, the journalists interviewing him seemed so superficial and thoughtless—their intellectual constructs burst like bubbles as soon as they came in contact with what could immediately be perceived as the truth of experience. I had the same impression later about a few people with very different convictions, such as Sister Emmanuelle or Germaine Tillion—the very rare feeling of a total commensuration between the different facets of a human being.

You are going to find this hard to believe, but the admiration that I had at the time was not enough of a motivation for me to read *The Gulag Archipelago*! As I said before, I considered that I had given enough of my time to Communism and I did not expect to find any revelations in the book. This lack of interest lasted for a very long time . . . until the end of the eighties.

That is to say, until the fall of Communism! As long as Communism lasted, you did not feel free to think about it?

It wasn't that simple. First of all, I was not free in actual fact because the rest of my family was still living in Bulgaria. It was a safe bet that, if I became an anti-Communist activist in France, my parents would suffer the consequences. This thought was always at the back of my mind—that I do not have the right to complicate the lives of my parents and my brother. It would have been intolerable for me to stir up trouble in Paris if they had to pay the price for it in Sofia. I felt a kind of personal engagement towards my family.

But, in a more profound way, it is true—and this I realized afterwards—that I partly remained a subject in a Communist country, a little deaf to the world around me. The Wall had to fall and Zhivkov had to be overthrown before I, who had been living in France for 26 years, could feel liberated. In any case, my professional interest in the subject only came to me at that time. That was when I started to think and write about the totalitarian world. It was in those years that I was able to conceive of *Facing the Extreme*, a study of moral life in the concentration camps, and it was for the needs of this book that I finally read *The Gulag Archipelago*. Right after *Facing the Extreme*, I prepared a collection of documents about the concentration camps in Bulgaria, entitled *Voices from the Gulag*. A more recent book, *Hope and Memory*, also deals at length with the subject.

You can see how much time it takes sometimes for the interior to catch up with the exterior, for circumstances, encounters and events to transform you deeply. In my case, it was as if totalitarianism had to die in the real world for it to come back to life in my mind as an object of knowledge.

You are describing one of the effects of totalitarianism on individuals and it sounds very much like a traumatic experience. Sometimes people will only talk about a serious traumatic experience 25 years later, when a member of the family has died or some other event has occurred that releases the past.

Similarly, many of those who were deported could freely speak about the concentration camps only 30 years later. To answer, finally, your question about whether *The Gulag Archipelago* was a liberating event, I would say, historically, yes, it definitely was. It accompanied, in France, the most important ideological change in the post-war period. But as far as my personal biography was concerned, it wasn't. The events that occurred in my personal life in those years were much more decisive for me: in 1973, I became a French citizen; in 1974, I became a father. This is what led to my full entrance into the world.

How did these two events in your personal life change your way of seeing the world? For a start, how did the young Bulgarian student, who had arrived in Paris one morning in April 1963, first become a real immigrant and then a French citizen?

At the beginning, I only had a temporary resident permit that I had to renew regularly and that depended on the validity of my passport. Consequently, each time I had to go to the Bulgarian Embassy to prolong my passport. In April 1964, a year after my arrival, I only asked for three months because I was persuaded that I'd be going back to Bulgaria once the school year was over.

At that point, I received a letter from my father that was without a doubt the most decisive letter in my life. He told me, in substance, 'Your life is there, you mustn't come back.' These words must have cost him a lot—I was very close to him because of my line of work which was akin to his, but also simply because we got along well together. And he was 63 years old at the time. Encouraging me to stay in Paris was a little bit like giving up his son. My mother agreed with his reasoning. I find that such a selfless deed. Given the content of the letter, he entrusted it to someone to give to me instead of sending it by ordinary mail.

It shows that he was deeply aware that political freedom is a priceless thing.

More so than I was. He must have thought that what mattered to me most, that is friendships, could be recreated elsewhere, whereas my public and professional life under the Bulgarian regime, in the line of work that was to be mine (teaching, writing, researching around literature), risked being poisoned forever. He was, in this respect, more clear-sighted than I. At the time, the order of priorities for me was the opposite.

It was a difficult letter to receive. I thought about it carefully and I accepted my father's advice, which turned me from a visitor into an immigrant. So at the end of the three-month period, in June 1964, instead of going back to Sofia, I asked for a one-year extension. First I asked my aunt, who was providing me with a 'grant', then the Bulgarian Embassy and finally the Prefecture of Paris.

My aunt said yes immediately. She supported me for three years in all, which, even if it was minimal support, was a huge gift. I could count on her check every month, which meant that I did not live in the anxiety of ending up on the streets. The Bulgarian Embassy was more difficult. They gave me a lecture. Why, they asked me, did I want to stay here when my home was there? The education I had received had to benefit the Bulgarian people and so on. They shilly-shallied for quite some time without refusing my request. If they had done so, I could have declared myself a refugee. And a half-hearted Bulgarian was better than a vociferating refugee! In the end, they gave in. Much later, I learnt that there had been an embassy employee whose unique job was to collect information about me and follow me everywhere. There must be a thick file on me in the Bulgarian State Security's archives. If I wanted to, I could consult it now. One of my friends did so, with the results you can imagine: he found letters of denunciation written by his friends. But for me, all this is too remote; it's a past that is over and done with. It doesn't interest me.

Finally, the third phase was the French Prefecture: this was a trying but not a dangerous phase. In administrative offices, one is often confronted with a generalized xenophobia and with a contempt of sorts for all those who are on the other side of the counter, the contempt of low-ranking employees for the people who depend on them.

Even you, who were not in a particularly precarious situation, seem to be still revolted by this bureaucratic violence.

Let's say that these experiences made me more sensitive to the distress of foreigners. Petty humiliations such as these are afflicted by people who, in reality, have very little power but who, for that very reason, want to make as much use of it as they can. They stress the distance between you and them precisely because it is small; making you feel that you're at their mercy gives them the feeling that they exist—and from this experience, that is necessary to all, it is those who are weaker who are made to suffer. Foreigners, because they have no rights, often find themselves reduced to the role of foils: the long lines waiting in the cold or rain, when it would be so simple to provide a covered reception area; the pushing and shoving; the curt, often incomprehensible, remarks tossed out in a disdainful tone. This creates, in reaction, a certain sense of solidarity between foreigners. Everybody knows that he or she will be mistreated. No comparison with real persecutions, of course, but these group phenomena, these attitudes of petty tyrants, the indifference of the administration, the gratuitous humiliation inflicted on those who cannot protest—all of this can so easily become much more serious! No group of people is immune to the rise of discriminations and to the impulse to exclude others. And even very small deeds can bring great evil.

Foreign, assimilated, estranged

Besides this administrative aspect, what was your experience as a newcomer? In what way were you a foreigner and are you still a foreigner?

I suffered little from being a foreigner; often, I even benefited from it. There may have been a few administrative humiliations and a few sidelong glances from xenophobic concierges but in the end I was white, European, multilingual and had a diploma; therefore I was not exposed to a tenth of the racial or social prejudices that French people reserve for foreigners. In intellectual circles, being a foreigner was even a plus. It gave me a slightly exotic touch, which must have made me more interesting. By the way, André Glucksmann used to tease me about it, saying, 'Sometimes you come out with commonplace remarks but your accent makes them sound very deep.' In any case, I had the leisure to carry my foreigner status in France lightly. Although I must say that, in this respect, I went through several stages.

At the beginning, I wanted to become as French as possible. It was both an existential need and an intellectual challenge. A great many foreigners go through a period like this, of wanting to be as much like the 'natives' as possible, to master all the codes, to be like the other in order to feel accepted. After a year in France, I claimed that I had tasted all the cheeses, that I could distinguish a Bordeaux from a Bourgogne with my eyes closed, even determine the vintage year. I wanted to know the geography of France well so I took advantage of every occasion I had to visit all its regions. I wanted to learn French history (contemporary politics did not interest me yet) and master all of the subtleties of the language (which I'm afraid I did not accomplish).

This period of immersion and total mimicry lasted for a while. I must say that my integration was very quick indeed. By 1964, I was publishing (bad) articles in French. In 1966, I defended my thesis with Barthes. The same year I got married for the first time—obviously, to a French woman. In 1967, I was admitted to the CNRS where I still work today. I had already published my translation of the Russian formalists, had directed the first issue of the journal *Langages* entitled 'Semantic Research'; my first book, *Littérature et signification*, based on my thesis, was published the same year. My resident permit had changed colours: it was green, not orange, and I renewed it a little less often. I was not particularly nostalgic for Bulgaria, even though I did not have a negative picture of it. I deplored its political regime but I quickly realized that my Bulgarian education had been quite decent and I was very much at the same level as the other students, French or foreign, whom I could meet at Barthes' seminar or in the other classes. My Bulgarian complex of inferiority had faded. But Bulgaria was no longer of relevance.

Did your naturalization confirm your desire to be a Frenchman among others?

Quite the opposite. This ultimate step to integration is what, paradoxically, enabled me to abandon this desire. I strongly wanted to be naturalized in order to mark my integration in French society and, at the same time, to be free to travel outside of France. You cannot imagine the obstacles a Bulgarian had to get around to go to Rome from Paris!

I discovered on that occasion the great suspicion of the French administration towards Eastern European nationals—so great that it almost prevented me from being naturalized. And so I found myself, once again, having to meet the minister. I first sent all the documents, as I had for my Bulgarian passport, and waited. No response. And this even though I met all the specifications: length of stay, marriage to a French woman, degree obtained in France. One day I received a summons. The man who received me asked if I knew why I had been summoned. I said no. He told me I was at the DST, the French counter-Intelligence service. Then he started to interrogate me: 'At such-and-such date, you were at Orly airport to meet a Bulgarian. Who was he? What did you talk about?' I realized that not only the Bulgarian Embassy, but also the French secret service had a thick file on me . . . one as empty of any real substance as the other since I preferred poetics to politics by far at the time. So there were two guys tailing me, one from the DST and one from the Bulgarian Embassy. I hope they stopped to have some drinks together, at least; if not, they must have been bored to death. When I looked behind me in the streets to see it anybody was following me, it wasn't pure paranoia after all.

Between you and me, I would never have been a spy for Bulgaria. I was filled with a sense of loyalty to the country that had opened its doors to me. But the official in front of me had his geopolitical categories and did not care a wit about my psychological frame of mind.

foreign, assimilated, estranged

At one point, the conversation took an unexpected, and for me, a completely fantastic turn: my interlocutor started to insinuate that I had instigated the May 1968 revolts. This was rather comical considering what I thought about them—revolution was really not my cup of tea. Moreover, I had spent the entire school year from 1967 to 1968 teaching in the United States. How could I have prepared a popular uprising? But this official stuck to his idea, and I'll tell you why. It so happens that, when I left France in September 1967, I had left the apartment in which I was living with my first wife to a young girl, Bénédicte, whom I had met at Barthes' seminar. Little did I know at the time that Bénédicte lived with a boy who taught sociology at Nanterre; even less did I know that this sociologist would become, nine months later, one of the leaders of the May 1968 movement!

So here I was being accused first of spying for Bulgaria and then of having led a revolutionary conspiracy! To my great dismay, I saw my chance of being naturalized slipping away as I was talking to this DST official—and all because of an apartment I had left, sadly by the way, since I was also leaving my wife. I protested vehemently, but my interlocutor did not care. 'They all deny,' he said placidly. It was an infernal mechanism, even though what was at stake was not a matter of life and death. My cries of indignation were also interpreted as 'denials' by this man who was used to unmasking enemies; the more I spoke out, the more I proved my guilt. I was becoming the living illustration of the kind of character we read about in books—the victim of a misunderstanding. I was coming up again the wall of the administration's certitudes. I left the DST building feeling very depressed.

The imbroglio was resolved, I must say, in quite a 'Bulgarian' way. I told Barthes how upset I was. He knew somebody at the École des hautes études who had 'connections'. This person intervened — I don't really know how — and my application was taken out of this absurd impasse. One day, to my great joy, I received a letter confirming my naturalization. Like in Bulgaria, personal intervention, not impersonal law, had unlocked the situation.

In this case, it was a matter of 'pulling strings'!

That's what did it! And I think with compassion about those who have no 'strings' to pull. There's no doubt about it — we are not all really equal before the law. Besides, I had the confirmation, through a rather burlesque epilogue, that without this 'friendly' intervention, my application would have been thrown into the bin. A few weeks after I received my naturalization letter, my doorbell rang. I open the door to find these two young guys, wearing jackets and trainers. One of them tells me: 'We work at the Prefecture. We know that you've asked to be naturalized. There's a good chance you'll be refused, but, if you want, we can give you a little hand.' Like a fool, I immediately responded, 'But I've already obtained my naturalization, a month ago!' They looked at each other and rushed down the stairs before I had the time to ask for their names and addresses.

They were just low-ranking civil servants who wanted to supplement their income. It was like finding myself back in Bulgaria — all differences notwithstanding, of course. In France, there are two clearly distinct entities: the law on one side and on the other, the individual who embodies the law at a specific point in time. The abstract authority and the holder of power. There can be interferences, we all know that, but when they are discovered, they are denounced and eliminated. In France, it is conceivable, as we have seen on several occasions in the recent past, to condemn a former minister on legal not political grounds. This was not the case in totalitarian Bulgaria where authority and power were one.

foreign, assimilated, estranged

That was how it happened. I have been French since then. Since exactly 5 June 1973, 10 years after my arrival.

What did this new national identity card change for you as far as your inner identity was concerned?

First of all, it regularized my relationship with Bulgaria. It's like a divorce. Generally, by the time the divorce is granted, the separation has been effective for a long time; the feelings are dead and consequently, we think that it is a mere formality. But this is not true—the gesture enables you to say goodbye to the relationship because it provides a legal translation for personal experience. At that point you can even re-establish calm relations with the ex-spouse, on a new basis, with neither reproaching the other for the lack of love. This is something like what happened for me with Bulgaria. From that point on, I had left it in the eyes of the law.

And what about your relationship with France? What did this document change? You mentioned the paradoxical effect of your naturalization.

Once I had obtained French citizenship, and because 10 years had gone by since my arrival in Paris, I realized that I would never be altogether French like other people. I would always have a distance vis-à-vis the national identity that people born and raised in France would not have. No, what I'm saying is a little presumptuous—it is not due to a personal quality, it is a matter of fact. To put it another way: my biographical background has offered me this distance, whereas people who have never left the culture they were born into have to make a personal effort to discover the arbitrariness of their habits. As for me, try as I might to be integrated, the difference will never vanish. The sign of this difference is the accent I have kept. And, at bottom, it's better this way. At the same time, the integration that was mine, the assurance that I was similar to the people among whom I lived, enabled me to deal with my new French identity better and no longer react solely as an ex-national of a totalitarian country.

That is how you became a 'homme dépaysé', *to borrow the title of one of your books. What exactly does the expression mean?*

I was a foreigner at first who strove to become assimilated; once I obtained my naturalization, once my integration was accomplished, I found that I was in fact a *homme dépaysé* (an estranged man). I prefer this expression to 'uprooted' which I find inappropriate and even nonsensical, to be perfectly frank. Human beings are not plants; their flexibility, their capacity to adapt to a variety of environments is even what characterizes them, among other living species. In the term *dépaysé* I hear at the same time the departure from one's country of origin and the surprised, new and different gaze that one brings to one's host country — an estranging (*dépaysant*) effect this time. And I experience this condition as something enriching, not impoverishing.

Towards the end of The Conquest of America *you quote a passage from Hugh of Saint-Victor: 'The man who finds his homeland sweet is still a tender beginner; he to whom every soil is as his native one is already strong; but he is perfect to whom the entire world is a foreign land.' Whatever Saint-Victor's original meaning might have been, we can take this today as the credo of the stateless and the nomad. Do you see yourself in it? Is that what being an 'estranged man' is?*

Hugh of Saint-Victor, in the twelfth century, was obviously referring to detachment from all earthly life. I do indeed like the passage and I especially find significant the way it reached me. I read it in a text by Edward Said, a Palestinian living in exile in New York who picked it up himself from a study by Erich Auerbach, a German philologist of Jewish origin who was living in exile in Istanbul during the

Nazi period. It thus suited the Bulgarian in Paris well! But I do not take it literally. I have a homeland today, and that is France, and I am happy about it. Being stateless is only desirable in the abstract, not in the real administrative world where it is essentially a source of annoyance, if not worse. Another victim of the Nazi persecution of the Jews, Stefan Zweig, writes in his memoirs, *The World of Yesterday*, that he used to like thinking of himself as a cosmopolitan, an individual who simply inhabited the planet Earth, until the day he lost his Austrian passport and discovered the distress of being truly stateless.

It is not only on the administrative level that the indifference to a homeland is deceptive. Cultures are, by definition, particular and local, and to acquire a culture takes time. In a lifetime, one can acquire a second culture, perhaps a third, but not more. In that sense also, France is not a foreign country to me any more and it is better this way.

The meetings of cultures

You started writing in French even before you had perfectly mastered the language. How do you like French today? Have you established a kind of personal order between the five languages you speak or do you feel linguistically estranged (dépaysé)?

At first, I would get a friend to reread and correct the texts I wrote in French. But it came to me quickly. I lived totally immersed in the language and practising it helped me. I still make small mistakes here and there—I'm counting on you to remove them from the transcript! On the other hand, I'm now incapable of writing correctly in Bulgarian, whereas I continue to speak it without the slightest difficulty (although with a vocabulary that must be out of date; I'm unfamiliar with the way young people express themselves these days). If I publish something in Bulgarian, I have to get it translated from the French by someone else. I feel at ease in English too, but here again I confine myself to speaking, much to my regret. I like the style of certain English publications, and I would have enjoyed writing for them directly. The order, therefore, established itself, by force of circumstance.

I am not sure I 'like' the French language. I try to use it as well as I can, to express my thoughts and feelings with utmost clarity and precision, but it remains an instrument to me, not an object of affection. It is probably in this sense that I am not a real writer. And yet I personally know people who spoke another language originally and who are now French writers; I guess I must not have been destined to become one.

Did you also find food to nurture your experience of integration into another culture in books, as intellectuals are wont to do?

Of course! During that period (the end of the seventies), I read and studied Mikhail Bakhtin a lot, a Russian thinker who probably influenced me and who certainly helped me go beyond formalism in literary studies. Bakhtin had introduced a category, using a Russian term that is a little difficult to translate, *vnenakhodimost* (which I translated as 'exotopy'). It helps us understand what I call *dépaysement*. He talks about it in particular when he describes the work of interpretation. Interpreters are, by definition, exterior to the text they analyse but, according to the classical conception, they must endeavour to get as close to the author as possible, to immerse themselves in the author's universe and become one with him or her. Bakhtin suggests that the reader's exteriority is both irreducible and useful, that meaning stays alive only because there is a continued dialogue, because a second consciousness meets the first. The reader's exotopy is an advantage, not a handicap. That does not mean that all interpretations are equally accurate, neither does it mean that a misunderstanding is necessarily at work, but rather that, conscious of what I am, I engage in a dialogue with the work I am reading. And a dialogue always involves a confrontation of differences.

At the time, I began studying Bakhtin's work and thought because I wanted to understand it better. He is an author with a chaotic biography, for both political and personal reasons. He taught his disciples in the manner of Socrates, by talking rather than writing. As a result, it was his disciples who published the first books formulating his thoughts—as if he were hiding behind pseudonyms. Then he was condemned by the Soviet regime and deported; he continued to develop his ideas but still did not publish anything. His own writings did not appear until decades later, some not until after his death. For all these reasons, getting into his thinking is a difficult enterprise, a real challenge for the interpreter. I fell for the game and did not come out unscathed. Whereas I was counting on integrating his thought into mine, Bakhtin was the one to attract me towards him, not so much by his way of reading texts as by the very fact that he was both a subtle analyst of literary texts and a thinker. Moreover, his thinking allowed me to formulate in a clear way what I had confusedly felt until then.

What attracted you in his thinking?

It was not only the idea of a positive 'exotopy' but also his insistence on our irreducible social dimension. The human being as a dialogic being, a dialogue that assumes very different forms with interlocutors, present or absent, individual or collective, agreeing or disagreeing. Dialogue appears to be the locus par excellence of the emergence of meaning, and is itself governed by the ideal of truth, without this truth ever being able to be established in it. It is rather the ultimate horizon of the dialogue—for us to be able to talk, to agree or disagree, the possibility of truth must be postulated. But this horizon can never be appropriated; after all, what characterizes the horizon is that it is unreachable. My study of Bakhtin thus also led me to works of a new nature.

Before we come to the consequences of this 'exotopy' on your work, I would like to return to everyday life. In what circumstances do you feel this dépaysement *that you've been talking about?*

In all sorts of circumstances. Let's take the professional world, for instance. A very powerful model of intellectual excellence has taken hold in France, a model that young French students are encouraged to imitate. I'm thinking of brilliant students, just out of one of the *grandes écoles*, capable of absorbing a lot of information in very little time and regurgitating it all in the form of a dissertation — that fine rhetoric that all too often (poorly) replaces direct observation, authentic experience and original thinking. There is also the fondness for striking, slightly paradoxical statements that have such a hard time passing the translation test . . . Not to mention the cult of wordplays! I am not saying that these are deficiencies to avoid absolutely, but they are choices that are not compulsory. It is a handicap that is inherent to all forms of education — professors teach students to be like they are. We are threatened by reproduction. If students do not always imitate teachers, it is because they are confronted with multiple influences from a variety of sources and they have to recompose them in their own way. In France (or should I say, in Paris?), there is an excessive amount of self-satisfaction. People don't realize that they are maintaining in this way a rather conventional, monotonous discourse, stamped with the seal of conformism.

Marginality and singularity can sometimes be a weakness; it can also be an asset in escaping stereotypes and getting back in touch with the world, beyond conventional grids.

Do you think that French culture is especially exposed to the danger of conformism?

Possibly a little more than others, as a result, I think, of the country's extreme centralization and its rarely assumed heritage from the monarchy. The seventeenth-century moralists were aware of this. La Bruyère, for example, observed that the court creates a model that the rest of society hastens to imitate. Montesquieu had one of his characters in *Persian Letters* say, 'The prince communicates his own sentiments to the court, the court to the city, the city to the provinces.' This need to conform to a model is promoted in a country with a unique centre, like France; it has thus survived the Revolution and takes on the form today of imitating this model of excellence.

Did you try to change this state of affairs?

Indirectly, by making it one of the subjects of my research. I also took part in an interesting group experiment, in the *Lettre internationale*, created in Paris in 1984 by a Czech emigrant, Antonin Liehm. The journal was international in two ways: it had contributors from a wide variety of countries and it also had a series of national editions, with a partially autonomous content, in Italy, Spain, Germany and Eastern Europe. I started getting involved in the *Lettre internationale* in 1986 and for five years contributed a regular column, a 'correspondence', commenting on new books and events, a number of which were reprinted in *L'Homme dépaysé*. Liehm's project showed great openness; the texts that were translated in the *Lettre internationale* were of a very high level and they were generally unknown in France. Yet, the review had to shut down a few years later.

It wasn't because of a lack of quality contributions. I believe, rather, that Liehm underestimated the self-centredness of French culture, more specifically of Parisian culture. A journal that did not speak of what was going on here had no chance of success. Parisians do not act like the people living in Prague, happy to know what is going on in the rest of this huge world. The international section of the journal would have had to be counterbalanced by a strong French section — which never came. I draw a lesson from this: rare are those who see themselves in pure internationalism and escape nativism.

Do you think you need to actually undergo the physical experience of exile to acquire this 'outsideness' (dépaysement) of the gaze?

No, of course not. One can arrive at this 'outsidedness' by way of other paths altogether. When I talk about singularity, I am not only thinking of the status of foreigner. It can result from crossing social barriers or simply from a personal path in
life that, for various reasons, leads the person outside the norm. Montesquieu was
perfectly French. But he took the trouble, through reading and travelling, to put
himself into the other's place and see himself from the outside, whence this very
refreshing book, the *Persian Letters*. We gain from self-detachment, because it
enables us to become more aware of ourselves. And this consciousness is precisely
what sets our species apart in the living world.

I am not completely Bulgarian myself any more nor am I entirely French like
other people; I am a hybrid. But this mix is not peculiar to exiles alone. You yourself make adjustments between your provincial side and your Parisian side,
between feminine and masculine traditions, between your parent's social world
and your own. We are all cultural hybrids. Certain cases are simply more visible
and more telling than others.

My awareness of this condition left its mark on my personal life. During those
years, in 1978–79, I met the woman who would become my wife and still is: Nancy
Houston, an English-speaking Canadian. Few things link Calgary and Sofia. But,
like me, she had been living in France for years, was writing in French and was
active in the French public arena. Whereas the year before I could apparently only
fall in love with French women, this time I chose to live with a person like me,
both outside and inside: an 'estranged' (*dépaysée*) woman.

This encounter contributed to reorienting my life, no less than naturalization
or paternity had. We have a strong intellectual bond, not only an emotional one.
We influence each other, so much so that I sometimes have a hard time knowing
what is my own. She certainly contributed to detaching me from the academic

world, helped me accept the continuity between life and thought and enabled me to say 'I' in my writings. Estrangement (*dépaysement*), maternal caring and high moral standards are a few of the themes our books have in common, even if we deal with them in very different ways. We each draw our individual strength from this bond.

To come back to the effects of cultural hybridity — we have noticed that a good number of our friends and acquaintances have a similar status, that they too are foreigners who have settled in France. Don't get me wrong — this is not a conscious choice based on these criteria. Friendship and love develop not for generic reasons but because of the person, 'because it was he, because it was me'. We simply notice, after the fact, that these invisible affinities must have had a role.

Once again, others feel this distance and difference for reasons other than immigration. It's simply that immigration offers it to you as a gift.

Fully entering the world

In talking about the change in direction in your life in the years 1973–74, you mentioned another event, even more personal, that one would not expect to see figuring as decisive in the biography of a public man: the fact that you became a father. How did this child change you?

It changed me in several ways. For a variety reasons, I felt strongly concerned by the arrival of this child and I wanted to live this experience fully. And unless you plug up your eyes and shut your eyes, an infant forces you to live here and now. Children will not be reduced to abstractions—they cry and laugh for you, and ask you for a response. They force you to accept the continuity between material life and spiritual life. Loving them in your heart also has to take the form of washing their bottoms, changing them, preparing their bottles—not too hot and not too cold.

In reaction to this brutal intrusion of new preoccupations and gestures, so different from what I was used to, two attitudes were possible. Either I firmly separated my person and my life into compartments and, in this case, my becoming French or my becoming a father would have had no impact on my way of thinking and hence on the content of my work which is a work of thought. Or I tried to establish, if not a perfect coherence, at least a communication. Now, I was averse to the first option because it resembled too much the attitude of the Bulgarians whom I had known who elevated hypocrisy and thus also discontinuity to a mode of life: good drinking companions at night, obedient conformists during the day. I opted to search for continuity and my way of thinking was transformed as a result.

In that sense I felt at odds not only with my former compatriots but also with a good number of French intellectuals. And I'm not merely talking about the bourgeois intellectuals spouting revolutionary doctrines whom I had met when I came to France. You know as well as I all the philosophers and writers for whom only the life of the mind, only their research and creations exist, and who would love to reduce their physical presence in the world to a minimum or who, in any case, would rather not take it into consideration in their work; from material life, they retain only the body, itself reduced to sexuality. Personally, I do not believe, to borrow Mallarmé's terms, that 'everything in the world exists in order to end up in a book.' Exchanges in friendship and in love and material life matter a lot to me. I like to work with my hands, to fix up my house, cook for my friends and family, take walks in the forest and smell the soil. And I absolutely do not want to isolate these experiences from the work of the mind. My thinking must not ignore the pleasure of my senses.

You are going to think that I have a score to settle with Sartre, which is not the case, but once again he is the one who comes to my mind as a counter-example.

You know, the attitude of, 'I live in a hotel, have no children, and no day-to-day concerns.' A lot of less famous intellectuals adopt the same attitude, sometimes without realizing it. I take exception to it on two points: first of all, I feel that they are missing out on fundamental life experiences (how I pity all these young men who did not see their children growing up because they had to finish their thesis!); secondly, I believe that no impenetrable wall should separate thinking from these aspects of life. Otherwise, you risk producing an image of the world in your work that has no relation to the world in which you yourself live.

So you learnt to live in the concrete reality of the world. That could have changed your way of approaching work without modifying its content. Yet, it was precisely during those years that your enthusiasm for the structural analysis of narrative waned. What relationship do you establish between these changes in your private life and the development of your work?

Before this twofold change—my naturalization and my paternity—I was floating in a rather abstract, imaginary world, that of my work, or else I would let my different lives develop parallel to one another, without any interaction. My feet were not really on the ground. Without realizing it, I continued to be shaped by my Bulgarian past. The public arena in Bulgaria was 'uninhabitable', so I acted as if it didn't exist. The public arena in France did not suffer from the same shortcomings, yet I kept the same avoidance attitude. The content of my work changed the day I took the world that existed around me into consideration. Admittedly, I could have noticed it earlier! I realized that the criticism that I was (silently) addressing to militant French comrades or to political life in general—the empty talk and the lack of correspondence between words and deeds—could be applied to me in another way, because I had let this distance grow between my professional work and the person I was in private. From then on, I strove to establish continuity between my identity and my ideas, to bring my subjects of study and my existential concerns together. The 'I' that I was to use in my writings was not going to remain purely rhetorical.

After this turning point, my books took another direction. The apprenticeship was over. I did not know at the time that, like Goethe's hero, Wilhelm Meister, I was about to embark on my 'years of journeying' that would be longer still than my 'years of apprenticeship'.

You talk about this change in direction as if, faced with a real dilemma, you had made a clear-cut decision, almost an ethical choice. Wasn't your full entrance into the world simply due to psychological factors that escaped your control? Your becoming a French citizen and a father were two events that naturally removed you from a temporary context and situated you in the long-term, in a place, in an history. Or, more simply still, you were then at the age when people 'build their homes' as we say.

It is true that none of this occurred to me at the time. And it was not a free choice: I could not do otherwise. I also like the idea that after a certain age, say 40, your identity becomes more stable. You have already made some major choices that you won't go back on any more and this was my case. Also, knowing how to make the temporary permanent and the relative absolute is one of the characteristics of our species. On the other hand, one cannot set down such a clear-cut boundary between the voluntary and the involuntary, the conscious and the unconscious. Decisions, in cases like this, are partly conscious. External determinations do not explain everything: all 40-year-old men do not react the same way, nor do all fathers or all citizens of the country they live in. Circumstances influence you, but they do not decide for you. I was looking to satisfy demands that were already in me but where did they come from? Be that as it may, ever since then, my life is poor in outside events, even though my interests continue to evolve (I'm still 'journeying').

In sum, your biography ends exactly at the moment your autobiography begins! Would you agree that it is possible to read your books from that time on as autobiographical? In what way are you present in them?

Precisely not in an autobiographical way! That is absolutely not what attracted me. Actually, it is our interviews today that come close to an autobiography. At the end of the seventies, I was not ready for that at all. I have always had a strong distrust of narcissist attitudes, of people who take pleasure in talking about themselves and, a fortiori, in saying good things about themselves. You know, like those people in the limelight who are interviewed on television and respond to compliments by glibly explaining why they are so terrific! I feel ashamed for them when I see them succumbing to the childish desire of being flattered. Yet, even without bragging, introducing autobiographic narrative into research can be quite irritating. Self-knowledge cannot replace knowledge of the world.

Then what do you mean by bringing your subjects of study closer to your life? Here again, if I understand you correctly, you are talking about an intermediary position between inside and outside, presence and absence.

As is often the case, both extremes are to be avoided: an impermeable separation as much as the invasive presence of the author as a person in his or her work. Autobiographies are obviously legitimate in their own right; their quality simply depends on the interest of the events recounted and the writer's talents. In the human sciences, in history, in philosophy, the author's intervention can assume more discreet forms. It remains the hidden driving force behind the research, the motivating factor governing the very choice of the object of study and of the perspective that will be adopted.

You cannot truly progress in the knowledge of the human without being deeply engaged in it, with your whole being. Otherwise, what you produce is, at best, a variation of what already exists, with the addition of new information or a more brilliant presentation. I would like to quote in this regard a statement by Simone Weil to which I subscribe: 'The acquisition of knowledge brings one closer to the truth when it concerns knowledge about what one loves, and in no other case.' The difference is here described as one between knowledge and truth, with the search for the latter requiring total involvement: it has to cost you personally. Thinking is a struggle against your own mental habits; their transformation alters the very identity of our being.

The result is not necessarily blatant. The engagement of the subject in what he or she writes can remain nearly invisible, but it is essential nonetheless. It can be a matter of minor appearances of the author in the book. When François Furet tells us, in the course of a sentence in *The Passing of an Illusion*, that he himself once shared Communist hopes before renouncing them, it helps us read the book better. In my writings over the past two decades, my personal interventions have been generally limited to a preface or a few scattered passages that serve to remind readers that they are dealing with an individual who is trying to think, not with a form of impersonal knowledge as in physics or biology.

5. Human Diversity

The Conquest of America — *Cultural plurality, moral unity* — On Human Diversity — *A culture that does not change, dies*

The Conquest of America

CATHERINE PORTEVIN: The Conquest of America, *published in 1982, is the first book in which you leave the confines of literary studies and turn your attention to the world. Through a look at the history of the conquest and accounts by Cortés, Columbus and the Aztecs, you address the theme of the foreigner, of the encounter between two cultures, the 'question of the other'. This is a theme that was directly inspired, as we have seen, by your experience. Were you looking for a subject like this or was it a coincidence that you understood later?*

TZVETAN TODOROV: It was not by accident that I chose to examine the history of the discovery and conquest of America, the most spectacular encounter between two parts of humanity. All of the accounts also spoke to me about me. In this way, my identity as an 'estranged man' (*homme dépaysé*) confronting the encounter between two cultures, yet keenly aware of the unity of humankind, came to be introduced into my field of interest. The history of Mexico's conquest became, in that respect, a wonderful allegory, written in majuscules, of my minuscule history.

But you could have chosen another place and time in history to study. What was the origin of your interest in the accounts given by the conquistadors and the Aztecs?

My interest was sparked by circumstances. I went to Mexico in the spring of 1978. I gave courses on the history of criticism, literary genres and symbolism in language — that was what I knew how to do. Finding myself in Mexico, I wanted to learn more about this bewitching culture that possessed an intensity that is seldom realized. It was more or less by chance that the chronicle of a Spanish conquistador fell into my hands. It was written by Bernal Diaz, a man of the people, a simple soldier who, with incomparable narrative skill, using countless funny and moving anecdotes, recounts his extravagant impressions of the conquest of this country. Try to imagine the Spanish soldiers discovering this exotic kingdom, streaming with gold and splendour and, at the same time, practising human sacrifice.

I could not put the book down. Thereafter I read Cortés' letters to Charles V, which were equally fascinating, then a small anthology called *The Vision of the Vanquished* which presented the testimonies of Aztecs recorded by missionaries at the time. Little by little, a project took shape in my mind. The field was entirely new to me, but the subject — an encounter between cultures — irresistibly attracted me. As to how to approach it — I could make use of concepts with which I had become familiar in previous years.

Thereupon, I plunged into the study of texts describing the encounter between the Spanish and the Amerindians at the end of the fifteenth century and the start of the sixteenth. I was able to do so thanks to the flexibility offered to me by the CNRS. I spent three years working on the project—I read a lot of texts in translation, in English, French or German, and I learnt a little Spanish to be able to decipher the writings that had never been translated and to check the presence of this or that term. I also went back to Mexico and was able to work in the El Colegio de México library where I found texts that were unavailable elsewhere.

In what respect did your knowledge about language and symbols help you?

I maintained a semiotic perspective at the beginning. I even thought of using 'The Semiotics of the Other' as a subtitle but my publisher at Seuil felt that it was too abstruse. I decided on 'The Question of the Other', which corresponded well to the subject. The semiotic perspective enabled me to enter the subject—it was the reason why I did not feel too alien to the field. I turned to semiotics, in particular, to help me answer an old question, the one every reader of these accounts spontaneously asks: how could Cortés defeat Moctezuma when he had 200 men in his pay against the 20,000 on the other side? Of course, the Spanish were good soldiers and they had a few rifles but those were not machine guns, they could fire with them maybe once every half an hour. The technological superiority could not suffice in itself to explain the victory. It was here that the semiotic perspective turned out to be useful to me. One can say that Cortés' victory was due in part to the fact that he communicated better. Before I wrote my book, I published an article that contained the seeds of this hypothesis, entitled 'Cortés and Moctezuma: On Communication'.

What do you mean by communicating better? Are you speaking of communication in the sense that consultants to politicians would use the term?

Not so very differently, as you will see. A broad distinction has to be introduced here between communicating with men and communicating with the world.

Communicating with the world is an odd form of communication, since the world is not a subject but a complex of signs to be interpreted. A society may cultivate and favour one form of communication or the other. My hypothesis was that Cortés won the confrontation thanks to his extraordinary skill in communicating with men.

If you take an interest in such questions and in this type of behaviour — which has seldom been the case with historians working on the subject — you notice, for example, that his expedition began with a significant and very original gesture: the search for an interpreter. His soldiers wanted to embark on an immediate foray for gold — an eminently desirable commodity at the time and which they had heard could be found in those parts. Cortés stopped them from doing so. On the other hand, having heard Indians pronouncing a few words in Spanish one day, he concluded that there must be some Spanish survivors from a shipwreck living among them. This time he was interested, and he hastily sent his men out to look for them. His intuition proved accurate: a few days later a Spanish man dressed as an Indian was brought before him and he became Cortés' first interpreter. Later, Cortés had an Indian mistress, La Malinche, who spoke several local languages and who quickly picked up Spanish. These interpreters were to play a decisive role in the conquest. The difference between the other conquistadors and Cortés was that he wanted not *to take* but *to understand*. Or rather, to understand first, the better to take after!

Thanks to his understanding of what was going on around him, Cortés discovered the weak points of the Aztec Empire: the internal conflicts between populations and local dissatisfaction with Aztec hegemony. He was able to efficiently exploit it because he had learnt not only how to decipher the messages of the others but also how to send back to them the signals he wanted to transmit, that is to say, those determined by the effect he wanted to obtain.

The culminating point of this semiotic manipulation, of this war of signs, was the use Cortés made of the Quetzalcoatl myth. According to traditional accounts, this god of the Aztec pantheon had left the country promising to return one day. When the Aztecs learned of the appearance of the Spaniards on the coast, they immediately began asking themselves whether this could be Quetzalcoatl returning. Far from dissuading them, Cortés did everything he could to lend credence to this interpretation, thereby providing a local legitimacy for his aspirations to power.

How would you historically situate Cortés' way of practicing communication?

First of all, Cortés was the spiritual heir to Machiavelli. He had absorbed the great lesson: emancipated from religious and moral imperatives, political action, to be successful, must adapt to the circumstances and not conform to pre-existing rules. His way of communicating was an illustration of this—he learnt to interpret signs in order to use them and achieve his ends. Cortés' victory was the victory of effective communication, of the capacity to understand the other, to comprehend foreigners so as to bring them where you want them. We have here a consummate model of the art of communication in which we can find some aspects of our modern communications strategies. What characterizes Cortés' communication with human beings is precisely the fact that it was exclusively strategic. He was continually anticipating his interlocutor's reactions so that he would behave in a way that would help him attain his goal. All in all, he had a perfectly pragmatic, utilitarian outlook.

At the same time, Cortés exemplified another trait of the Renaissance man: he was keenly aware of individual differences and changes. He recognized the signs of the passage of time, the appearance of the new and death of the old; he was not imprisoned in a repetitive, cyclical conception of history. Thus, he knew how to innovate and how to improvise when faced with the unexpected. The foremost characteristic of the contemporary European culture that Cortés represented was its capacity to adapt to changes. Renaissance men inaugurated a world that was no longer necessarily one of reproduction, a world in which novelty had its place.

Cortés is a very modern character. He prefigured at once the ethnologist, the colonialist, the manager and the modern tourist.

He embodied above all the new figure of the politician, a disciple of Machiavelli's Prince who also possessed a rational framework for interpreting his experience. He thus knew how to enlist the missionary as well as the ethnographer in his service, without neglecting the interests of the businessman.

In comparison with this human communication that Cortés practised, what characterized Moctezuma's communication?

In a society dominated by rituals, as the Aztec society was, the gesture is not only conditioned by the effect that is sought—it is there because that is the rule. For this very reason, it contributes to integration in the cosmic order. The Aztecs had established a harmonious relationship with nature, with the gods and with themselves. The arrival of the Spanish, which was an absolute novelty, deeply disturbed them and it took them 10 years to internalize this change. Unprepared to mentally grasp the new, they tried to find a place for Cortés in their system and so identified him with something they already knew: he was a Quetzalcoatl returning or another god. During this 10-year period, the Spaniards managed to subjugate them entirely.

The way you present Christopher Columbus, he resembles Moctezuma in a way more than Cortés.

tzvetan todorov

Columbus' strength did not reside in communication with human beings — which is why, by the way, he did not have a brilliant political career. To our minds, Columbus remains a naive, credulous and superstitious man who never understood the true significance of his discovery. He was no better equipped than Moctezuma to perceive the new and the different. Not only did he think he was in Asia but, when he did not understand the language of his interlocutors, he doubted it was a language at all. On the other hand, this deeply religious man knew how to interpret the signs of nature well. After all, he managed to cross the Atlantic four times, which meant that he knew how to decipher maps and the elements. One could say that Columbus and Moctezuma, each one in his own way, practised communication with the world better than with human beings.

And are we heirs to Cortés rather than to Moctezuma?

Cortés succeeded beyond his wildest hopes and his model has taken hold among us. However, modernity's victory had its price: Cortés crushed the Aztecs, but we have lost, in part at least, the ability to live in harmony with the world, with our society, with ourselves. We have introduced the instrumental model into communication with human beings, thereby reducing everything to the actor–action–goal paradigm. Take a look at the school system to begin with, where it is the instrumental capacity of performance alone that is valued. Witness as well the immense importance of the economic model in our world, since economy typically works on this paradigm. It was as if our actions were essentially directed to producing an effect when, in fact, three quarters of them escape this model. If I go to visit a friend, it is not with an exterior goal in mind or it would not be friendship. I go see him because I like being with him. The end purpose is in the act itself, not beyond. I have the impression that my own professional interests have changed in relation to these two models: I am less interested today in works than in the process of their making.

Now, in the dominant discourse, 'gratuitous' activities, precisely like friendship, have no place, as if knowing how to listen, to care about your loved ones and to be a good friend count for nothing. This dimension of existence, because it is not named, remains the blind spot of life in society. This does not keep each one of us from experiencing beautiful friendships, of course, but these activities are absent from our common representations and thus from public discourse.

Cultural plurality, moral unity

Communication is not your only focus of study in The Conquest of America. *La Malinche, whom you just mentioned, was not only Cortés' interpreter but also, significantly, an Aztec who was sold as a slave to the Mayans and who, perhaps partly out of vengeance to her own people, embraced Spanish culture. Would you agree that La Malinche is the main character of 'your'* Conquest of America *and maybe the one in whom you recognize yourself the most?*

The theme of cultural hybridity was new to me and I was dealing this time with a theme related to my very identity. I wanted to address the subject through a portrait gallery: one encounters some truly extraordinary characters in the history of the conquest of Mexico.

La Malinche was an Indian who got close to the Spaniards. When the Mexicans rejected Spanish sovereignty and became independent in the nineteenth century, they sought to marginalize the image of the conquistadors and to stigmatize or repress the memory of these traitors to the nation who had contributed to the subjugation of the Aztecs by facilitating communication between the two cultures. In Mexico, pride of place was given to Cuauhtemoc, Moctezuma's successor, for having fought valiantly until the bitter end unlike Moctezuma who remained undecided. As for La Malinche, people preferred to pass over her in silence. But for me, La Malinche was, if not the main character in the book (there is none), at least one of its most engaging. She figures on the cover of my book, in an engraving from the sixteenth-century Mexican manuscript, the *Lienzo de Tlaxcala*, where she is depicted on a throne between Cortés and Moctezuma; she played a central role for the Indians of the time as well. I wrote this book with the feeling of 'rehabilitating' La Malinche. I might add that Octavio Paz, in *The Labyrinth of Solitude*, devoted a chapter to her, regarding her not as the traitor, as the villain of the story, but simply as the embodiment of what the Mexican people would become: a syncretic, hybrid people, like we all are, but more conspicuously so.

Interestingly enough, at the same time in Mexico, many Spaniards were, in a symmetric way, becoming closer to the local populations, some in their way of living, like Gonzalo Guerrero and Cabeza de Vaca, both shipwreck survivors, and others in their intellectual work, like the monks Bernardino de Sahagun and Diego Duran. Various modalities of cultural hybridity were eloquently illustrated in the very first decades following the conquest of Mexico.

A few years later, I was able to pay a part of my debt to these texts that had taught me so much when I co-edited with Georges Baudot, the best French specialist on Nahuatl culture (that of the Aztecs), a collection of accounts of the conquest written by Aztecs (*Récits Aztèques de la Conquête*). These texts, sometimes written in

tzvetan todorov

Spanish, sometimes in Nahuatl, offer us a unique view in history—the Europeans seen from the outside by those who had never even suspected their existence. It is a fascinating book, illustrated with period drawings.

A third theme that can be found in The Conquest of America *is that of ethical judgements. It appears here for the first time in your work, but certainly not for the last.*

This is why the book represented a turning point for me. In *The Conquest of America*, I addressed ethical questions through the agency, in particular, of Las Casas, a generous and courageous Dominican who distinguished himself by defending the Indians. Yet Las Casas' position is not without ambiguity. He defended the Indians against the Spanish because he felt the former corresponded better than the latter to Christian ideals. It did not occur to him not to implicate them at all in Christianity. He asked not for their autonomy but for their more complete integration into the Spanish Empire. I dwelt on his position because it seemed to me to provide a good illustration of the general nature of ethical choices. One does not opt for black or white, and the best-intentioned deeds have their negative counterpart. Of course, Las Casas was right to vehemently protest against the cruelties of the conquest; but his protests disregarded the very identity of the Indians, which is another form of violence. Admittedly, towards the end of his life, his outlook shifted towards one of greater recognition for each tradition's independence.

During a confrontation between two cultures and two peoples, one can put the accent on the equality of their rights and their dignity or on the differences that separate them. The first category is ethical and legal, and describes what ought to be. The second is anthropological and historical, and refers to what is. But neither position is simple. The principle of equality surreptitiously brings with it an anthropological hypothesis, that of identity, which also often translates into a policy of assimilation. This is, to a certain extent, the history of French colonization, conducted in the name of Enlightenment ideals. According to Condorcet, a precursor on the subject, all men have equal rights, including the right to become civilized. Since the French and the English are the most civilized people on Earth, they have the right — even the duty — to bring civilization to the savages ('the duty to interfere'). If the latter resist, and persist in their ignorance, they must be forced to improve. European populations must 'either civilize or peacefully remove the savage nations,' he wrote.

The second attitude has its own pitfalls. Scientific interest in the description of differences could lead us to forget that we all belong to the same species. All groups see themselves as norms of social behaviour. Value judgements creep in here too, as differences tend to be interpreted in terms of hierarchy, of superiority and inferiority. This is the danger that threatens all differentialist ideologies, be they on the Right or the Left. When differences are not seen within an egalitarian framework, apartheid and xenophobia emerge on the horizon. In fact, the same goes for gender differences.

You approach these ethical questions not as a philosopher but, rather, as an historian, a somewhat peculiar sort of historian . . .

What profession should I put on my business card? Historian? Anthropologist? Philosopher? I'd rather not have to choose. I do not see myself doing pure philosophy; I do not master this posture and am not at ease in the entirely abstract discourse. Philosophical anthropology would suit me better, but it does not exist as an independent discipline. Historian could also fit the bill, provided that moral life and aesthetic life can be considered historical subject matters. There was a time when I used to say that I was seeking the 'moral meaning' of history.

But this moral reading is also what gives rise to the catechism!

Catechism is doctrine reduced to precepts, to easily memorized formulas. 'Moral meaning' is something else. It stems from an ancient exegetical doctrine that originated with Saint Augustine and was later codified in the Middle Ages. For centuries, the Bible was the only book to be interpreted, it was thus around the Bible that a doctrine of interpretation was developed. According to this doctrine, the Biblical text always had four levels of meanings to it, one literal and three transposed meanings: the anagogical is related to ultimate ends, the Last Judgement and eternal life; the typological concerns the relation between the Old and the New Testament; and the moral level seeks the meaning of the Biblical message as it relates to the present, to daily life, to the moral practices of believers. To interpret on the level of 'moral meaning' is to choose a framework of interpretation, not to pronounce prohibitions and recommendations.

You present some of your works as 'exemplary narratives'. Does this mean that they are uplifting narratives?

It's a manner of writing history. First of all, the events must be reconstructed as precisely as possible (this is the requirement of factual truth, the truth of adequation). Then, you examine their 'moral meaning', as I was just saying, which means without losing sight of the use that the reader could make of the text in his or her own life.

This form suits me for several reasons. Narrative, unlike abstract analysis, is accessible to a public of lay people; moreover, it proposes rather than imposes, so it provides more leeway to the reader. Narrative history stays in the mind of readers in a way that allows them to come back to it later, on their own terms; it is addressed to their present consciousness but also acts through the agency of memory. Storytelling may be the only way of bringing home an experience that was not ours. Therein lies its great power. We can project ourselves into the characters, real or imaginary, and come back transformed. Arendt said: 'No philosophy, no analysis, no aphorism, be it ever so profound, can compare in intensity and richness of meaning with a properly narrated story.' It seems to me that, from this point of view, an historical narrative possesses the same power as a novel.

I add the term 'exemplary' to indicate that I am not restricting myself to reconstructing the events. It is a reminder to the readers that the past has something to teach them about the present. To remind without teaching a lesson, to raise questions without offering fixed answers—the boundary between the two is sometimes difficult to define with precision.

On Human Diversity

The Conquest of America: the Question of the Other *and, seven years later,* On Human Diversity: Nationalism, Racism, and Exoticism in French Thought [Nous et les autres: la diversité humaine; *lit., 'Us and Others: Human Diversity'*] *are works that are both similar and very different. They are similar thematically, as evidenced by their French titles, in particular, and different by subject matter and the way they are treated.*

I liked (and still like) the stories that I brought back to life in *The Conquest of America* because they do a good job of fostering reflection. The characters that inhabit these stories have stayed with me. However, I had the feeling that my conceptual analysis was not thorough enough, that I had to take it farther. It seemed to me that the most appropriate means of doing so was to confront my own thoughts with the history of thinking on this question—to take advantage, so to speak, of the work of our predecessors. This led me to engage in a 'dialogic history of thought', my second favourite genre, if you will. *On Human Diversity* is written in this spirit, as are *Literature and its Theorists*, *The Morals of History*, *Imperfect Garden* and my studies on La Rochefoucauld, Rousseau, Goethe and Constant.

If I qualify this history of thought as 'dialogic' — an adjective inherited, as you will have noticed, from Bakhtin — it is to distinguish it from an history that is entirely subordinated to the author who is being studied, with the commentator trying to be as invisible as possible and thus disregarding his or her 'exotopy'. The goal is not to talk more about yourself than about Rousseau but to establish a dialogue with him, which implies not stepping aside completely. This is the necessary condition for your study to be a search not only for meaning but for truth. This dialogue is obviously asymmetrical, since your author is usually dead and cannot contradict you. But you can still go quite far in this direction in an attempt not to betray him and to avoid imposing your own ideas on him.

You say history of 'thought' rather than of 'ideas'. What is the distinction?

I would rather speak about the history of 'thought' because 'ideas' are disembodied; they go from one author to another, whereas 'thought' is always bound up with a subject — a person with a biography, a body and a complex of interests. Maybe this is one of the reasons for my affinity with the writing style of French thinkers. I am ill at ease in academic philosophy, in German-style metaphysics, where it is often a matter of pure 'ideas'. I have read Kant, whose thinking is central in the tradition I am interested in, and a few others, but I could never feel as close to these philosophers as I do to some of the French thinkers whom one may very well hesitate to qualify as 'philosophers': people like Montaigne, Pascal, La Rochefoucauld, Rousseau, Diderot and Constant. Beyond labels, it is the thought that draws me and

tzvetan todorov

it goes well beyond the confines of the philosophical tradition per se; it can be found in the works of novelists, scientists, politicians, memorialists and so on.

For *On Human Diversity*, I was following my inclination when I limited myself to French authors from the outset. Besides, it was a way of furthering my integration into French culture, of becoming more familiar with the traditions of the country that had welcomed me. All in all, I was paying a debt I had incurred when I was naturalized.

I open-mindedly set about reading or rereading the 'standard authors' who had thought about this question of human diversity confronted with universality, about how 'we' is defined when situated in relation to 'others'. I was teaching a seminar at the time at the École normale supérieure on rue Ulm in Paris and we read all of the influential French authors, in chronological order, from Montaigne to Barrès and Lévi-Strauss. After a few years, the issues became clearer and I decided not to follow a chronological order and to structure my book instead around a few important questions about which these authors conversed across the centuries: relativism, races, the nation and exoticism. I made an exception for Montesquieu, to whom I devoted the concluding chapter because he seemed to me to be the most convincing thinker on all of these subjects. Rousseau's clear-mindedness was also of great help to me on this occasion. These two authors answered other thinkers, anterior or posterior, in an imaginary dialogue to which I was sometimes so bold as to add my voice.

Do you think that reading the works of thinkers from the past can really shed light on subjects such as nationalism, cultural hybridity, cosmopolitanism and immigration, whose current apprehension depends at least as much on social and political contexts as on conceptual matters?

Racism and nationalism are also current practices. They are dangers that threaten us today, which is why I try to analyse them. I do not think we need to choose between concept and context, between the abstract and the concrete; both are necessary if we want to understand social facts. My contribution was in areas in which I had a certain competence, not in conducting sociological surveys.

These collective passions have resurfaced recently, whereas twentieth-century Europe was dominated by ideological movements that led to totalitarian regimes: Communism and Fascism. Nazi racism itself was more ideological than 'physical': nothing distinguished Jews from 'Aryans', which is why they had to stick a yellow star on them. Taking over from religions, these movements allowed people to recognize themselves in a political programme, moral principles and rules of social life. Nationalism and racism, for their part, confirm the general need for collective belonging but in a much more superficial way. They bring together those who resemble us physically, those who are like we are in linguistic or administrative terms, in opposition to the others. I wonder whether the new situation is truly preferable to the one before, when ideological passions prevailed.

But is the nation always 'bad'?

Of course not! First of all, the nation has a 'republican' sense to it, which opposes it not to other nations but to other means of legitimating politics. When the French proclaimed 'Long Live the Nation!' during the Revolution, it was a cry in support of the people over the king or tradition. But even when it designates the entity by which nationals are distinguished from foreigners, the nation remains perfectly justified. It is the ground on which collective solidarity stands — our health and retirement systems would collapse if they were not restricted to the residents of the country. Every government in Europe today gives a privileged place to its citizens to the detriment of those who aren't. Finally, the nation consolidates our collective identity, our particular culture and all of us need to have at least one.

But criteria of nationality need to be established. It is not so much by its concept that the nation is problematic as by the rules that define nationality. You speak of a country's 'residents' but it isn't so simple: many laws of nationality are more restrictive than that and take into consideration bloodline or religion, for instance.

From a democratic perspective, the state rests on the will of individuals, not on their nature. French citizenship today is based not on blood, skin colour or religion, but on the nationality of one's parents, the place of birth or, in the case of naturalization, a deliberate choice. Residents, even foreigners, should share responsibility for the local life they are leading and participate in local elections. If they do not wish to be naturalized, they should stay out of political life on a national level. The legal problems of the nation do not seem insurmountable to me.

Why then is there a nationalist danger? In other words, what becomes of the reference to the nation when it is posited by an extreme right-wing party like the National Front?

First of all, extreme right-wing nationalists pretend that there is no distinction between private affections and public justice. It is perfectly legitimate to love and prefer those who are close to you; public affairs, on the other hand, must be settled on the basis of equity, not sympathy. I love my children more than my neighbour's but, when they come over to our house, they all get an equal portion of cake. The policies of discrimination conducted in towns governed by the National Front are unacceptable. The foreigners in question are taxed and pay their dues just like French citizens; they should therefore have access to all social rights, without exception: schooling, housing and medical care.

These nationalists are only demagogues looking for a scapegoat. All of your problems, they say in substance, from unemployment to insecurity, if not from pollution to global warming, are due to a single cause: immigrants! This is both false and pernicious.

Demagoguery is the foremost characteristic of extreme right-wing movements today. It usually involves identifying a few social ills, on which everyone agrees — such as insecurity, unemployment and corruption — and proposing seemingly simple remedies which are, in reality, both inapplicable and ineffective. For a start, expelling all foreigners from France and closing the borders is impossible; if it were possible, the result would be disastrous as much for the economy as for the culture, for the demography as for the 'grandeur' of France, to say nothing of morality.

Therefore, one can defend the nation and criticize nationalism. That is why I adopted a critical attitude in my book towards certain nationalists whom many people consider good company, like Jules Michelet and Charles Péguy. On the other hand, one cannot ask of the nation what it cannot give. It has to provide political direction but it has nothing to say about morality. Neither does the nation suffice to found justice.

Is there something to defend in the idea of race?

The idea of race is not shocking in itself and, in any case, it belongs to the sphere of knowledge, not morality or politics. Contemporary biologists establish subdivisions in the human species according to the distribution of physical traits. Note that races have a legal status in the United States, and a given number of positions in the administration and in universities are reserved for members of each one. What biologists have never managed to establish, on the other hand, is a stable correlation between those physical characteristics and mental capacities. Even if such a connection could be established, there would be in this no racism, merely the acknowledgement of a fact. Racism begins when existing differences become the basis of morally unacceptable policies or conduct, when certain races are designated 'inferior', when they are mistreated, when they are massacred. Now, equality is a value for us, not a fact; we want all the individuals in a country, regardless of their characteristics, to have the same rights.

No scientific discovery can shake this ideal. It is not because biology has proven that all races are equal that we are against racism. If that were the case, the opposite could be true. Imagine scientists discovering tomorrow that, after all, races are 'unequal' — well, do we enslave black people again? Take gender equality. Like all mammals, human males are physically stronger, on average, than females. This by no means legitimates male domination — even though it has been exercised for centuries. What 'ought to be' (*le devoir-être*) does not follow from what 'is' (*l'être*). Equality, in rights and in dignity, between all human beings is our ideal because we can reasonably argue that it is superior to any other, not because men are equal in actual fact.

However, we must recognize that human beings — and our fellow citizens are no exception — generally react to visible physical differences without trying to know whether or not they correspond to a biological category. It is a fact that is not to be ignored on the pretext that it is 'politically incorrect'.

Is it vain then — maybe even counterproductive — to attach value to differences in order to defend the ideal of equality?

The defence of universality is the only means of promoting respect for differences. Without it, our distinctive identities can become deadly. Only the law applied to each and every one allows us to assert our singleness without it becoming a reason for aggression. Let us, therefore, first defend the equality of rights, including the right to be oneself.

Nowadays nobody overtly claims to advocate racism, or even nationalism, yet there is no scarcity of acts that fall into these categories. What would be the present-day relevance and validity of the fight against racism?

If we start by morally stigmatizing people, we bar the way to comprehension. Nothing is explained by saying that the French are racists (as they themselves sometimes say in opinion polls). Some sort of innate malice or infirmity cannot explain the tensions and reactions of exclusion that can be observed here and there. They result from the superimposition of physical or cultural groups on the one hand, and social practices on the other. If 'Africans' bump into you three times in a row on a train line running from the suburban slums, you may quickly jump to the conclusion that they are all 'brutes'. The racial response usually hides a social question that we haven't the right to brush aside with a wave of the hand.

The same holds true for national and immigration issues. An immigrant myself, I am not in a position to be impartial. Yet, I think that deculturation can be a real handicap and that it can become a source of aggressive behaviour. Deculturation involves the loss of a first tradition—because your parents did not transmit it to you—without the acquisition of a second culture in its place. When you feel excluded from society, from its usual codes and regulations, the only avenue still open to you is violence.

I find it shocking that, notwithstanding all the great anti-racist rhetorics, there are still so few men and women in politics who are visibly of foreign origin, say, from Africa—North Africa in particular. There are also very few journalists of foreign origin in the media, on television, on the radio, or in the major newspapers and magazines.

Very few renowned professors or intellectuals or heads of major firms too. Is it that the elite, so prompt to denounce ordinary racism in the suburban slums is more racist, deep down, than the 'people'? That they practise a sophisticated form of racism, never declared as such, not murderous but no less responsible for much of the resistance to the integration of immigrants (North Africans and Muslims, especially), since it is this elite that shapes the picture that French society has of itself?

I agree with you completely. It's one heck of a problem that you're raising.

A culture that does not change, dies

In On Human Diversity *you take a stance in favour of a certain form of universalism. Can one say that cosmopolitanism represents your ideal?*

No, although I did go through a phase, at the beginning of the seventies, when I liked to regard myself as a cosmopolitan man, a citizen of the world. I was at ease in Bulgaria, I am in France, I could be in the United States; I am at home everywhere, or precisely nowhere; I am always just passing through, catch me, desire me! From now on, I inhabit the entire world! But it did not last for long. I still understand this attitude but I think it is lacking in lucidity. First of all, because it underestimates our need to have a culture and culture is necessarily particular. No one is neutral in relation to his or her cultural identity, if only because we necessarily speak one language. Of course, you can change languages—I am living proof of this—but you always speak only one language at a time. A universal language will never exist, despite the dreams of certain philosophers, and there is no reason to imagine that such a language would be the guarantee of universal harmony between humans — far from it!

At the political level, cosmopolitanism is also pure fiction. Our human rights are not worth much if they are not guaranteed and defended by a particular state. We obviously all have a simply human, universal side to us that is precious, but it does not come into play at this level. Lastly, I am wary about the cosmopolitanism of economic decision-makers, the media stars and famous authors who make up the jet set. The poetry of airport terminals and international palaces is not my cup of tea.

But, yes, I do consider myself an advocate of universalism, both in the obvious sense of the unity of the human species and in the more problematic sense of a universal understanding — an understanding about what the world is and even what it should be. But I describe this universalism in *On Human Diversity* as being a universalism that is ongoing and flexible and not rigid. Differently put, this universalism posits the possibility of communication and dialogue instead of arguing in favour of unification and standardization. I can confront my worldview with that of a human being who is very different from me, and we can understand each other and understand why we are different. What is fruitful is the meeting of cultures, not cultural eclecticism. This avenue to the universal involves being deeply immersed in the particular. Here again, I diverge from what we usually call cosmopolitanism. Dostoyevsky, who is the most Russian of all Russian writers, is also Russia's most universal writer.

Isn't your view of dialogue a little idealistic? Don't you have a tendency to underestimate the relationships of domination that make such dialogue unequal, regardless of the good-

will of the participants? To put it otherwise, isn't advocating cultural dialogue, when you belong to the dominating culture, a comfortable and not very risky position to take?

I do not disregard relationships of domination, both because I come from a relatively minor culture, that of Bulgaria, and because I studied such relationships, in the case of Cortés, for example, who was a partisan of a strongly slanted dialogue. But if the alternative is isolation and the temptation is to be self-sufficient (which is but an illusion), I would rather take my chances with dialogue. Dialogues are never reduced to pure domination. Even in the case of the colony, the colonists need the colonized and are thus dependent on them, and the colonized know how to appropriate what suits them in the colonizer's culture.

What do you think of what we today call 'globalization'?

I cannot deplore globalization if by that we mean increased communication between people. In this too, I diverge from the opinion of Lévi-Strauss who believed that an acceleration in contacts was dangerous. How can I be against the opening of borders and more frequent encounters? I'm delighted at the greater ease in circulation of people, ideas and information. I think that the extremes that we have been seeing in relation to this will disappear over time. The fact that we are suffering today from certain harmful effects of economic globalization is due to the fact that we have infringed upon one of the great democratic principles — that of pluralism. Politics must not be subordinated to economics, and neither should economics be subordinated to politics as was the case in Communist countries. The political bodies of a country or of a group of countries, like the European Union, must correct the pernicious effects of economic globalization; that is what they are there for. But today we use the word 'globalization' as a synonym for 'capitalism'.

Unless you can specify how these pernicious effects can be corrected, it sounds like wishful thinking.

You're asking me to demonstrate greater versatility than I can, I'm afraid. But this is the purpose of joint projects: philosophers, anthropologists and historians, for instance, should work together with jurists, economists and politicians to search for an adequate response. To each his or her share of the job.

You draw a distinction between the universality of judgements and the particularity of cultures. But what exactly do you mean by 'culture'?

It is in human nature to have a culture. This is, then, a paradoxical nature indeed because the identity of the species resides in the fact that we can be different. To me, culture, which is always collective, is a way of conceiving of the world, a way of organizing the chaos in which we are all immersed. Hence, it also imposes a code of conduct. Culture is not necessarily composed of books and shows, even though we can hardly do without them in our societies. 'We can be men without being scholars,' says Rousseau, but without a culture we are incompletely human. The philosopher Marcel Conche speaks in this regard of 'essential culture', as the culture that exists prior to particular forms of knowledge and which enables us to perceive the world and designate it, to recognize our feelings and express them.

Language is an essential element of culture. You have to master it to make your way successfully through society unless you have another form of interaction with the world, say, visual or corporal. The group's non-verbal traditions, its ways of being and doing are also part of culture. But so are the works of the mind, of course. From this point of view, the Christian heritage is evidently an essential ingredient of European culture.

a culture that does not change

By insisting on the necessity of culture as you do, isn't there a risk of imprisoning people in their individual traditions, in their 'communities', as we say more and more often today? Isn't there a risk of seeing 'culture' play the same role as race once did?

Culture has two characteristics that should stand in the way of this conflation; every individual harbours several cultures, and every culture is constantly evolving.

First characteristic: several cultures. As I was saying before, we are all cultural hybrids. The different layers that constitute individual human beings and human groups do not coincide with each other. Some of your reactions are due to your education, others to the fact that you are a woman or a journalist or French, still others to your age or your personal background. These affiliations do not all perfectly overlap.

I find it rather disturbing to see the old dream of homogeneity resurfacing in the current division of ex-Yugoslavia, with each small territory wanting its independence because of one cultural difference or another. One group wants it because they speak Albanian, another because they are Muslims and a third because their nineteenth-century history was different. This dream of one state, one people, one land has never been a reality; if it became one, it would be more like a nightmare. This movement goes against the tide of all of contemporary history, and I find it regrettable.

The solution to this type of conflict is not in the exercise of a would-be right of each people to self-determination. It is not to be found in the creation of small homogeneous states but in the protection of the status of minorities. That is what should be the great political principle of the twenty-first century. A nation furthers its own good by respecting and protecting its minorities. Why? Because minorities are a particularly dynamic element in a society. They have to be, in order to assert themselves and survive. Take a look at the place that Protestant and Jewish minorities have in France, which is out of proportion with their numerical importance — they strongly contributed to the development of French culture and society.

Second characteristic: every culture is mobile. This is another obvious fact that we all too often forget. A culture that does not change is a dead culture, in the same way that we call a language that no longer changes, like Latin, a 'dead language'. What is French culture? That there has been continuity is unquestionable, and yet not a single element has remained intact. The language has changed, as has the religion, the customs and, of course, the physical types. The extreme right-wing nationalists cry out against the invasion of immigrants in an attempt to arouse fear and cause panic. But the Christians were invaders, as were the Francs and most certainly the Gauls, not to mention the Romans. There is no reason to let ourselves be unduly impressed by the existence of population movements and new influences.

Change and plurality depend on one another. We change within a country because it comprises manifold cultures with shifting hierarchies and interactions, and because contact with other cultures is inevitable. A culture is like Argo, the legendary ship: between its departure and its return, all the planks and all the sails had to be changed yet it was the same ship that came back to port.

If this is the case, why do people hold onto their culture to the point of being willing to get themselves killed for it, as we have seen around us in recent years?

First of all, it's important to say that struggles for power are often disguised as cultural conflicts, in the same way that the social difficulties we were talking about before are disguised as immigration problems. But it is also true that the history of recent decades has shown us the illusory character of a certain individualistic view of the world. In their great majority, human beings need to have a collective identity and to feel that they belong to a recognizable group. As long as the group is not threatened, we do not realize it; we even believe we can do without it. When the group is the object of discrimination or persecution, or simply when it is forced to change very quickly, its members feel they are in danger and try to protect themselves by attacking others. This can happen to any group.

I might add that recourse to this form of recognition—bound up with a sense of collective belonging—is ineluctable when all other paths are blocked. You can see it in the Balkans. The people there would love to be living peaceful lives like ours, getting rich and having time for leisure activities, rather than killing each other in the name of obscure collective identities; but this option is not open to them. When you have no other prospect, you fall back on this last resort. I suspect that the same is true in Algeria: the rise of Islamism, that the government pretends to fight, is in reality fuelled by this same government when it deprives its people of the means to live decently. These are not individuals from another species; they are simply in a situation with no way out.

One can readily follow you as far as principles are concerned. But couldn't the sharp increase in movements of migration and in the number of refugees all over the world turn this mix of cultures (which takes time) into a clash of cultures?

We must not, out of fear of being politically incorrect, act as if immigration had no consequences on the life of our society, or assume that these consequences are necessarily positive. They are in certain respects, in others they are not. The current movements of populations, which are greater than in any other period in history, could endanger social structures. In their new country, fathers turn out to be under-qualified, and thus lose their prestige and their authority over their children.

The mothers, confined to their homes, have a hard time learning the codes of the new society and controlling their children. Neighbours reject the newcomers and their offspring and give in to xenophobia. The upshot is the disorientation of the older generation and the revolt of the youth that often makes headlines. The family of origin cannot assume its regulatory role any more. These youngsters have the feeling that the surrounding society—that looks so appealing to them on TV—rejects them; and so they have no desire to respect its rules and are willing to break them without hesitation. In the place of the social norms that failed comes a form of 'respect' that is, in fact, a submission to force or an admiration for outward signs of wealth, such as cars. In the place of the traditional religion that was never learnt and that is identified with the humiliation of their parents, comes fanatical indoctrination, blind submission to a few slogans learnt by heart, reassuring by their simplicity. From here, the future martyrs and fighters for the holy war will be recruited. In a vicious circle, the marginal situation leads further and further into marginality.

This is a very serious situation, of which the violence is only a visible symptom. It is a situation that requires in-depth treatment of the causes. We must help restore the authority of the parents (or of the 'uncles' or 'big brothers') and patiently repair the social fabric, so that people will appreciate and protect the setting in which they live instead of destroying it.

For someone who defined himself as an anti-political man upon his arrival in France, you have certainly changed. You are smack in the middle of a political debate here.

Thank you, democracy!

6. The Humanist Bark

Universalism with moderation — From Tocqueville to Dumont — What is humanism? —
Loving human beings — Elective affinities — Between the terrorism of truth
and the selfishness of freedom

Universalism with moderation

CATHERINE PORTEVIN: *After abandoning structuralism, you set to sea in a pretty unsure vessel[1] when you became a humanist. One journalist even awarded you the title 'apostle of humanism'! And this, at the end of the seventies, right at the time when everyone was learning at university that humanism was dead — and that man was too, for that matter — and that this was cause for celebration. Was it your non-conformism again that drove you to bring this corpse back to life?*

TZVETAN TODOROV: I am afraid that it is the peasant from the Danube in me again who is to blame. In the sixties and seventies, I was not interested in the debates on the 'death of man'. It simply did not enter my field of vision. I would have been

---

1 '*Vous vous êtes embarqué dans une sacrée galère*': *galère* is a galley, but is used colloquially to refer to a mess or a difficult situation. The sentence could be translated as, 'You've got yourself into one hell of a mess.' My rendering keeps the metaphor of a frail ship at sea that is the title and conclusion of this chapter. [Trans.]

quite incapable at the time of defining what corresponded to the 'humanist' label. But while reading the canonical authors to prepare *On Human Diversity*, I developed the greatest admiration for Montesquieu and Rousseau. I found many of my own intuitions in their works. That was when I discovered the name given to this philosophy in textbooks: 'humanism'. And so I discovered that I too was a 'humanist'. At the beginning of the eighties I also met Luc Ferry, a brilliant young philosopher with whom I became friends. He brought to my attention the critique of the French 'anti-humanism' of the sixties.

Who in particular?

A variety of approaches can be grouped under the label of French anti-humanists: those represented by Foucault and Derrida in philosophy, by Bourdieu in sociology and by Lacan in psychoanalysis. These are French variants on theories developed, for the most part, in Germany, in the thinking of Nietzsche, Heidegger, Marx and Freud. They share a common critical aspect: the refusal to see a responsible subject behind human action (seen as the effect of class affiliation or unconscious structures); the rejection of universality (necessarily a mask for ethnocentrism); the rejection of the distinction between facts and the discourse on facts, between truth and interpretation. Humanism indeed opts for the opposite position each and every time.

I should immediately add that the output of these authors cannot be reduced to an 'anti-humanist' stance. Lévi-Strauss, for example, is close to this line of thought in his general statements, but his description of kinship systems or of American myths does not depend on it at all.

The history of thought resembles a zigzagging movement: every movement corrects the excessiveness of the one before. The 'anti-humanists' were right to criticize the naive confidence and triumphalist discourse of some of their predecessors, but their discourse became excessive in turn.

The humanist theme in On Human Diversity *is universality, which we have already discussed. But is that enough to characterize humanism? Wasn't the universal idea present in European culture long before what we can historically call 'humanism'?*

It is true that the idea of universality, of the unity of humankind and of the equal dignity of all was not advanced for the first time by advocates of the Enlightenment in the eighteenth century, nor even by the humanists of the Renaissance. In the European tradition, we already find it formulated by the Stoics, and then by Christianity. We also find it outside of Europe, particularly in China.

But the European humanists transformed this general idea and specified it. On the one hand, they extended it to the whole of human life, and not only to the human relationship with God; they thus made it independent from the religious framework. Whereas Christian universalism meant that all human beings have access to the same god, the humanist perspective sees them as also having the same rights in the eyes of humans. In addition, and no less importantly, these humanists wanted to unite the idea of human unity with an acknowledgement of the extreme diversity of humankind. Because, as we have seen, the affirmation of unity can surreptitiously become an affirmation of the sameness of all men. In the middle of the sixteenth century, we find, for example, some magnificent declarations by Las Casas on the unity of all nations and all human beings; but he understood this in the old Christian sense and it enabled him, as we have seen, to ignore or, in any case, to disregard, differences.

Now, from the Renaissance on, several developments rendered this interpretation impossible: the great geographic discoveries, the proliferation of journeys to distant lands and the Reformation, with the division of Western Christianity in two and the religious wars. It had become increasingly imperative for a few tolerant great minds to conceive of universality without obliterating diversity.

It is, then, a more problematic universalism because it is no longer pure principle but put to the test of reality—of the 'world', as you like to say—but without lapsing into relativism?

The pitfall or perhaps the temptation is indeed to insist on differences to the point of renouncing unity. The thinkers of religious tolerance, Spinoza, Locke and Pierre Bayle, incurred this reproach from the guardians of Catholic orthodoxy. Accepting that each one prays in their own way, and even that they address themselves to their own god, is this not accepting a plurality of gods, and hence of ideals? How then is it possible to imagine that men are alike everywhere? The plurality of gods would be explained then by the plurality of human groups, by their differences, what was called polygenism.

Those who fought for religious tolerance did not go to that point, but the relativist position has its defenders today and they are not necessarily racists. Relativists today are right to say, for example, that people think differently because they think with the help of language and that the many different languages that exist divide and organize the world in different ways; or that people perceive different worlds because they are conditioned by specific customs, by the social organization peculiar to each people. The unity of the species is not denied, but it is reduced to the biological; at the same time, it is argued that culture is what produces each person's identity. Consequently, there can be no universal values; a common world does not even exist, since every culture construes the world in its own way.

Yet, we have the feeling that there is some truth in relativism, in the recognition of differences in order to resist imposed uniformity. How do you interpret this 'desire' for relativism?

It gains ground as soon as surrounding dogmatisms are undermined because, deep down, the immediate given of existence is diversity: the diversity of individuals, backgrounds, desires, judgements, cultures, historical destinies, choices imposed by language and by each country's history, etc. The refusal of unity is a spontaneous attitude. But this attitude was long held in check in Europe by the existence of a theologico-political system that joined the spiritual and the material in a single structure. Or, if you prefer, temporal power and spiritual power were conflated. This led to dogmatism rather than universalism. Relativism is thus the assertion of human diversity in opposition to dogma. It is tempting, therefore, to fight not against dogma, but in the name of tolerance for diversity — against any absoluteness and any all-encompassing, unifying principle.

In sum, universality and tolerance do not go well together.

Their cohabitation constitutes a real challenge. How can you practise tolerance without lapsing into indifference, without renouncing the universal framework? In *On Human Diversity*, I enjoyed analysing the difficulties that thinkers in the past had in reconciling the two. Montesquieu was the one who achieved the best synthesis. Yet, in the eyes of his contemporaries, he was a relativist. Understandably so, since he first distinguished himself with the *Persian Letters*, which was interpreted as a demonstration of the relativity of viewpoints: the Persians seem ridiculous to the Parisians, and vice versa. And his greatest work, *The Spirit of Laws*, is presented as a sum total of knowledge on the world's different countries, particularly their laws, without judging any from a unique standpoint. Montesquieu says he seeks to reveal reasons for customs, not to condemn or justify them. This is why he is sometimes seen as the founder of modern sociology.

But he is not really a relativist, you say, because his entire analysis is guided by absolute principles, in particular, by the idea of 'moderation'. In what way does moderation, in

Montesquieu's understanding of the term, enable him to conceive of universalism and diversity together, and to defend what is at bottom a quite moderate universalism?

In Montesquieu's writings, the presence of these absolute notions is discreet, but it constitutes the true framework of his analysis. The case of 'moderation' is the most interesting. It never becomes the object of direct examination; it does not even appear overtly as one of the structuring concepts of the argument. It is, notwithstanding, at the root of his study of political regimes, and he clearly uses it as a universal category. The good regime, he asserts, is not necessarily republican or monarchical or aristocratic, but it is necessarily moderate. What does this mean? At bottom, a moderate regime is one in which power is not unlimited; it is shared. Moderate is opposed to 'tyrannical' — the tyrant concentrates all powers in his own hands. What Montesquieu dubbed a 'moderate' regime, we would today call 'pluralistic'. Whence the idea of the separation of powers, to which we are attached, and which is scorned precisely by totalitarian regimes which are 'monist' and not 'pluralistic'.

Montesquieu's teaching here is twofold. First he shows how diversity can be accepted on one level (monarchies or republics, for example, have their reasons and their coherence) and refused on another. Tyranny is to be banished under all climates. Moreover, it is diversity itself that he elevates to the rank of a universal category. It is because each society is itself plural, manifold and made of divergent ingredients and interests, that moderation is a logical political necessity. The balance of powers will preserve every individual's interests.

In a modern democracy, this pluralism is exercised on many levels, not only between the legislative, executive and judicial powers, as Montesquieu advocated. Political reason is separated from morality and religion; politics and economics must remain independent, to which one may add the separation of the private and the public, the plurality of political parties and the media and so on.

You have thus brought Montesquieu back into fashion, when he was not very popular any more. Of the eighteenth-century 'philosophers', Montesquieu is rarely regarded as a seminal reference today. There is a preference for Diderot who was more of an artist, or for Rousseau who was more passionate and more paradoxical which suits our times well.

Yet, Montesquieu had an important posterity—the great liberal philosophy—but it was hidden from view in France during the post-war period, because of the hegemony of the Marxist doctrine. Thinkers like Constant or Tocqueville were greatly indebted to him.

When you take this liberal thinking as a reference, does it mean that you no longer condemn liberalism in the forms that it has taken today?

It seems to me that the word does not always designate what is really at issue. The liberal thinking that I value—in France, Montesquieu, Constant and Tocqueville—is the affirmation of individual autonomy. How could I be against it? Liberalism is a political ideology before being an economical one. We have a tendency today to reverse the hierarchy formed by the two senses of the term, which is regrettable but this regret does not concern the classical authors. We can also criticize present-day liberalism for forgetting the other ingredients of the democratic structure: common affiliation, general will and universal law. We cannot defend liberty alone and set the autonomy of the individual above every other value. Liberty and autonomy must remain coordinated with an equal concern for the common good.

Sometimes, the word 'liberalism' is employed in an even broader sense to refer to the use of might against what is right. This is an eternal struggle. The powerful in this world—whether their might is military, economic or cultural—have always sought to free themselves from the constraints of law, and to reduce common rules to the role of a fig leaf covering up their oversized appetites. Democracies are no exception in this respect. Rich people who would like to be even richer turn democracies into plutocracies. Could a man with a modest income become the president of the United States today? I share the indignation regarding the arrogance of force, but I refuse to reduce liberalism to that.

From Tocqueville to Dumont

Tocqueville's work is a look at America through the eyes of a Frenchman. Was it, once again, the experience of outsideness [dépaysement] *that appealed to you in his writings?*

Tocqueville effectively accomplishes in the real world what Montesquieu outlined on a fictional level in the *Persian Letters* — to see the world through the prism of another. This, to me, is what makes *Democracy in America* the masterpiece of 'exotopy'. It proves the extent to which this approach can be productive, since we continue to be impressed by the accuracy of his descriptions today, a hundred and seventy years after the book was published. But it is not only 'America seen through the eyes of a Frenchman': for Tocqueville, America becomes an incarnation or, if you prefer, a laboratory of the democratic regime. He was in a position to discover this new order with surprise because he was still familiar with the categories of an aristocratic regime, the Ancien Régime — contemporary France being situated midway between the two. Tocqueville thus perfectly understood the logic of the democratic process and he illustrated the possibility of accepting difference without giving up unity; he saw each world from the viewpoint of the other, but his judgements remained coherent. His book offers a genuine typology of political regimes and, beyond, of conceptions of the world.

Yet, you are rather hard on Tocqueville in On Human Diversity, *since you remind us that he also defended his nationalist sentiments and that he was one of the first French ideologists of colonization.*

Tocqueville did not only write theoretical studies. He was also a man of action for a time, a deputy and even a minister. In that capacity, he did a lot of thinking about the relationship between France and Algeria, since his political activity was situated at the time of the conquest and colonization of Algeria. In his writings on colonization, we discover another Tocqueville: the subjugation of one people by another is no problem to him; everything that might be in France's interest seems worthy of approval to him. Humanitarian principles –philanthropy, as it was called at the time—are discarded. This raises another big problem: the relationship between theory and practice, between abstract considerations and political action. Reading Tocqueville, one wonders whether it is at all possible to conduct a foreign policy consistent with the great democratic ideas. Tocqueville, in any case, did not manage to do so. This could be a bitter lesson indeed: would the intellectual, the beautiful soul, be condemned to choose between inaction and betraying his or her own ideals?

We could discuss this very serious lesson later, but right now I would like to return to Tocqueville. His texts on colonization are not as well known as his major books. How was it that you became familiar with his thinking?

tzvetan todorov

Even his major books were rarely cited in intellectual debates at the beginning of the sixties. This was because of the omnipresence of the Marxist outlook, which marginalized this in-depth reflection on political structures. Things have changed since, notably at the instigation of Raymond Aron and of Louis Dumont.

The discovery of Dumont's work was important for me. Lévi-Strauss was the most prestigious name in the field of human sciences in the sixties, but, for me as for a number of others, Dumont's work had a more decisive impact. His first major book, *Homo Hierarchicus*, was published at that time, and already I was impressed. It dealt with the caste system in India, a subject that was quite remote from my interests but its aim was more general. Dumont was showing us the inner coherence of the hierarchical model, pushed to an extreme in India but present to a lesser degree all over the world. As a result, our own society, founded on the principle of equality and not of hierarchy, could be conceived as simply another model, equally coherent and not necessarily better in all respects. As Dumont wrote in the introduction of his book, he was picking up where Tocqueville had left off. Just as the latter had described democracy from the perspective of the aristocracy, so Dumont was describing hierarchy from the perspective of equality and, in so doing, was leaving open the possibility of describing our world, our European society, from the outside: equality perceived and analysed from the perspective of hierarchy.

Dumont started this latter project—describing the Western tradition from the outside—but obviously could not see it through to completion. The task was too immense, too much for one man! He took the first steps though, in his essays in *Homo Aequalis* on the history of individualism and on the German and French traditions.

In the end, all ethnological studies teach us the same lesson—that we can be human in different ways and that there is nothing natural in our habits since another population right next to ours has entirely different ones. The problem is that when the society that the ethnologist studies is too distant from our own (for instance, micro-societies of hunters and gatherers, without writing, living techno-logically in the Stone Age), it is hard—maybe even pointless—to avoid projecting space on time; or, to put it otherwise, to avoid seeing the elsewhere as ours before establishing a line of evolution from them to us. Comparing ourselves to the Indians in the Amazon can be striking, but we would have a hard time perceiving them as a possible avenue, as a prospect of development for us in the future. On the other hand, using the Indian tradition as a starting point, Dumont held out a mirror to us, somewhat distorting but revealing nonetheless, which allowed us to understand ourselves better; it was all so different from us and, at the same time, it was still us.

In what respect was his contribution to our knowledge of societies useful to you?

It is really from Louis Dumont's work that I learnt to grasp diversity within unity, because he did not content himself with positing the two models, hierarchical and egalitarian; he also queried their interaction and the choices that we, as Europeans today, could be brought to make. Dumont used to say that the universalist, egali-tarian model should remain our global framework but that, within it, numerous sectors of our social life continued to be grounded in the hierarchical principle. The interconnection between the two needed to be rethought each time. We already mentioned this theme when speaking about the demagogical attitude that prevailed in 1968 and that consisted in thinking of education in egalitarian terms. Dumont had, for example, analysed totalitarianism as a monstrous combination of the two models which he also called 'individualist' and 'holist.'

tzvetan todorov

It was thanks to Dumont that I was able to turn to history and relinquish the remnants of the naive egocentrism that makes us see our predecessors as mere steps on the way to our own wisdom. I could not have written *Theories of the Symbol* without having internalized the fundaments of his typological thinking. To be precise, these are the acceptance of plurality, the refusal to line up all forms of society on a single axis from the most primitive to the most developed, the refusal to attach a value judgement to an observed difference and, finally, the arrangement of particular forms into coherent groups.

And today, do you still read Louis Dumont?

His thought continues to inhabit me. I still draw from it a certain way of approaching the complexity of the world and of admitting the impossibility of bringing everything together in a single perspective. Dumont was quite irritated, for example, by the ease with which anti-racist activists in the early 1980s acclaimed 'difference in equality', refusing to realize that choices always have a price — that you can't have your cake and eat it too. He aptly showed how we are often brought to choose between hierarchy and war, and that we can legitimately prefer hierarchy because the principle of equality — one must be bold enough to admit — often spawns competition and conflict. In other words, and to return to our starting point, universality and tolerance do not always go well together. But this is precisely the form that the universality of the humanists takes, tempered by an understanding of the heterogeneity of each society and the difference between societies.

What is humanism?

So moderate universality, to use Montesquieu's category, characterizes humanism. But I come back here to my earlier question: does that suffice? Perhaps, before defining the essence of the doctrine, we should specify the historical period in question. The humanists you refer to—such as Montesquieu and Rousseau—are those of the eighteenth century. But humanism, as it is taught in school, is basically the humanism that emerged in the Renaissance. When would you say that humanism was born?

As far as the history of thought is concerned, it is hard to give a precise answer to the question of 'when' because each thought has its premises in the preceding thought. But let us start from what defines this worldview. As the term itself indicates, 'humanists' are those who ascribe to human beings a more important role than they had until then—more important, in particular, than what was attributed to them in the Christian worldview.

But weren't the first humanists in the Renaissance mainly specialists in Greek and Latin authors?

It is true that the term 'humanists' was initially used to designate the scholars in the 'humanities' who rediscovered the Greek and Latin heritage and translated and wrote commentaries on these texts. But the focus of their study — texts and monuments outside the Christian tradition — implied a more radical choice. By concentrating exclusively on reading Plato, Aristotle, the Stoics and even the subversive Epicureans, by singing their praises, openly or indirectly, the early humanists defended the right to place value on a part of the past for its strictly human interest without being directed in any way to the worship of God. In their own way, they were already proclaiming human autonomy. This autonomy later assumed two distinct forms: the importance of the human being as the source of knowledge and deeds; and the importance of the human being as the goal, as the destination of acts. The human being becomes the starting point and the end point. Moreover, thanks to their studies, the Renaissance humanists discovered the plurality of forms that human civilization could assume; thus they also participated in the humanist approach to universality.

Only recently, in 1998, did you feel the need to devote a book, Imperfect Garden, *to the history of French and European humanism. This work seems to close a cycle opened with* On Human Diversity, *pursued with your studies on Rousseau, Constant or Tocqueville, among others. In short, it absorbs, completes and synthesizes the work published in previous years. One has the impression, with* Imperfect Garden, *that you are reconstructing the tradition from which you yourself come.*

I knew, since *On Human Diversity*, that I recognized myself in humanist thinking. I wanted to understand it better. This led me, 10 years later, to *Imperfect Garden*. It took up the same canonical French authors but this time I restricted my examination to the humanist tradition, leaving aside the questions of universalism and relativism so as not to repeat myself.

To me, the more general category, of which humanism is one of the variants, is 'modernity'. But what is modernity? The crucial issue here is whether, on the material level itself, the human world and the divine world are one. They certainly were not (not entirely, at any rate) for the ancient Greeks and Romans. No matter what, in the Roman Empire, religious convictions were not affairs of state. Neither were they for the early Christians—'My kingdom is not of this world,' Christ affirmed, remember? The idea of uniting temporal and spiritual power is even attributed by the Evangelists to the Devil, since he is the one to tempt Jesus in the desert by promising him all the kingdoms of the Earth. Yet this is precisely what the first Christian emperors established, from Constantine in the fourth century onward: the unification of human and divine affairs, the instauration of a unitary theologico-political order. Henceforth the state was to act in the service of religion, if not the opposite.

But Christ's original precept was not totally forgotten: the pope did not become the emperor nor vice versa. This duality is what permitted the emancipation of this world here below from constraints coming from the Heavens. The first thinker to forcefully assert the autonomy of the material world again was William of Ockham. In the fourteenth century, he took sides with the emperor against the pope and defended the autonomy of the temporal in relation to the spiritual.

Is modernity the separation of the two?

Yes. And in this sense it was truly a renaissance, since it was the rebirth of what existed before. But in another sense, it was an innovation. In traditional societies, or in holist societies, to borrow Dumont's term, the idea persists of an order imposed on human beings from outside, by divine word or by nature itself, dictating the order inherent to the cosmos. Knowledge of this order is precisely what constitutes tradition, and it is transmitted from generation to generation. The novelty consisted in the fact that henceforth human beings themselves would have the job of deciphering the world and deciding their destinies. The idea of modern science, liberated from religion and morality, as well as that of popular sovereignty, rushed into the breach opened by William of Ockham and a few others.

You begin Imperfect Garden *with a short fable, a modern version of the temptation of Christ in the desert. In your telling, the Devil offers man neither power (as he did to Christ) nor knowledge (as he did to Faust), but free will. Is this the birth of modernity? The affirmation of human freedom, freedom of judgement and the autonomy of will, whatever the laws of the gods might be?*

Emancipation comprises several steps. The idea that human beings are responsible for their own destiny, that they are not just pieces of clay in the hands of the Creator, an idea that was already present in the thinking of the early Christians, took hold again in the sixteenth century. Then came the scientific revolution, with Bacon, Galileo and Descartes, and the idea that the truth concerning the world is not necessarily what was transmitted to me by tradition but, rather, what my experience and my reason teaches me.

Literally, truth does not drop out of the sky!

Precisely. It is up to us to discover it. Finally, came the aspiration for political autonomy and popular sovereignty, the claim that laws have their foundation in the collective will. This too was an older idea but it reached its consummate form in the eighteenth century, notably with Rousseau, and it served as ferment to both the American Revolution and the French Revolution.

One could effectively say that modernity consists of a conquest of freedom: freedom of reason, freedom of will and freedom of self-government.

All the same, in your fable, you suggest that the Devil may one day ask us to answer to him for all his generous gifts, or even that he may have already taken his due — in short, that there would be a price to pay for freedom. That's a rather sacrificial outlook, isn't it?

It is not I who suggest this but the critics of modernity, whom I group together in my book under the heading of 'conservatives'. And incidentally, I do not use this term as an insult in my writing; I think that we are all occasionally conservative, at least at certain levels. The crux of the matter is to know the hierarchy of our values, and whether it is the affirmation of modernity or its criticism that prevails. Conservatives are moderns themselves, but reluctantly; when a problem arises, they readily bring up solutions from the past. These prophets of doom consider that the present is off to a bad start, and that we are heading for the worst when everything was going so well before. The past in question differs: for some it is the Third Republic, for others the Ancien Régime, for others still it is Ancient Greece.

So, according to the conservatives, the Devil has taken a triple tithe from the moderns: he has deprived them of their social signification and condemned them to individual solitude (modernity is necessarily 'individualist'); he has deprived them of values, forcing them to live without ideals or religion, in the pursuit of their sole material interests (modernity is 'materialist'); finally, he has deprived them of the stable, solid subject who was thought to reign supreme over the world. In reality, human beings are prey to subterranean forces, to unconscious impulses over which they have no control.

tzvetan todorov

Among all the moderns, the humanists are, more specifically, the ones who refuse to admit that one must give up sociability, values or the self to preserve freedom. They believe that man's social dimension can be transformed, but not eradicated; that common values must be preserved, even if they are not based on God or on the structure of the universe any more; and finally, that the self may not be able to control everything but that it remains free, as Rousseau said, 'to acquiesce or to resist'.

Loving human beings

You mentioned earlier that the autonomy of the human was twofold: that human beings became at once the source of their knowledge, deeds, laws and the destination. In what way are we to understand this second requisite?

We find early formulations of this idea in the Middle Ages. But this time, we will not turn to a monk like William of Ockham for help but, rather, to a woman who led a religious cleric into sin. I am talking, of course, of the famous Héloïse who loved Abelard and who was loved by him. In their letters (which are impossible to determine as either authentic or fiction), Héloïse goes far down this path of conceiving of the human being as the ultimate goal of our actions. The letters, as you recall, were exchanged after the lovers were separated; their purpose was to make sense of their past relationship. Abelard, who submitted to the official Christian rule after the catastrophe, sees terrestrial love for the creature as merely an avenue to the celestial love for the Creator. Héloïse returns to the subject several times, insisting: 'No, it is not God or Jesus whom I loved and still love in you, it is you, yourself, your being, your individual person, irreplaceable, unique.' One could say, in this sense, that humanism is a way of assuming what human love has taught us, since the beginning of time.

And there the break with Christianity was inevitable. Christianity could accept the autonomy of the will, especially in a moderate form (otherwise, one could lay oneself open to accusations of Pelagianism, a theory named after the fourth-century monk Pelagius who maintained that humanity could achieve its own salvation without God's help). Erasmus, for instance, who was a real Christian thinker, left room for free will as did the Jesuits later. But the idea that the human being is the ultimate purpose of our actions, and that this purpose could be put at the same level as the purposes that were usually attributed to us, or even on a higher level — this is idolatry from the Christian perspective as it is from any other religious perspective.

Does that mean that a true Christian cannot be a humanist? Many Christians consider themselves humanists.

If the term is understood in the sense given to it by authors such as Nicolas de Cues or Erasmus, who prepared the groundwork for the emancipation of humanism, very well. But if we are talking about the consummate doctrines, the incompatibility is patent. The lucid Christian thinkers are clear on the point. Pascal is an anti-humanist author, which is coherent with his general position — he only wants to love human beings as a way of loving God, and he wants to eliminate all purely human attachments. We are also familiar with the eloquent letters written by Francis de Sales on this subject: those who love God must give up even their friends and their children, not to mention physical love. The Jansenist author

Nicole said that no creature should become the end for human beings. There is no room here for Héloïse's choice.

Obviously, this does not prevent the individual Christian from becoming attached to individuals but, to such a person, God always remains the ultimate justification. Saint Paul says that loving God is nothing other than loving your neighbour. This equivalence can be understood in either sense: thinking only of God or thinking only of one's neighbour, helping people, doing charity — which is another form of love.

From this point of view, humanism is necessarily secular since it refuses to seek any other justification for loving human beings or loving an individual. The ultimate purpose is the human being, not God, not the harmony of the cosmos and not the victory of the proletariat.

But loving human beings in the name of what? Because they're so 'terrific'? If that were true, we would have heard about it by now! Simply because they are human beings? That would indeed be a form of idolatry! It is this 'good sentiment' side of humanism that troubles me.

But humanists do not claim at all that human beings are 'terrific'. It is a corruption of the term to use 'humanist' to refer to someone who thinks that human beings are good, that they can be trusted or other sentimentalism of the sort. It was long thought, absolutely wrongly, that Rousseau saw the original man as a 'good savage' — which made Baudelaire snicker in derision: how naive of Rousseau to believe in the existence of goodness! (Which is proof that Baudelaire never read Rousseau.)

The humanists are perfectly aware of all the harm that human beings can do, especially to themselves. Besides, in the contemporary period, there were people who became humanists in response to the darkest episodes of our history: Auschwitz in Primo Levi's case, Babi Yar and Kolyma in Vassily Grossman's and the Second World War in Romain Gary's. Mind you, they do not, for that matter, resign themselves, no matter how great the temptation, to saying that it's a dog-eat-dog world. Humanism is not a sentimentalist ideology, but neither can it be grounded in a radically pessimist anthropology. Its conception of human beings is of indeterminate beings on a moral level; that, constantly in need of others to affirm their own existence, they can contribute to their happiness as to their misfortune; that they possess a degree of freedom in their choices, and that they are therefore responsible for the good and the evil that they do. By the way, this is why humanists have always been interested in education. If human beings were good (or evil), educating them would be pointless.

When humanists give pride of place to love, it is not because the object of love is always perfect but because loving someone is the best one can do. In the mother's love for her child, the child is not the one who is admirable but the love.

Do you think that humanist values are more in keeping with reason than others? Do you think that they make us any happier?

Max Weber referred to the impossibility of choosing between different value systems as a 'polytheism of values' or a 'war of gods'. Aron, in his text on Weber, points out that certain values are not more rational but are closer to reason in as much as such values can, like reason, be shared by everyone. This is the case for peace but not for war, for equality but not for submission. Of course, certain individuals and certain cultures may prefer war and aspire to victory. But all cannot be victorious at the same time, whereas all can live in peace. This value is therefore universalizable, unlike the aspiration to supremacy.

In other words, what counts is not rationality but universality. In that sense, Aron says, 'two times two equals four' and 'thou shalt not kill' partake in the same movement, because they are potentially acceptable by all and always. Humanism is not truer or more logical, but it has a more universal vocation and is addressed to all human beings.

For you, who is the first true humanist in the French tradition?

Montaigne, unquestionably. It is a significant coincidence that he seems to have been the one who introduced the term in its current meaning. And he did so in a telling context. Faithful to William of Ockham's tradition, he wanted to mark the boundaries of two separate areas: one reserved for theologians, who deal with matters of God and religion; the other reserved for 'humanists', specialists in purely human matters which must be treated, he says, 'in a lay, not a clerical manner'. His *Essays* are an example of this new attitude. What is important here is the very possibility of treating the knowledge of humans separately.

All of the ingredients of the new doctrine are found in Montaigne's writings: universalism connected to tolerance (he even puts too great an emphasis on tolerance for my liking, often to the point of verging on excessive relativism); a preference for acts accomplished in freedom (acts of will, acts of choice); and, lastly, the affirmation that the individual as such constitutes a respectable end for our actions. And this not only in physical love, like with Héloïse. Montaigne similarly extols friendship, refusing all justifications for his feelings beyond 'because it was him, because it was me' but also, in the very enterprise of the *Essays*, he finds it legitimate to analyse his own moods and thoughts at length 'because it is me'.

All these writers whom you read and admire are men who lived withdrawn, far from action and far from politics: Montaigne in his tower, Descartes in the anonymity of Amsterdam, Rousseau in hiding on the estates of his friends. They were all exiles, in a way, exterior or interior. Is this the destiny of all humanists?

It was, in any case, the destiny of the great humanists preceding the Revolution. They were not seeking to provoke social upheavals; they were even rather conservative, politically speaking. They aspired to educate individuals, and for this purpose it is better that order prevails in the country. Montaigne says simply that he bends his knees, not his reason. Internal freedom, external submission—this separation had meaning, I might add, under a non-totalitarian regime. Descartes, frightened by Galileo's condemnation, locked his *Treatise on the World* in a drawer—a work inspired by the same principle, that is to say the freedom of reason in the search for knowledge—and abandons the project of publishing it in his own lifetime. The first rule of his moral guidelines is, as we know, to obey the laws of one's country. Even Rousseau had nothing of a revolutionary—he would have been more outraged than anyone to see the use that Robespierre was to make of his theories. Then, things changed. This does not mean that humanist thought is unrelated to political practice. Modern democracies have adopted the principle of universality and equality before the law and protect individual autonomy—proof that doctrine can turn into action.

Elective affinities

Out of all the French humanists after Montaigne, you obviously have a preference for Rousseau and Constant. In what respect do you feel close to them?

Actually, my favourite humanists are two Swiss Protestants (at least they were at first).

There is nothing original about admiring Rousseau today. His *Confessions* were like the discovery of a new continent — that of the personal life of an individual. Before Rousseau, it was not thought to be worthy of attention; ever since, it is deemed of utmost interest — just look at the literary output in this vein today. Montaigne examines his innermost being but, in point of fact, there are very few personal anecdotes and revelations in his *Essays*. Rousseau, on the other hand, describes the details of his life. I also admire the brilliant accuracy of some of his statements, the way he has of putting profound thoughts in a nutshell: 'Iron and wheat have civilized men and ruined the human race'; 'Man is born free yet everywhere he is in chains'; 'We would rather not be than not be seen.'

These are surely legitimate reasons for appreciating Rousseau, but there's more to it with you: he really 'hooked' you. How and why?

It was first the power of his thought that attracted me to Rousseau. Marked by the absence of concession or complacency, Rousseau never turned a blind eye to the tragic aspects of life. His thinking was far from naive.

Another more superficial reason for my attraction was the very difficulty in interpreting his thinking. I saw him, as I had Bakhtin, but on a different level, as a challenge. As I said earlier, it is always tempting for the interpreter faced with numerous rich and manifold works to jump to the conclusion that its author is contradicting him or herself on one point or another and leave it at that. Now, the question of coherence is a long-standing problem in the interpretation of Rousseau's thought. How can the theses in his political writings be reconciled with what we can infer from his autobiographical texts? How can the Social Contract be reconciled with his *Confessions*—not to mention such other books as *The New Héloïse* or *Emile*? Many articles on Rousseau bear the word 'unity' in their title, often in interrogative form. It is sought, its apparent absence or its secret presence is announced. So I in turn got down to the task in a short book on Rousseau's thought, *Frail Happiness*, which also served as preparatory work for *Imperfect Garden*. It seemed to me that Rousseau was exploring alternative, successive solutions to what he saw as a single problem, the great problem of human existence: the reconciliation of individual and social requisites.

Your Rousseau seems much more 'social' than the Rousseau with which we are familiar. Are you sure that you are not dragging him a little too much in the direction that suits you?

All I did was read him carefully. We usually attach too much importance to Rousseau's laments: he complains that nobody loves him and then adds that

that's okay by him since he doesn't need anybody. One must not confuse his persecution mania—which was not, moreover, totally unfounded, since he was really persecuted—with his thinking on humankind. He himself clearly differentiates between the two. There is also a tendency to misinterpret certain statements in *Discourse on the Origin of Inequality*, in which Rousseau pictures the beginnings of humanity and claims that men were alone at the start. First of all, this is not, strictly speaking, an history; rather, it is a hypothetical construct employed to analyse human identity. And, above all, it goes to show that, without social interaction, human beings would not be what they are.

The shaping of our identity, according to Rousseau, starts when we notice the existence of others, of others looking at us, when we acquire an awareness of this. Human beings who think they are alone are not quite human yet. Those who, on the contrary, recognize the existence of others, are stepping at the same time into the world of morality since, henceforth, they can do good or evil and such notions only have meaning in relationships between individuals. They are also joining the world of freedom—because the practice of good and evil presupposes that I am free to choose—and the world of language and culture, shared with other human beings. For Rousseau, individuals without an awareness of the self and the other, without morality or freedom, without language or culture—in short, without social life—are not really human.

This insistence on our social nature is decisive in the humanist doctrine—it is what differentiates humanism from individualism. This is a difference that the conservative critics I was telling you about before did not want to see (I diverge on this point from Louis Dumont's historical hypotheses). For humanists, 'the others' are like the oxygen of existence, impossible to conceive without them. The individual can live without others; he cannot exist alone, without the gaze of others that he internalizes. Such is Rousseau's lesson.

Why did you choose Rousseau's expression 'frail happiness' as the title for your work on him, as if you saw this as his main 'message'?

Rousseau's reasoning is that since our happiness depends on others, it cannot be absolutely guaranteed. If our fulfilment depended solely on the natural order, everything would be fine; since the natural order is always true to form, it would suffice to know it in order to conform to it. If it depended on God, everything would be fine too, since God is there, infinitely merciful. If it only depended on the self, everything would be fine again: 'self-love', the necessary defence of one's being, would surely lead individuals in the direction of their greater interest. Alas, we need others to achieve happiness, and this inborn incompleteness defines our very identity. Our need for others, Rousseau says, is born from our 'infirmity'. 'If each of us had no need of others, he would hardly think of uniting himself with them,' he writes. And because we need others, our happiness can only be aleatory; or, as Rousseau concludes: 'Thus from our very infirmity is born our frail happiness.'

So we have to accept this tragic dimension of the human condition. We cannot be guaranteed that others will always grant us this love, this respect, this recognition. Promises are useless in this respect — people change, love dies. Our children's love for us, one of the most intense emotions that exists, is destined to change, even to disappear. Our love for them is not in a better boat; if we truly love them, we must accept the distance that grows little by little between us and, ultimately, stop taking care of it. We promise undying love to our partners, although we know that this love can fade. As I grow old and change, I will not be the same lovable person I was for a particular somebody in my life (you know

Pascal's famous passage on this topic), and yet the attention that person gave to me constituted my own life.

This is why happiness is 'frail'; but that does not mean that it is insignificant. Human finiteness is one of the great themes of humanism, because humanists have relinquished the expedient of eternal life. Yet, they do not neglect the search for happiness; they simply remind us of its frailty. They know too that our consciousness has discovered infinity; and this is how I, in turn, understand the human condition: the tragic disparity between our need for infinity and our de facto finiteness, but also the respect that our attempts to remedy this situation deserve.

Your attachment to Constant is more surprising. I don't know why, but he does not figure in the pantheon of 'great authors'. We all read Adolphe *at some point in school but, as far as the rest is concerned, I think he is considered a bit, might I say, inconstant. Yet your interest in him, one could even say your affection for him, has been unflagging.*

For Rousseau, my overriding feeling is admiration. With Constant, I feel a true sympathy, almost a personal attachment. Unlike Rousseau, Constant does not make a display of his vulnerability and does not take pride in it; he contents himself with admitting it. His melancholy moves me. Which does not mean that I do not admire him. He is no less rich and manifold than Rousseau. He was a great political theorist, a remarkable scholar and historian of religion and the author of penetrating analyses of sentimental life, his own and that of others. He was never very fashionable, maybe because he did not like to set himself up on a pedestal. He too was persecuted for a long time by a few mediocre minds who must have been bothered by what Stendhal, on the contrary, admired in him and which he termed his 'extreme truth'.

What was his contribution to political theory?

The first trait that distinguishes him is precisely that he was not a pure theorist: he was also a man of action who energetically participated in the political life of his country under Napoleon and during the Bourbon Restoration. And, unlike Tocqueville, there was a true continuity between theory and practice in Constant's life: practice nurtured and corrected theory, and, in return, abstract ideas guided particular choices.

His great contribution to political thought comes precisely from his observation of politics in practice. The Revolution took place in the name of a principle to which he himself subscribed — namely, popular sovereignty — yet he observed that individuals did not live more freely and that the Terror was even worse than anything prior to it. In trying to explain how the Revolution could have gone off course like it did, Constant discovers that the politics of the just state, that which we call 'liberal democracy', is based not on one requisite but on two: alongside the sovereignty of the people comes the freedom of the individual. His great political text, which remained unpublished at the time, is called *Principles of Politics*, in the plural. The relationship between theory and practice is significant and the example of Constant demonstrates that the humanist thinker need not necessarily stand on the sidelines or go into exile. But I still think he was a better thinker than a politician.

One could also say that his contribution consisted in creating a synthesis between Montesquieu and Rousseau. According to Constant, the good political regime must be legitimated both by the manner in which it is instituted (by the general will of the people, or Rousseau's heritage) and by the manner in which it is practised (by limiting each power and preserving pluralism, or Montesquieu's heritage). In the Western world today, we all live in liberal democracies, the broad outlines of which conform to Constant's ideal.

Rousseau, in his La Profession de foi du vicaire savoyard (Profession of Faith of a Savoyard Vicar), *proposed a new religion to take the place of the religion commonly practised around him. Constant, on the other hand, spent his life working on a treatise on religion, but it was a study rather than a profession of faith. You wrote the preface to the new edition of this work. Do you feel closer to Constant on this subject than to Rousseau?*

I am very happy to have contributed to this new edition, the first since the original edition was published, which just goes to show how little success this fascinating work achieved! The problem is that Constant appeared to be too much of an unbeliever in the eyes of the defenders of Christianity, and too attracted to religion in the eyes of the anti-clerical militants.

The position he adopts in this book is more that of an anthropologist and an historian than that of a believer. He thinks, nonetheless, that religious experience is one of the most important experiences that exist in the history of peoples as in the life of the individual. First of all, there is in his attitude a confirmation of the separation between the theological and the political, in other words, of the need to keep the religious experience in the realm of the individual's personal life. He also examines the nature of religious sentiment and sees in it a form of contact with the absolute, with the unlimited, which is indispensable for human beings, if they are to feel that their lives are worth living. Only, this contact can also take on other forms: the contemplation of nature, ecstasy before beauty . . .

This need for spirituality—a variety of which is manifested in religion—seems right to me. Like Constant, I think it corresponds to an indestructible dimension of our existence on earth. Like him, at certain moments I have the impression of opening up to a dimension of experience that is over and above everyday life. It only happens sporadically: such moments escape the control of the will yet their role is essential. I do not know what it is like to speak with God; but I recognize this connection with the absolute when I am in contact with beauty: the beauty of a landscape or of a work of art, a *Crucifixion* by Grünewald or Titian, a gesture by Suzanne Farrell in a Balanchine ballet, a simple melody by Schubert that takes my breath away. And also in my love, attachment and tenderness for my friends and family.

Nothing in what you have just said about Constant gives us a clue to the vulnerability you were talking about before.

It is particularly present in his private writings but can also be glimpsed in his novel *Adolphe*. Constant, like many others in his day, suffered a violent shock at the very beginning of his life—his mother died in childbirth. This was also Rousseau's fate, but his trauma was softened by the presence of a loving father and other relatives. Nothing of the sort happened in Constant's case. In a sense, he never got over this bad start in life. It is a commonplace to say this today, but our inner selves are built on the love and attention that we receive from those around us in our early childhood, from our parents above all. A child who was loved during those years faces life well armed and well protected. Constant entered adulthood with a gaping hole in his armour that nothing could fill—not the love of the women he met, nor his successes in society. He was therefore a constantly dissatisfied person; he did not like himself and always had the impression that he was on the brink of an abyss. This makes him, at the same time, particularly clear-sighted about himself and about others. *Adolphe* can be read as a treatise on the impossibility of love. I do not share these feelings or this outlook on the world, but I find their expression in his writings very moving.

Between the terrorism of truth and the selfishness of freedom

Modernity, as you were saying, is a much broader concept than humanism. What are the relationships between humanists and their neighbours, the other 'moderns'?

In 'modernity', thus defined, we find several families of thought. I speak of families because they are not philosophies, or even perfectly coherent ideologies, but a somewhat eclectic gathering of ideas. And these families often enter into wedlock. Great thinkers cannot be pigeon-holed into a single category — the likes of a Montaigne or a Rousseau spill over any label. In fact, categories are only useful in so far as they give us an understanding of the broad lines.

I have already mentioned the conservative family which participated in modernity only reluctantly. There are two other great families, aside from the conservatives: scientists and individualists. Both opposed humanism, but in different ways. As a result, the humanists found themselves fighting on two opposite fronts at the same time. We saw this for the idea of universalism: they had to set themselves apart as much from a dogmatic universalism as from a generalized relativism. The humanist is a little like the good knight Bayard, defending himself on both his left and his right.

The term 'scientism' can be misleading, because of its proximity to 'science'. Could you explain what scientism is, and in what respect it differs from science, knowing that some scientists can be said to be scientistic?

Scientism corresponds to a worldview that is very widespread and strongly influential in our society, even if the word itself appears only rarely. Its starting point is the idea that the universe is already completely, exhaustively known— this is the 'transparency of reality' postulate. The next step consists in saying, 'Since I have uncovered the secrets of all natural processes, I can reproduce them in my own way, and take them in the direction I want to go. I know the secrets of the living, so I can create new species; I know the secret of the atom, so I can use it for both war and peace.' The following step occurs when this knowledge becomes the basis not only of technology, of the means of transforming the world, but also of morality and politics since it makes it possible to establish justice and injustice, legitimate and illegitimate ends. And, the final consequence: since we know the truth, why burden ourselves with asking people their individual opinions on the question?

If scientism turns into a political project, it ends in totalitarianism where, in the name of historical 'laws' the bourgeois and the kulaks are exterminated or in the name of biological 'laws' the Jews are murdered. If scientism remains only a force among others, without becoming a state ideology, its partisans will tolerate for a while the erring ways of those who do not agree. But, ultimately, even in a democracy, political choices adorned with the prestige of science are the ones that end up prevailing. In our societies, scientists have been invested with the aura that once belonged to representatives of religion or the nobility. We all have a tendency to defer to scientists when they speak — be they biologists, physicists or economists.

You're not going to tell me that you're against science?

But, as you were suggesting in your previous question, scientism is not science. I might even say that it is the opposite. Let us start at the beginning, with the initial hypothesis of the transparency of reality, of the possibility of an integral knowledge of the world. This hypothesis has nothing scientific about it. It is a pure act of faith, totally alien to the spirit of science. Scientism does not distinguish between 'everything is knowable' and 'everything is known'; they confuse the abstract principle with the actual state of science — a knowledge that real scientists, for their part, know is temporary and incomplete. It is religion, ideology and, eventually, philosophy that pretend to be able to explain everything. Science never offers anything more than partial, temporary knowledge, and it knows it. Science begins by abstracting, fixing limits and excluding, not by encompassing everything.

That technology is based on science, that the transformation of the world follows scientific knowledge, so be it. But to think that ideals derive from knowledge is a mystification. Ernest Renan, one of the nineteenth-century thinkers of scientism, declared, 'The great work will be accomplished by science, not by democracy.' I believe exactly the opposite: it is democracy, hence popular will and the great principles to which the latter subscribes, that must direct public life, not science. An ideal and a value can never be true (or false), only more or less elevated. The prestige of science is used to avoid examining choices that remain strictly political. It was not physicists who decided to bomb Hiroshima and Nagasaki, and it is not biologists who choose to invest huge sums of money to successfully clone a human being.

tzvetan todorov

Even so, it is their discoveries that define what is possible.

Yes, and a dangerous trend is emerging in our societies: ability becomes will, which then turns into duty. I have the ability to do something, so I want to do it; I have an instrument at my disposal, so I use it. With social conformism playing its part, we are here submitting to technology and to technological thought.

But it is not science that is to be blamed for what could be called the 'terrorism of truth'. Science encourages critical thinking, the re-examination of dogmas and open debate. The totalitarian regimes that claimed to be scientific were actually scientistic, and stifled real science. In Nazi Germany, Einstein's 'Jewish physics' was stigmatized and so the Theory of Relativity and the Quantum Theory were banned. In Russia, Mendel's 'bourgeois biology' was condemned and preference was given to Lysenko's rantings. How can anyone talk in a case like this of a regime inspired by science? For the same reason, the Soviets missed the computer revolution.

I insist on this point because I simultaneously or successively adopt both attitudes: I aspire to knowledge of the human world and I assert the superiority of certain values. But there is continuity between the two. A scientific policy or morality does not and will never exist; politics and morality are directed by will, not by knowledge. We have to be wary, in both areas, not to put our desires in place of our perceptions. Human sciences must study human beings as they are, not as they would like them to be. Knowledge can enlighten the will; it cannot dictate its decisions.

What then do you think of the makeup of the National Ethics Committee: firstly scientists (doctors, biologists and geneticists), and then philosophers, most of whom are known for their religious affiliations—a committee of 'scholars and priests'.

I can only deplore it. Obviously, you need to know what you're talking about when taking up the subject of abortion, embryos and assisted reproduction. But this is within the reach of any good high school student; you don't need to be a Nobel Prize winner for that. When it comes to ethics, scientists are in no way better equipped than any other citizen—unless, that is, we presume that morality results directly from science, in other words unless we practise scientism. As to the tendency to call on a priest every time there is a question of morality, it's enough to turn you into an anti-clerical militant! Our humanist ethic, implicitly present in the democratic project, affirms the universality of human beings, promotes the freedom of subjects, refuses to reduce individuals to the role of instruments— none of these choices requires faith in God, or a constituted religious doctrine. I deplore this tendency all the more in so far as I consider the existence itself of this committee a good thing, very much in the democratic spirit: an authority respected by all, offering enlightened recommendations.

If we follow your reasoning in distinguishing so strongly between humanism and scientism, there is reason to wonder whether current criticisms of humanism are not, in fact, based on a false idea, on an understanding of humanism as human omnipotence over nature, a power based on science. Would anti-humanism be criticizing humanism for what it is not?

The dream of total control is not a humanist dream; besides, I maintain that it is not the dream of scientists either. From the humanist perspective, there is always something that eludes determinations, an element of chaos, of mystery, of freedom. That is the meaning of Montaigne's expression 'imperfect garden' which I chose as the title of my book. Such is human existence—the garden can be worked but it can never be turned into an Eden. Perfectibility exists, but not perfection. It is Sisyphus' boulder that keeps tumbling down again. This is the human condition—always having to start over, again and again, nothing is ever acquired once and for all.

Yet, this dream of perfection permeates the mentality of our contemporaries. I see a somewhat marginal example of this in the current tendency (even stronger in the United States than in France) to look behind every event for someone to pin the responsibility on, and eventually to sue. If someone gets killed in an avalanche, it's the natural park supervisor's fault for not having anticipated it. If you break a leg walking down the street, it is the municipality's fault for not having kept its streets in a state of repair. When a tree falls on a tent and kills 12 people, instead of seeing it as an accident, as an unfortunate combination of circumstances, we immediately wonder: whose fault is it? Who will we be able to condemn for this accident? Since everything can be controlled, all risks can be eliminated. There is nothing scientific about this attitude; it has more in common with a magical view of the world. I wonder whether we were not closer to science when we attributed such events to the inscrutable ways of divine providence?

Humanism is nonetheless being challenged today by advances in biotechnology. Cloning, the possibility of creating a living being without sexual reproduction, puts into question the very definition of the human being. Do you share the concern of those who fear the prospect of a new form of eugenics?

What is preoccupying about any project of physically improving the individual, and then the entire species, is that the transformation in question is irreversible and independent of the future subject's will. Education's goal is to make us better, more learned, more human, but it is a practice that can be reassessed at any point in time and in which the subject who is being educated takes a growing responsibility as time goes by. Eugenics determines the future without consulting those who are going to live it, of course, and without even really consulting the parents who are obliged to trust the holders of knowledge.

Humanists accept human beings the way they are. They do not participate in political or biological utopias, in a search for perfection. They recognize, to put it simply, nature's part. A human being is naturally born with a penis or a vagina; a child is naturally engendered by sexed organisms. We can change sex, we can artificially produce a child, but we cannot act as if the natural norm did not exist. I sometimes have the impression that we are heading in the direction of a total reversal of the strict precepts of Catholic morality. Earlier we were told, 'No sex without procreation'; soon we'll be hearing, 'No procreation with sex'! I am not saying that different individual choices should be prevented, but I think we should think twice before investing public funds in this direction. I cannot get the fact out of my mind that the world today is threatened by the prospect of too many children rather than not enough.

Admitting that nature exists does not mean sitting back with our arms crossed and doing nothing about what exists. We are not condemned to choose between utopianism and conservatism. How can one not rejoice at the ability of these same biotechnologies to locate and eliminate malformations and to cure genetic diseases? But they must confine themselves to this role, rather than launch into an enterprise of improving the species. As far as biology is concerned, it seems difficult to me to give up the very idea of a norm—it is another question to know how to establish it. The collective effort must be aimed at repairing what is inferior to the norm, not replacing it by a superior norm—curing sick children rather than producing more intelligent children. This is another version of Montesquieu's lesson: only limited power is legitimate.

Examining the dangers of scientist thought is important because of the potentially serious consequences, such as the subordination of the economy to what are purported to be its own laws (as if it was not there for the benefit of human beings), nuclear contamination and eugenics.

So that was humanism defending itself on the left. How about on the right? Humanism also has to defend its position on its conception of the individual against the surrounding individualism. Isn't the fight, in this case, milder than against scientism?

It is not situated at the same level—we move here from the life of societies to that of people—but the consequences are equally omnipresent. What distinguishes individualists above all is their conception of the individual as a self-sufficient entity and their disregard for the necessarily social aspects of human life, our membership in a community and our dependence on friends and family. According to this conception, the individual (the subject, the self, the being) exists by and for him or herself and only optionally enters into relationships with others. Family is a hindrance, useful only as long as one does not earn one's own living; community is good in so far as it promotes the individual's development. What needs to be contested here is less the values advocated than the entirely   fanciful underlying anthropology. For the autonomy of human beings is not a starting point; it is a late acquisition and an optional one at that. The relationship precedes the individual: children need their parents or other adults to survive but also to acquire a conscience and thus become real human beings. And children are necessarily born into a language, which means into a community, surrounded by rules of life established long before them. The fiction of the self-sufficient individual is dangerous because it fuels acts that destroy the social bond and which are therefore potentially suicidal. On principle, individualists accept no restrictions to their freedom.

Whereas you, as a humanist, are in favour of censorship?

Here we go! And what are you in favour of? 'Forbidding is forbidden'?[2] Let's be serious. There is no society without proscriptions, without norms, without rules—

---

2 *'Il est interdit d'interdire'* was a famous May 1968 slogan. [Trans.]

which does not automatically lead to the creation of this very particular institution that is censorship. Individual autonomy is a good thing, and it is part of the humanist agenda but it is not unlimited. First of all, because it exists alongside collective autonomy — general will, if you prefer — and because common interests impose restrictions on the individual's desire. Furthermore, there are certain general principles that we want to respect, regardless of the collective or individual will. For example, the death penalty is a barbaric act even when it corresponds to the will of the majority.

'I have the right to say (or write) whatever I want' — put that way, such a claim is untenable. One would immediately have to specify where, when, to whom and how. The law sanctions slander as well as racist propaganda. Why shouldn't it? We do not express ourselves the same way to children as we do to adults, in the popular dailies as in a specialized publication, in fiction as in an article, on the radio as at home. My freedom is limited by the freedom of others around me: they must be free not to listen to me. It is in this respect that public pornography, for example, is reprehensible: all I have to do is step out on the street and I'm subjected to it. Saying that should not cause an outcry. No need to start shouting 'the priests are back!' in typically French style.

Scientism deprives us of all freedom, individualism gives us too much. How do humanists find the right balance?

They do not know it in advance. They simply want to have the right to look for it. That is why they object to absolute, unquestionable decisions. 'It's right because it is true' or 'It's right because it pleases me' are replies that close the discussion when the point is, to the contrary, to keep it open.

What, in your opinion, is outside the scope of humanist thought? In other words, what are the limits of humanism?

tzvetan todorov

Humanism sets a framework, but it does not tell us how to fill it. It teaches us that it is better today to live in a society that grants equal rights to all its members, that promotes the expression of their will and prevents the individual from being reduced to the role of an instrument, of a bolt in a machine. However, just as it does not define a political approach, conforming to its requirements does not guarantee a happy and fulfilled life. Humanism does not teach us why certain experiences are so deeply moving, why a landscape or a piece of music can transport us into ecstasy. Humanism does not impart meaning to each individual life or fill it with beauty, and this contact with meaning and beauty, this communion with beings and with nature, is precisely what makes life worthwhile. Humanism may not do all that, but it doesn't promise to either. So let us accept it for what it is.

When it comes to unsure vessels, humanism is a frail craft indeed to choose for setting sail around the world! A frail craft that can do no more than transport us to frail happiness. But, to me, the other solutions seem either conceived for a race of superheroes, which we are not (we should be wary of our tendency to confuse goodness with truth, our ideal of humanity with what we know of it), or heavily laden with illusions, with promises that will never be kept. I trust the humanist bark more.

7. Humanism: Practices and Works

From principles to action – Thinking/acting – Listening to your conscience –
Can art be humanist?

From principles to action

CATHERINE PORTEVIN: *Your thoughts on humanism were nurtured by your reading of classical authors, from Montaigne to Constant and Tocqueville. Nowadays, can one be a humanist in the same way?*

TZVETAN TODOROV: Yes and no. History has brought us knowledge that our great ancestors did not possess. In relation to Montaigne, Montesquieu, even Constant, our knowledge of civilizations that differ from ours has increased greatly and, as a result, the idea we have of what is universal and what is particular to each culture has changed too. Before observing the ravages of nineteenth-century colonization, who could have imagined that the act of 'civilizing the savages' could have so many pernicious effects? Even in Rousseau's times, it would have been impossible to foresee that the rationalist projects to improve social order risked producing the Terror, even turning into the totalitarian nightmare. In this respect, we are much warier than our predecessors. If tomorrow clones also inhabit the Earth, our idea of the human being will change. All the same, the great lessons of the classic humanists, if only we make the effort of understanding what they meant, remain pertinent. This is my wager: I believe that the thinking of these authors from the past has greater present-day relevance than the morning newspaper. They allow us to step out of our automatic responses, to go beyond appearances and into the innermost depths of the present. For this purpose we must not lock them into their specific historical context. We have to believe in our common humanity and, thus, in our capacity to enter into a dialogue with them across the centuries. Dwarves, we can stand on the shoulders of giants — such is our privilege as readers.

At bottom, aren't the principles of humanism a secular version of the evangelical commandments, in the sense that, as Simone Weil said, the Gospels contain a conception of human life (a theory of Man) more than a theology (a theory of God)?

In certain respects, we Europeans, whether or not we are believers, are all Christians; we have been shaped by this tradition if only to oppose it. We have already talked of the different affiliations that link humanism to Christianity. The presence of a human-god, of an embodied divinity, also brings this religion close to a humanist perspective. Nevertheless, the break seems decisive to me. Humanism is not a religion and it does not involve an act of faith. It is not a scientific theory either, but a set of principles that enables us to better understand and judge human affairs.

Isn't it playing with words to oppose religious faith to what you call the 'humanist wager'? In both cases, one does not know, one isn't sure, and so a form of belief is solicited. After all, Pascal too spoke of a wager.

When we subscribe to an ideal and act on reality in the name of this ideal, we are making a wager; in this sense, there is a similarity. In both cases, there is a belief in transcendence, in the necessity of conceiving of something 'beyond' or 'above' our particular existence. In both cases, people deem self-sacrifice legitimate, in the name of a value more precious than their own lives. But the content of the ideal, that in which it engages us, is not the same. Humanists do not ask us to believe that human beings have to put themselves in the hands of an infinite, all-powerful God because without Him they are but dust. They take human beings as they are, however they are. And they do not promise them miracles: no eternal life, no reward in the Hereafter for their suffering on Earth. It is a wager on the perfectibility of humans (which is entirely different from a belief in final salvation or, for that matter, in linear progress) and on the possibility of happiness, which we know is very fragile. And the sacrifice that is contemplated in this case would benefit other humans — not God, not the Church — no more than it would benefit the Revolution or Universal Justice.

So you are not a Christian who has not yet had the courage to come out of the closet?

Communism presented itself as an enemy of religion; I could have become a Christian in reaction to this. But I grew up in an agnostic family; I think my grandparents already were. I knew nothing about Christianity as long as I lived in Bulgaria. As an historian of thought, on the other hand, I could not ignore it any more. The debates between the Pelagians and the Augustinians, the realists and the nominalists, Erasmus and Luther, the Jesuits and the Jansenists are as relevant now as they were then and continue under different names. I read Pascal and Dostoyevsky with great admiration. But I only know of Christian faith from the outside. Spiritual experience fascinates me. The religious attitude remains alien to me.

What would be the action of a 'humanist' today, in concrete terms? In recent decades, there has been reason to see its principal figure in what has been termed 'humanitarianism'. Do you see yourself in this?

Humanitarian action starts from a humanist idea: the unity of the species, and hence the solidarity that links all its members. It is also heir to Christian charity — here, as there, one helps the suffering, the sick and the poor. Only this time the justification is grounded in humanity, not in God. Therefore, humanitarianism enters the humanist framework even if it only occupies a part of it.

It is perfectly understandable that in a time of disenchantment with regard to the great political projects — after May 1968 and after the decline of the Communist ideology — humanitarian action has emerged as a desirable alternative. I have no objections to the human rights ideology or to the satisfaction that can be obtained from turning convictions into acts, even though humanitarian action does not always manage to avoid political instrumentalization. I hope that humanitarians will not stop acting the way they do. It's just that experiences in recent years have shown us that humanitarian action has its own pitfalls and today, these are well identified. One of them concerns media coverage. Indispensable to attract the attention of governments and collect funds, it can easily lapse into indulgence towards the macabre or into self-promotion. Humanitarian agents must also be wary of the perverse effects that result from the fact that they occupy such a superior position. With no ulterior motives, they are helping others, sacrificing their time and their energy; the pride of the donor is a well-identified trap in the Christian history of charity. The position of the beneficiaries of humanitarian aide is not the best in the world either: they are condemned to shoulder the role of powerless victims. As I've heard said, 'a mouth that eats does not speak.' An exchange of words implies reciprocity between the two partners, not food given to one by the other.

Do you see a victory of humanism in the fact that political actions today claim to follow humanitarian principles, an example being the intervention in Kosovo in 1999? Do you think that the 'duty to interfere' is a translation of humanist principles into foreign politics, into relations between countries?

On the contrary, I see it as a corruption of humanitarian action. Nothing illustrates this better than the expression 'humanitarian bombs' used to describe the bombs that the NATO forces were supposed to have mercifully dropped over the Yugoslav population. The phrase was used in defence of the intervention by Vaclav Havel, President of the Czech Republic, whose writings I admired when he was a dissident. What an eloquent demonstration of this textbook case—the means used preclude the attainment of the stated end. Humanitarian bombs indeed!

I am not a pacifist. I am convinced that war can be legitimate, even necessary. In my opinion, this was not the case in Kosovo in 1999. The NATO intervention was not justified. Even supposing that it was, it would not have been a humanitarian intervention in any respect. In this case, it was simply a convenient mask for a political action, a play of powers. Colonial wars were also conducted in the name of good principles. The humanitarian idea must not be compromised this way. I kill you to teach you a lesson—that is not my conception of philanthropy. War is never humanitarian, and humanitarian action is never violent.

Moreover, this war contributed to what it claimed to be fighting—ethnic purification. Now all the Serbs are on one side and all the Albanians on the other, with enough resentment to last for decades if not centuries. Nothing to be proud of.

Then we should let people die in their countries without lifting a finger, simply because it is happening outside the confines of our borders? Are you not brought in this way to tolerate crimes that remain unpunished?

What interests me above all is the prevention of crimes; their punishment is another story. Keeping the Yugoslavian government from discriminating against and persecuting Kosovo's Albanian population seemed to me to be a legitimate goal, but I remain persuaded that it could have been achieved by exerting pressures other than military. After all, we are not compelled to choose between Munich and Dresden, between capitulating to the arrogance of the enemy and annihilating the enemy, civil population included. In this instance, politicians were singularly lacking in imagination—or in goodwill. Let us not forget that the carrot is at least as effective as the stick. If some people have to be killed to save others, the result is, you will readily admit, mixed. That is why I prefer speaking of a duty to assist rather than a right to interfere—a moral duty that excludes recourse to bombs.

I am more guarded about the question of punishment. In the case of Kosovo, the responsibilities seem to me to be more divided than has been said. The situation bore greater similarities with an inter-ethnic civil war than with a unidirectional persecution. The brutal actions of the Serbian army generally came in response to provocations by the pro-Albanian army, the UCK. We have been seeing a repetition of this scenario in Macedonia: provocations, repression and a movement of solidarity with the victims. In these conditions, punishing people on one side and not on the other is not, to me, an illustration of principles of justice.

I have already spoken of my misgivings in general with regard to political trials, where the victors will not content themselves with their victory but insist that the defeated be found guilty. To travesty politics in justice is odious: it is taking advantage of one's might to humiliate, even eliminate, the adversary. The very possibility of such perversions, which are all too often real, should suffice to make us abandon in advance the idea of such trials. And it is not because the people have chosen new leaders that they should repudiate their preceding choice. For a politician to lose power is already sufficient punishment. I am not arguing in favour of absolute immunity for politicians: they remain responsible before the law like everyone else. But to condemn them penally because the policy they conducted is different from the one that prevails today seems indecent to me.

Furthermore, the majority of the population often supported the culprits of today when they were heads of state, which means that the people are guilty too! How is one to punish the population of an entire country? This would have less to do with a humanist policy than with God's justice in laying Sodom and Gomorrah to waste.

Aren't you afraid that your fine humanist principles will be perceived as noble intentions with which one cannot help but agree, but which remain powerless to change reality? Isn't there a risk, in other words, of being reduced to the role of the beautiful soul?

Powerlessness to change reality is indeed the first feeling that grips me when I read the newspaper. I go from one country to the next, from the Near East to Indonesia, from Chechnya to Texas, and I can only acknowledge that, no, indeed, the world is not doing well. And there is no hope that this will change in my lifetime. I cannot say that I have much faith in the new world order. Do you know of a quick way to improve the world?

This does not mean that I disregard the really positive global changes. For example, human beings have a longer life expectancy today than a hundred years ago. Exhausting physical tasks that used to be accomplished by humans are handled by machines today. Slavery and racial discrimination have diminished. It is the individuals themselves who have not improved.

I do not advocate resignation for all that, even if it is a serene resignation. There is no such thing as perfection, but better and worse do exist; I am certain of that. Not to entertain too many illusions does not mean doing nothing. My action on the world is by way of language: I write to seek the truth, but also to influence the minds of my contemporaries.

Humanist thought does not define a political agenda; rather, it establishes reference points that allow us to judge different policies. Saying that all human beings are equal in dignity, that the autonomy of the will must be respected, that people must be the ultimate goal of our actions does not suffice to constitute the platform of a party. Saying that right is preferable to might because law is universal does not suffice to explain why the democratic state relies both on right and on might; that it does so is to manage its relationship with other states or even to become a reality (the French Revolution was not in itself a democratic act, nor was it especially in keeping with humanism). Neither can humanist principles determine economic strategies and choices, even if they can provide a few safeguards. It is incumbent upon politicians to take charge of this difficult and, ultimately, noble task: converting principles into concrete measures, translating the general framework into acts, arranging requirements hierarchically, finding suitable compromises between conflicting interests. To each his or her own role.

Am I a 'beautiful soul' because I do not work in a ministerial post, or demonstrate at Place de la Bastille with a banner in my hand or sign petitions every day? I am not sure that I would have helped change the world more by choosing these other paths.

Yet, on certain subjects, you do take a position. I am thinking, for example, of your article in Le Monde *on the 'Debré laws' in 1997, in which you cite your beloved Constant at length. Was that a humanist intervention?*

I quoted a beautiful passage by Constant that established the basis for the right to civil disobedience when one judges that the law goes against the very principles of right or of universal ethics. The laws in question concerned the status of foreigners in France: it was a bill, so expressing one's opinion could still have an effect and, in fact, the draft law was modified in the end. The initial text proposed that all those who did not denounce the presence of an illegal foreigner would be punished. This constituted a flagrant encroachment by the public sphere on the private sphere. First of all, when I welcome foreign friends I do not ask them whether their documents are in order. Secondly, even if I know that they aren't, I am not going to denounce them: being a foreigner is not a crime, is it? So one could say that, yes, in this case, protesting against this bill involved judging political action by the yardstick of humanist principles, and pointing out the discrepancy between the two. But humanism is more an education of the mind than an incentive to intervene in day-to-day political life.

Ultimately, do you have confidence in human beings?

Not particularly. I think we are capable of the worst humiliations, and we are not very intelligent. The way the French population have taken what was said in the media and by the government at face value (be it about Chernobyl, Iraq or Kosovo) has given me pause for thought. After that, why be surprised that totalitarian propaganda worked so well? No, I do not have confidence. But I have tender feelings. We are such clumsy naive beings that we deserve a little compassion.

Thinking/acting

I would like to insist on what 'acting as a humanist' could involve today, since one of your foremost concerns is trying to bring in line ideas and acts, identity and work, discourse and life, how you think and how you live. That being the case, what is your position on intellectual engagement? Is intervening in the public debate — which you seldom do — a duty for you as an intellectual?

I would like to start from a distinction between 'engaged' and 'responsible'. Intellectuals are always asked the same question: are you politically engaged? Should you be? But it is of no interest! Engagement is the easiest thing in the world. It is a bit like Monsieur Jourdain's prose: everybody is engaged in one cause or another, glad to use their capacities and enthusiasm in the service of their ideals; there is nothing specific about the intellectual in this respect. Responsibility is a different matter altogether. Unlike mere mortals, intellectuals — writers, scholars and philosophers — propose an interpretation of the world in their oral and written words. When they become men or women of action, they have the moral obligation — it is their responsibility — to make sure that their action is consistent with their theories. Irresponsible intellectuals are those who do not do what they say, who simply take advantage of their reputation to attract others to the road that suits them at one moment or another. Their profession being 'to think', their obligations are heavier than those of others.

When Robert Brasillach was sentenced to death after the Liberation, men and women of letters circulated a petition asking for his pardon. François Mauriac, who had courageously sided with the Resistance during the war, was one of the initiators of the petition. Camus signed it, pointing out in a short judicious comment that, in all likelihood, Brasillach would never have signed a petition if the Germans had sentenced him, Camus, to death! The fact remains that de Gaulle refused the pardon and Brasillach was shot. De Gaulle is purported to have referred, on this occasion, to 'the sin of an intellectual'. To him it was a particularly serious sin: the fact that Brasillach was an intellectual was regarded as an aggravating circumstance. A man, who was purported to know and to enlighten others, had led them to disaster. Arendt developed this same theme in a fine essay on Brecht's political career. According to her inversion of the Roman proverb, what the ox may do (that is to say the individual, the common man), Jupiter may not. The more power you have (political, intellectual or symbolic), the greater are your responsibilities.

Who epitomizes for you the figure of the responsible intellectual?

Take the case of Albert Camus. What attracts me to him is not that his choices suit me better than, say, Sartre's, but that he changed political convictions and emotional attachments based on what he considered to be true. Let us recall the biggest issue in the forties and fifties, namely, the attitude towards Soviet Communism. Because of his ties with Resistance circles, Camus was close to the

Communists, to the French Left, which was more or less pro-Soviet. Little by little, he realized that the 'land of socialism' was a lie; so he broke with his former friends, at the risk of incurring ostracism, sarcasms and hostility. In so doing, he took seriously his responsibilities as a writer, a man of letters and a thinker; he felt compelled to tell his readers what he deemed was the truth.

Now think of Aron, who took positions similar to those of Camus vis-à-vis totalitarianism but who understood his responsibility in other terms. The parallel between Camus and Aron seems to me to be more interesting, in this respect, than the one that is usually drawn between Sartre and Aron.

Responsibility always involves coherence between the discourse one produces and the world. But what world are we talking about? For Camus, individuals had to firstly remain true to themselves, to their innermost being and to their conscience, never lie to themselves and be scrupulously honest even if there was nothing to gain from it. For Aron, responsibility consisted first of all in devoting oneself to the meticulous study of the world, in order to form one's opinion with full knowledge of the facts. It is, on one side, if you will, a subjective correspondence between the discourse and the speaking subject and, on the other, an objective correspondence between the discourse and the world that is spoken about. Or perhaps one could say, the responsibility of a writer on one side and of a scholar on the other.

Did you meet Raymond Aron?

No, he died before I began to take an interest in the field in which he excelled. The specialists in literary theory didn't think much of him! But I knew the stands he had taken with regard to totalitarianism and I approved of them. Unlike the young people I spent time with when I arrived in France, who were nice but unrealistic, Aron knew what he was talking about. He had kept a 'cool head', as people used to say, and he insisted on flushing out the realities lurking behind the fine words. In subsequent years, on the other hand, I devoted a lot of time to his work.

To my mind, Aron combines breadth of information with rigour of reasoning in a remarkable way. He was, to begin with, truly very knowledgeable, infinitely more so than Sartre but also more than most of his university colleagues. He knew political history, sociology and economy well, but also the history of ideas and philosophy. Yet, to him, this knowledge was not an end in itself, as it often becomes to specialists who are weighed down by their own erudition. He put his knowledge in the service of reasoning and of the dialogue with the reader — with all readers, by the way, since he wrote in a daily paper. He did a wonderful job at fulfilling his role, which consisted in putting into the hands of one and all the knowledge necessary for each person to think for him or herself. He would suggest a solution but without bombarding the reader with it, without erasing the question marks. It is the privilege of the greatest minds to be able to lead us by the hand like this. I have only had the same sensation, I believe, in reading Isaiah Berlin. Even today, whenever I have to write on a subject, I first check to see whether Aron has not already dealt with it, whether he has not already dissected it for me.

And you are not bothered by the dryness that sometimes characterized his work, by his virtuosity in pragmatism?

Bothered that he is dry? If he tells the truth, I'll take it. In general, I do not find him dry; I like his rigour and his probity — some of his pages are even dazzlingly brilliant. This does not keep me from disagreeing with him at times, and I do not refrain from saying so: differences between an author I admire and me seem more interesting to me than those between Hitler and me. In one of my recent books, *Hope and Memory: Lessons from the Twentieth Century*, I clearly benefit from Aron's analysis of totalitarianism, but I also criticize him when I am not convinced. In fact, he is even the only author I criticize, which is somewhat paradoxical, but it is precisely because I feel close to him that I do so. The criticism helps me formulate my own thoughts better.

Let's come back to the Camus–Aron parallel. What did each say about the other?

I do not know whether Camus wrote about Aron, but Aron spoke of Camus several times and not always in flattering terms. At bottom, they had quite different conceptions of their role. Even before the war, Aron had decided not to allow himself to condemn a political action out of hand unless he was capable of proposing a better solution. His interventions were thus closely bound up with contemporary political affairs. And he wanted to spell out the consequences of his fundamental choices. For example, since he was for democracy, he had to defend France's entry into the North Atlantic Treaty; he had to renounce every de Gaulle-ian flourish in his search for a third way between the Russians and the Americans. This type of involvement in everyday politics was alien to Camus who held the more traditional position of a detached commentator, discussing good and evil without offering recipes for present action. Aron reproached him a little for that; he thought that Camus was too much of an intellectual *à la française*, meaning, a beautiful soul.

They had different attitudes towards the Algerian conflict too.

Aron examined the economic situation above all, saw that the colony was a disaster for France and concluded that the war must be stopped and independence granted. He did not call upon moral principles — which would have served to convince only those who already were; he addressed political decision-makers, those for whom France's interest should be important, and proved to them that, economically, war and victory would be a catastrophe. Camus, a *pied-noir* himself, was thrown into a moral dilemma. He was torn between emotional attachments —

for the land, for his family, for his childhood friends—and the principles of justice in which he believed, and which led him to approve of the decolonization. He sought a compromise for a while—he had much in common, in this respect, with Tillion. Then, when the war became too intense, he made a strong decision—he chose to be silent. He continued to intervene in individual cases to save lives, but he stopped expressing himself in public. Aron judged this attitude rather severely; it was, he said at first, the attitude of the 'colonizer of goodwill'. Then he reproached Camus for abdicating. He didn't understand Camus' subjective responsibility, his exigency of truth to himself, and wanted him to assume an objective responsibility, to act according to what he knew was the truth of the world.

Maybe Aron did not have subjectivity or, rather, considered it a weakness to take his own emotions, his personal attachments, his identity into account.

It would seem so at times, but not always. During the Six Day War, between Israel and the Arab countries, he had a different type of reaction—he felt an emotional solidarity with Israel and was ready to fly (metaphorically) to its aid, without looking to be well informed or to examine the situation beforehand. He was himself struck by this difference in attitude when he was writing his *Memoirs*. And, oddly enough, at this point he evokes Camus' reaction to the Algerian War but this time to posit it as legitimate. He does not realize that, a hundred pages earlier, he had condemned the gesture; now he is the one to claim the right to have one's own truth. And he has an interesting way of putting it: at certain moments, he explains, an intellectual must give up logical arguments and rational analysis and react with his inner being, 'either he remains silent or heeds his demon'.

This statement has given me pause for thought. I say to myself that, confronted with this choice, Camus chose to remain silent and Aron to obey his demon; and I admire Camus' gesture more than Aron's. By making an exception in the case when his solidarity was engaged, Aron opens a breach in his own position and justifies in advance all forms of blindness, since one can always adduce an irrepressible solidarity. In this instance, he is opting for engagement, not responsibility. His objective responsibility was impaired when he found himself confronted with a situation in which he reacted not rationally but emotionally (his 'demon'). Camus remained silent because he understood that he could not choose, without repudiating himself; he remained true to the path of subjective responsibility that was his.

Another difference between the two is that, even though both wrote books, one was a writer and the other wasn't.

In this sense of the word, the writer is not a person who writes beautiful sentences—of this there is no dearth in Aron's books—but someone who invests himself personally in his writing. Aron did what he did well in his journalistic, historical or philosophical works but he is not personally present in them. Not even in the *Memoirs*, and scarcely more in the interviews published in *The Committed Observer*. This is surely due to personal reasons—education, family traditions, the milieu of the École normale supérieure and journalist reflexes—but we can regret the fact that he kept his 'demon' in the dark most of the time. Perhaps he was too hard on himself, too private. In that sense, he did not create an œuvre, even though he had so many good ideas. An œuvre is the meeting of thought and destiny, carried by a passion for form. Camus produced an œuvre.

Listening to your conscience

And which one of the two do you identify with most?

Firstly, I recognize in both of them a talent far superior to my own. Apart from that, I am torn. The kind of writing I do is obviously closer to Aron's. I do not write novels or plays like Camus, and, like Aron, I am interested in the history of ideas and in political history. But on the other hand, the criticism that Aron addressed to Camus could be addressed to me too. I do not participate daily in political life and I do not propose concrete solutions; I content myself with commenting on events from afar, without taking any risks. Thus I follow a path that combines the drawbacks of both. Let's say that I try not to forget who I am when I write, and at the same time I try to be as informed as possible. I'll let you choose the label.

Let me suspend judgement for the moment and come back to my initial question. What relationship is there between, on the one hand, knowledge and thought and, on the other, action? Has your work on the history of humanism made you more . . . human?

I remain a disciple of the Enlightenment in as much as I believe that education, knowledge and culture can make us better and more autonomous human beings. They make it possible for us to accomplish one of humankind's great vocations. But this general conviction—and without it I would not be writing books or working for the National Education system—must be accompanied by all sorts of restrictions and specifications. Rousseau was careful to do so in his own time: moral progress does not automatically follow from an accumulation of knowledge, contrary to the assumptions of scientism. There is no reason to be too surprised, as the judges in Nuremberg were, by the fact that the people who commanded the extermination of the Jews had received a higher education. We have also seen that as educated a man as Tocqueville, who insightfully and compassionately analysed the destruction of the Indians in America, did not hesitate to encourage the conquest of Algeria and the subordination of the Algerians. Such counter-examples do not, of course, compromise the idea of education. Consider a different example: a direct relationship has been established between birth control—which is more than a good thing, it's a necessity—and the literacy level of women. In this precise case, education is absolutely necessary to humankind if it wants to survive—in good conditions, at any rate.

We know perfectly well that reason, knowledge and high culture do not guarantee moral progress. But what then makes us act in the right way?

It is not knowledge, not in a mechanical way, in any case. It is not what we call reason either. Reason, Benjamin Constant said, is an infinitely pliable and compliable instrument, that can be made to say just about anything: 'In the name of infallible reason,' he wrote, 'Christians were fed to the beasts and Jews were sent to the stake.' We can logically argue in support of any thesis whatsoever; the world is complex enough to provide arguments in favour of anything.

If you do not possess within you a conviction in terms of justice and injustice, then all moral references can collapse. This may correspond to what Rousseau called the 'conscience'. This is how I understand his idea: each one of us internalizes certain fundamental experiences, related especially to our childhood and to the love of our parents. This gives rise to reactions that we do not need to think about. Mencius, a Chinese sage from the fifth century BCE, said more or less this: if I see a child fall down a well, I rush to save him first; the reasoning comes after. Without these basic intuitions, reason is not worth a thing—it can be made to serve any purpose. The great criminals of history, particularly in the totalitarian world, all had a problem with these fundamental experiences, and hence with their consciences. Yet, we cannot leave it at that. Our intuitions are sometimes mute, sometimes contradictory; we have to be able to compare our personal convictions with those of others. Certain solidarities—we were just talking about this—are more legitimate than others. I will spontaneously sympathize with my own family ('My country, right or wrong,' proclaims the famous English proverb), and this can lead me to commit great injustices. We need to be able to question our conscience. This is where reason, rational argument and conversing with others come in. I try to put myself in their shoes; I accept the principle of reciprocity. Rousseau speaks, in this regard, of the 'soul enlightened by reason', which seems to me an evocative expression.

As for me, I look for these arguments in my readings of others, and then I use them to try to convince my readers. But the force that motivates me probably comes from a few tiny incidents, like the ones I was telling you about. That is the source of my almost visceral attachment to the great principles of liberal democracy. I can criticize its weaknesses, but I can hardly stand to see it challenged.

But, beyond that, isn't there something that is inexplicable and unpredictable, as is the human quality, after all? Consider Tillion, whom you mentioned before. She had clear ideas, knowledge, a good sense of judgement, even convictions, but none of this explains why she immediately joined the Resistance in June 1940. She herself speaks of her engagement as a gut reflex.

Other scholars, other ethnologists, other French citizens of her age did not react the way she did, of course. She herself, if she had been asked before 15 June 1940, would not have known what to answer. Was she willing to risk her life to defend her country? She only knew that she was, and then she knew it immediately, the day Pétain declared the Armistice. She did not react the way she did based on reasoning, but 'because it was her'—like Montaigne's choice of a friend. However, right afterwards, she began to reason. And her first non-ethnological text—a text from 1941, which I recently discovered in her papers, written for a clandestine newspaper that closed before its publication—dealt with the cause of truth. In it, she declares that our intuitive solidarities and our commitment to our country's cause should never push us to manipulate the truth. As for me, personally, as long as the question is not raised by the circumstances, the response I could give is of no interest. My knowledge and my work enable me—I hope—to understand the world better; they provide no guarantee as to my behaviour facing the extreme. Maybe I would betray my convictions out of fear. I do not think that the firmness of soul that would be required in such circumstances depends on the books you have read or written, but it does depend on what you think of the world.

Can art be humanist?

So humanism cannot be politics, but can it be aesthetics? For you, what would humanist literature be?

Here, we must choose how we are going to interpret the term. Firstly, in the very broad sense, literature is almost necessarily 'humanist' in that, as a work of language, it addresses other human beings and, in so doing, it recognizes our common belonging to the same species. In this sense, all literature is universal; from Homer to Beckett, it gives meaning and shape to the life of all human beings. Beckett's message may very well be anti-humanist—let's assume that it is, for argument's sake. The clarity of his style, the rigour of his constructions and his irresistible humour evidence concern and respect for the reader. His writings are, I would say, profoundly fraternal, even when they describe the absence of all fraternity. Only if literature obstructed comprehension would it escape this vocation—and not entirely, for language always bears meaning, but let's say that, in that case, it would resist this vocation. I am thinking here of experimental poetry composed of linguistic sounds but not of words and, more generally, of the tendency to hermetism.

On the other hand, in a very narrow sense, a 'humanist' work would be one that expresses humanist thinking through what the author or characters say or through plot development. These writers sometimes publish essays, interviews or articles, alongside their novels, in which they directly state their humanist convictions. I studied two such authors in *Hope and Memory*: Vassily Grossman and Romain Gary. Literature is also ideology, even if it is not only this, and it can be humanist ideology.

Finally, there is the third and probably the most interesting sense: neither the general condition of literature nor the work's particular message, but the choice of literary forms themselves. These change, and the emergence of humanist thought also provoked an upheaval in the development of art.

This analysis of the meaning of forms (that is to say, how forms think) corresponds to an approach that, to my knowledge, you have not practised much for literature.

It is true that, when I was analysing literary works, this perspective was not a priority for me although I did apply it on a couple of occasions, for example, to works by Dostoyevsky and Henry James. The occasion never arose since. But others have done so. I knew of their work and admired it. For example, I had translated for *Poétique* the first chapter of a remarkable book by Ian Watt, an historian of literature whom I've already mentioned. In this work, Watt shows precisely how the new individualist and empiricist ideology that was emerging in the seventeenth century transformed narrative prose into what we call the 'novel'; how individuals appeared, how their irreducible diversity was recognized, how the phenomenal, concrete, unpredictable world supplanted the ancient universe populated by allegories and personified essences.

On the other hand, you have analysed painting from this angle in two books on art: Éloge de l'individu (In Praise of the Individual), *devoted to fifteenth-century Flemish painting, and* Éloge du quotidien (In Praise of Everyday Life), *which took up seventeenth-century Dutch painting. What made you choose this art form and these periods?*

I had long felt moved by painting. I have already spoken to you about my painter friends from my student days and my first visits to foreign museums in Russia and in Budapest. At some point I realized that my emotions drew me to the northern painters, Flemish and Dutch. This is, after all, how one's identity is built. In asking myself about my own spontaneous tastes, I was slowly discovering who I was.

I put the word 'praise' in the titles of both books because I believe the image always praises what it shows. A painting does not generally contain a clear affirmation of the kind that language produces, or it does so only in well-coded didactic genres. But the presence itself of what is shown, and the way that it is shown, constitutes an initial affirmation of sorts: this exists, it is worthy of being represented and in this particular way. It is like a sentence that would have only a subject and no predicate; it says, 'This is Joseph', 'This is the Virgin', 'This is a dairymaid', 'This is a sick child'—but always adding 'and this deserves to be seen'. To show is to think, and in painting too it is the thought that fascinates me. This is particularly true of figurative painting, for which I have a predilection. I wrote these two books to understand this painting better and why I felt so close to it. I learn by writing.

So how does fifteenth-century Flemish painting think?

Van Eyck, in the first half of the fifteenth century, was the first one to represent an object cut off by the frame of the painting. Pure whim, a 'gimmick' to set himself apart, you will say. Not at all! If objects are always shown to us in their entirety it is because they exist in and of themselves, independently of our gaze. Not having the frame of the painting coincide with the boundaries of the objects means reserving the painting to what is seen by someone and not to what exists in itself, in other words, it means recognizing the painter's subjectivity. For us, it goes without saying that representational painters show what they see: why, otherwise, would they set up their easel opposite the Notre-Dame or the Sacré-Coeur? But, in fact, it does not go without saying, and for a long time painting showed what things and beings are and not the vision that someone might have of them. The whole introduction of perspective goes hand in hand with this recognition of the subjectivity of the painter and, by this very fact, of the spectator and hence of the individual.

Or take the idea of time. We see for the first time in a fifteenth-century illumination that objects cast a shadow. What does this innovation signify? That the visible inhabits time, with a long shadow in the morning and a short one at noon. In painting shadows, one is also showing the time of day. Prior to this, objects did not have shadows because they existed in eternity, under the eye of God, not of men. Signs of ageing were not shown either. The point was to capture the essence of the object or the being. Another picture by the same Limbourg brothers, the illuminators of *Les Très Riches Heures du Duc de Berry*, depicts the first snow landscapes in Western painting. The subject was chosen because snow is temporary, a passing state of the world, neither essential nor immutable. Another illumination portrays two men smiling. People have always smiled, of course, but Christian art before the fifteenth century did not set out to represent the fleeting, the transitory, the instantaneous, and the smile is manifestly not a permanent state. These were inconceivable ideas a few centuries before, and they were ideas that were no less important than 'Workers of the world, unite!'

In praise of the individual, in praise of everyday life: one cannot help noticing that the themes you pick up on in painting coincide with the themes of your other works. What relationship do these ideas have with humanist thought?

The connection is obviously not fortuitous. The approach I adopted with painting coincides with a greater awareness of my choices in other fields. *Facing the*

Extreme, my essay on moral life in the concentration camps — a whole different world from seventeenth-century Holland! — was a reflection on heroic values and everyday values. The connection with *Éloge du quotidien* was direct for me, in this case. And *Imperfect Garden*, in which I examine the humanist conception of the individual, is in continuity with *Éloge de l'individu*. Indeed, I see a quite direct relationship between the thinking of fifteenth-century Flemish painters and humanism. What Montaigne put into words in the late sixteenth century — namely, justifying friendship by the individual identity of his friend and justifying the value of his *Essays* by his own identity — Robert Campin and Jan van Eyck had already grasped some hundred and fifty years before. They had painted the first modern portraits, those that portrayed people involved in everyday life. And they painted people not to represent their function, as in the case of a king or a prince, but simply because they had asked for their portraits, because they or their kin wanted to keep a trace of their appearance. It is also worth noting that these paintings, while they did not contest social hierarchies, emphasized humble people, thus prefiguring a theme of the Reformation, and recalling the equal dignity of all in the eyes of God.

At the same time, the uniqueness and the value of the individual were affirmed by the painter's subjective vision (the individual-as-subject as opposed to the individual-as-object). Finally, the painter-individual was henceforth appreciated for his capacity to innovate and not only to master tradition — in other words, for his autonomy. We thus find numerous humanist motifs in this painting — and, mind you, not so much in the titles of the paintings or in the comments written on the frame, which was fairly common practice, as in the very manners of representation.

On this level, what was new in seventeenth-century Dutch painting?

Robert Campin, in the early fifteenth century, represented the *Virgin with the Child* as if the Virgin was one of his Flemish neighbours. Pieter de Hooch, two centuries later, portrayed his own neighbours as if they were goddesses or saints. We thus go from the humanization of the divine to the divinization of the human; the religious dimension recedes to the background. The moral dimension too. At first, certain frequently represented scenes were intended to show what should not be done, the harmful effects of passion. But when Gerard Ter Borch depicted young women reading or writing letters, young people busy playing music and thinking about nothing besides exchanging long languorous looks, he was not making a negative judgement; thus, his representation extols human love and not theological virtue.

So emphasizing the value of everyday life is emphasizing the value of the utterly profane dimension of the human. Is this how praise for everyday life ties in with humanist values?

In this case again, as in the fifteenth century, painters were ahead of poets and philosophers. Until then the public arena was the only one to be highlighted; not everyday life, but a world of remarkable feats, heroes and extraordinary people: saints, kings and noblemen. This division coincides, to a great extent, with the division between masculine and feminine—the specific world is not held in high esteem and, for this reason, it is not an object of representation. Mind you, the quotidian was not admirable in its own right: with all the chores that had to be accomplished day after day—the washing, the sewing and the cooking—it could even be quite tedious, not to say depressing. But one could also choose to emphasize this world—the world of feminine rather than masculine values—to look for its beauty and to make it visible. Such a movement existed in Protestantism at the time, but it was in genre painting that it was crystallized most emphatically and brought into the full light of day. The most characteristic representatives of this new emphasis are not so much the painters who enjoy the highest reputation today, such as Rembrandt (who continued to humanize the divine) or Vermeer (who used the motifs of genre painting but transformed them into objects of pure aesthetic contemplation), as painters of somewhat lesser recognition, such as Pieter de Hooch and Ter Borch.

tzvetan todorov

To put it otherwise, instead of focusing on the canonical virtues, they presented the humblest of acts as virtues, even if it meant being relegated to the status of minor painters?

Exactly. Here are scenes of a mother removing lice from her child's head, women peeling turnips, a dairymaid or a fishmonger. Of course, these images are not meant to be heretical—traditional morality enjoins women to tend to their children, to keep their homes in order and to prepare meals. But it does not say that these acts are beautiful. And this is what these painters discovered; this is why they represented them. De Hooch painted two scenes in exactly the same place, the same courtyard of a Dutch house: a tidy light-filled courtyard with graceful plants. An idyllic scene! In the first we see a mother taking care of her child; in the other, a young lady, probably the same one, only now she has left the little girl to play with her dog and is getting drunk with two soldiers. 'Virtue' on the one hand, 'vice' on the other. Yet the same peacefulness prevails, the same happiness, the same enjoyment of the moment and the ground shines with the same brightness. So it was now the painter who had become the legislator of virtue, praising this world 'because it is him, because it is me'.

And, in this respect, he is in tune with the humanist message?

Yes, in the sense that he brings the absolute to life in everyday life, without having recourse to the supernatural and the beyond. One of Gabriel Metsu's paintings shows an elderly women, probably a maid, combing her young mistress' hair. An everyday life situation. Yet, the woman's attentive, caring gesture and the dreamy gaze of the mistress escaping through the open window bring us in touch with the absolute. It is a way of discovering meaning and beauty in the life of this world, which, as a result, becomes worth living—for true life is not elsewhere and later, it is here and now. I find that this painting helps us live.

8. The Moral Meaning of History

Facing the Extreme — *The heroic and the ordinary — In praise of rescuers — Evil: a political approach — Totalitarian evil — No reasonless evil, no unadulterated good — From* milice *to* maquis

Facing the extreme

CATHERINE PORTEVIN: *At the beginning of the nineties, you published* Facing the Extreme, *an essay on moral life in the (Communist and Nazi) concentration camps. In it, you pursue your ethical approach to history — inaugurated, as we have said, with* The Conquest of America — *but you also tackle politics head-on for the very first time and, more particularly, the subject in politics that is closest to your experience: totalitarianism. You have already described how the fall of the Berlin Wall led to the collapse of another barrier, this one mental, which kept you from examining Communism. But, more concretely, what was the genesis of* Facing the Extreme? *How did this extremely precise project of*

(1) approaching totalitarianism through its extreme effects (the camps), and (2) approaching the camps from the standpoint of moral values, take shape?

TZVETAN TODOROV: Concretely, *Facing the Extreme* emerged, as had *The Conquest of America*, from a trip. In 1987, my wife and I were invited to a conference in Warsaw, which I had visited already in 1961. At the time, the country was living under martial law: solidarity had been banned and opponents of the regime—they had always existed in Poland—had lost their jobs or had been imprisoned. We went to the church of the murdered priest, Jerzy Popieluszko, which was always packed. Meeting some of the intellectuals who had been marginalized by the government stirred a sense of empathy and I found myself thrown back into a situation that I knew well, that of the individual facing a totalitarian state.

I also discovered a country where the traces of the Second World War were hard to ignore. We were particularly disturbed by a visit to the Jewish cemetery in Warsaw. Those who are buried there died before the genocide, of course, but what is peculiar about the cemetery is that their descendants have disappeared too. It is situated right in the centre of Warsaw, but there is no one to look after it and so it is invaded by weeds. There is an air of unreality about it.

All of this had a strong effect on me. Back in Paris, to better sort out my own feelings, I read a few books about the history of Poland and I found myself identifying with it and understanding myself better. Once again, I got hooked. I spent three years exploring this dark world.

What was the experience that led you to take an interest in the world of concentration camps? You have told me about your visit to Auschwitz in 1961 but not about the camps in general. What exactly did you know about them when you were living in Sofia? Were you aware of the existence of the Soviet and Bulgarian camps?

Visiting Auschwitz in 1961 was an unforgettable experience, but I do not believe it played a direct role in the writing of *Facing the Extreme*. The decisive element was rather the renewed confrontation with the totalitarian system that was still alive in Poland in 1987 and, worse still, seemed eternal. In 1961, as surprising as this may seem to you, I did not know anything about the Soviet camps. The fact is that a totalitarian state has nearly total control of information, especially in that prehistoric age before Internet, e-mail, computers, faxes and photocopying machines. All public sources of information were in the government's hands. All that remained were the stories told by individuals. But, firstly, for us as Bulgarians, Russia was far away; in addition, the witnesses were frightened and avoided the subject; and, finally, you never knew whether the stories you heard were true or invented by someone who was embittered for who knows what reason. Even ordinary Russians, before *The Gulag Archipelago*, had difficulty acquiring a clear picture of what was happening—a fortiori, the Bulgarians.

On the other hand, we were well aware of the existence of a large labour camp, a penal colony, in Bulgaria itself, in Belene, located on an island in the middle of the Danube. Belene even came to be used as a common noun in the Bulgarian language at the time: we used to say 'You'll end up in Belene' to people whose behaviour deviated from the norm in one way or another, because they dressed in an eccentric manner or because they told too many anti-Communist jokes. Belene existed but it did not bother us. It is a characteristic feature of life under totalitarianism—and maybe, after all, of life itself, since custom is second nature—that what becomes a habit is not surprising or outrageous any more. There was a place where people who were mentally abnormal were locked up, 'a nut house' in Karloukovtsi, and there was a place where people who were socially abnormal were locked up and that was Belene. It was 'normal'.

But what exactly did you know about this 'normal' camp? About what life was like there?

Not much, probably because I did not personally know anyone who had been in Belene — and obviously newspapers made no mention of it. I only found out what life had been like in the camp much later, when I was in France and I read a few accounts that had been published. I learnt even more later, when I was preparing a collection of testimonies from former prisoners in the Communist camps, published in France in 1992 under the title of *Au nom du peuple* (and in English in 1999 as *Voices from the Gulag*). I then learnt that Belene had been closed (temporarily) in 1959 to be replaced by another camp situated in a stone quarry near Lovetch, where the conditions were equally harsh. This dreadful camp was closed in 1962 and Belene reopened its gates. Thirty years later, after the fall of Communist power, people began talking about it. The testimonies that I brought together in this volume can break your heart.

But in 1961, 1962 and 1963, my last years in Bulgaria, I was not aware of any of this, even though the former inmates who recount their experiences in this book were my age and most of them lived in Sofia as I did. Only we did not come from the same milieu. And, without fully realizing it, I was protected by the fact that I belonged to the intelligentsia, and by my close relationship to ex-Communists, who may have fallen from grace but who were still privileged, and to the children of Communist leaders. I never got into any trouble with the Militia and did not feel personally threatened. In hindsight, I might add that I did not really want to know anything that could have disturbed me; my life was exciting to me, and I unconsciously avoided any information that could have put a dampener on it.

And nobody you knew had ever been threatened by the Militia?

Nobody had been sent to Belene. But less violent forms of persecution existed—particularly internment, banishment, house arrest—and of these, I was well informed. House arrest consisted in obliging the person to leave Sofia and live in some godforsaken place, usually a village on the borders of Bulgaria. Bulgaria is a small country (the borders are not far from Sofia) but, with the bangers we were driving at the time (which took a day to cover 300 kilometres), it was quite an expedition. And banishment was tantamount to exile! There were mostly Turks living in these villages, a population made up mainly of farmers and the poor. The people who had recently been released from the camps were sent there, or those who were judged insufficiently guilty to be interned in the camps. In general, they were city-dwellers, people from Sofia who knew absolutely nothing about farming. Accountants, secondary school teachers and artists found themselves sentenced to live the rest of their days there. They had no family or friends, they had to find new jobs and check in with the Militia every evening. This was not a gentle exile—far from it!—but a quite brutal banishment that lasted for years.

I knew these people well. There were some of them in our family: uncles and cousins on my mother's side as well as on my father's. In the immediate post-war period, I remember preparing packages for them. But when it came down to it, they were not in camps.

In reading Facing the Extreme, *one comes away with the impression that the subject affects you personally and not only as a former citizen of a totalitarian country.*

The writing of this book coincided with a couple of events in my personal life, the echo of which is perceptible in the text, for me in any case. My mother died in 1989 after suffering from Alzheimer's disease for several years. I would go to visit her once a year; she'd recognize me but didn't know much else any more. She stayed at home and it was my father, at over 80, who took care of her (public medical care in Bulgaria was free but as bad as it gets!). This new role made my father unhappy and the atmosphere at home was heavy. I was travelling abroad when my mother died, and I only learnt about it after the funeral. A few months later, my father, then alone and distraught, came to live with me in Paris. He was in good health on the whole but doubly handicapped: he did not see well enough to read or write, and he did not speak French. I thus became the almost exclusive intermediary between him and the world. All this strongly rekindled childhood memories, both of the regime and of family life.

You evoke both of your parents in this book, in short texts in italics that punctuate the rest of your reflection, as if the latter leaned on the figures of your parents who were, moreover, very different from one another.

In a rather traditional way — as I mentioned in one of our first interview sessions — my mother's life was focused on the private arena, and my father's on the public. My mother had completed university studies, and had worked as a librarian before the war. But at the time of the conflict, as a result of all the privations and the additional efforts that it took to continue living decently, she fell ill with tuberculosis. She recovered after the end of hostilities, but she was retired as an invalid. She thus invested herself entirely in her private world — in taking care of her family and her home — and she put an enormous amount of energy into it. From then on, her goal in life could not be separated from her life itself. She had no project in terms of creation, or in relation to an institution or a public manifestation. Her sole purpose was to live through loving. She 'sacrificed' herself, in a sense, for others, but she never made anyone feel that she expected anything in return or that she felt hurt by the lack of reciprocity. We also regarded her attitude as natural — she had accustomed us to receiving. She did not derive happiness from herself but from the people upon whom she lavished her affection. And she acted like this not because it was the right way to act nor because it was her duty, but because that was her inclination. For her, what she did was the most natural thing in the world. She was not virtuous—she was good. At least, that is how I perceived her.

My father was essentially a public man. He headed institutions and this was at first a source of euphoria and then of endless worries. He gave lectures at the university, where he was admired by students, he published books and participated in different committees. In his private life, he attached great importance to friendship and was always surrounded by good friends. He loved talking with them, discussing politics, telling stories.

Would it be legitimate to see in the contrasting role of your mother and your father the distinction between the ordinary and the heroic that structures the first part of Facing the Extreme?

Let's say that it is a transposition—very indirect, to be sure, and recognizable only by me—of the values that my father and mother embodied in their own way. To be more precise, deeply affected by my mother's death so far from me, I wanted to put into words and concepts what had been but a matter of practice for her. I have always been irritated by these intellectuals, writers and philosophers who speak with contempt or condescension of people (usually women) who have not left an 'œuvre' behind them, who 'contented themselves', as is said in this case, with raising their children and loving their spouse. This was repudiating the path illustrated by my mother, one of the most admirable people I've ever known! I wanted to name and show the values she symbolized. I thought that such acts of caring and kindness were the best one could do for our poor humanity, far better than the great revolutionary projects. I recognized myself in the opposition Vassily Grossman draws, in *Life and Fate*, between Kindness and the Good, his preference going to the first (which he also finds exemplified by maternal love).

This is surely the origin of my attachment to what I now call everyday values, the values of the private sphere, reserved (or abandoned) to the feminine half of humankind for centuries. This specific interest had nothing therefore to do with the concentration camps. The proof is that I pursued the exploration of the same theme in an altogether different context—that of genre painting in seventeenth-century Holland. In this sense, as I said before, *Éloge du quotidien* and *Facing the Extreme* are closely related.

But what made you look for everyday values in the concentration camps? Why, to gain an understanding of the ordinary, did you have to go face the extreme?

I started from the hypothesis that extreme circumstances act, if you will, as a magnifying glass—things that stay hidden in ordinary life out of respect for conventions, out of politeness or out of hypocrisy are brought into the full light of day in the extraordinary situation of the camps. I also had a second key motivation for writing this book, which you noted at the outset, namely, studying totalitarianism. In a certain way, I tried to reconcile these two apparently very disparate lines of reflection.

The heroic and the ordinary

It is then, once more, as a moralist that you interrogate history. In this case, you approach the concentration camps from a brand new perspective: that of moral life. Let us start from the beginning: what do you call 'moral life'?

We step into the world of moral values from the moment that we do act not in our own interest but in the interests of another person or in the name of a principle. This statement is, of course, open to discussion. One could object, in the first place, that we always act in our own interests since, even when we are helping others, we gain something for ourselves, if only a clear conscience. But this extension of the notion of interest seems puzzling to me because it blurs the difference between clearly distinct acts. We could try to be more specific and add to our definition that we do not act 'directly' in our own interest. Another objection: some people, including Rousseau (and I believe that he was right), think that every moral act is accomplished in relation to a person. However, the 'principle' I evoked can also be with reference to people but in a more oblique way — if, for example, I give my life for my religion or my country or for science.

Let us suppose the following: morality starts from the moment that I am no longer motivated by selfishness and the instinct of self-preservation alone, from the moment that I am ready to sacrifice my life — or, in a less extreme case, my precious belongings and interests — in the name of something outside myself. If we suppose with Rousseau that humanity starts from the moment that we enter the space of morality, we can say that we become human from the moment that we are ready to sacrifice our lives. It is true that animals have this attitude too: the mother puts herself in danger to save her threatened babies, and individuals sacrifice themselves so that the group can live. But, on these occasions, we find that animals behave precisely like humans. The specificity of human beings, in this respect, could be due to one of the biological characteristics of our species, namely, that the human young cannot survive alone for a particularly long period of time. In order for the species to survive, the parents must take care of their child. Once could say that is a pure waste at an individual level because they receive nothing in return. The duration of this vulnerability of the young ones and of the concern internalized by the adults is such that it marks us within. One of our finest qualities may derive precisely from our weakness.

Humankind — and particularly its most illustrious representatives, poets and philosophers — has a tendency to disparage itself, to declare that we are an utterly selfish species. I do not believe that this is so. Without the possibility of sacrifice, humans would not be humans. To be sure, the reasons for sacrifice have changed but even today they are not lacking. What parents would not be ready to sacrifice their own lives to save their child? And what parents would not feel a burning sense of shame until the end of their lives if they did not do so — which would suffice to prove that our humanity depends on it.

I use self-sacrifice as emblematic of an attitude here, because it represents its most extreme form. This in no way means that the acts we consider moral are perceived by the people who do them as a loss of something they once possessed. On the contrary, such deeds usually provide us with a joyful and enriching experience. I am not sacrificing anything when I play with my child — neither my time nor my spirit.

Many concentration camp survivors cruelly recall how, in the camps, facing the extreme, morality was extinguished, how it became, out of necessity, a matter of 'every man for himself'.

This was one of my first challenges in *Facing the Extreme* — to counter the conventional idea according to which the camps were a purely Hobbesian world, that of the war of all against all, in which human beings act like wolves towards other human beings. It is an idea that is found in the writings of numerous survivors. I recall in the book an oft-quoted statement by a Jewish woman, a doctor in Auschwitz, saying, 'My principle is myself — first, second and third. Then nothing. Then myself again — and then all the others.' But I do not think that these declarations are to be taken literally. For reasons that we could analyse, the survivors tended to emphasize the deterioration in normal human relationships. It is quite understandable — they remember first what was most abnormal and cruellest. However, if you read their writings carefully, you see that, throughout their experience, acts that can only be described as moral subsisted, acts of mutual aid and of caring for others. It is clear that the rules of politeness disappeared and that the borders of generosity shifted but it is no less clear that, without helping hands, even fewer prisoners would have survived the camps. What makes these moral experiences so precious is precisely that they continued to exist when 'facing the extreme'.

What distinction do you make, within moral deeds, between the heroic and the ordinary?

The touchstone here is to know whether the beneficiary is an abstraction or an individual. Heroes act in the name of abstract entities. They fight and sacrifice themselves for humanity or for their country or for their village. Or, yet again, for an idea: honour, glory, freedom or justice. In the world of the ordinary, on the other hand, one acts for the benefit of another person, often for a family member or close friend, a lover, a child or a parent. And the same deed assumes a different meaning depending on the context in which it is accomplished. Heroes sacrifice themselves to defend their country. A mother sacrifices herself because her child is in danger of sinking into quicksand in the Mont-Saint-Michel bay: she jumps in, saves the child and perishes instead.

According to the Kantian doctrine, such a deed would have no moral value because the mother follows her inclinations in defending what is dearest to her. From Kant's perspective, morality begins when we overcome our natural tendencies and draw no pleasure from what we do. By this yardstick, my mother too would have been an amoral person. This brings me to doubt the pertinence of the Kantian framework. I find one of Rousseau's statements, once again, more convincing: he says that one can be virtuous 'out of duty or delight', by overcoming one's natural inclinations or, on the contrary, by yielding to them—after all, the human being is not entirely bad. Caring for our loved ones is at once a delight and a virtue.

In this opposition between the heroic and the ordinary, one can sense that you have a preference for the latter. You have been putting heroism into question in your works ever since.

tzvetan todorov

Does this mean that you condemn all acts that put ideals above human beings?

Putting aside my own personal inclinations, I have to say that each set of values suits a particular context. Heroism has its value in crisis situations. For Europeans, the last crisis was obviously the Second World War. To combat the Nazi invasion, it was not only legitimate but admirable to be ready to sacrifice your life for your country, for freedom and democracy. Even if this meant putting individuals to death, killing German soldiers. Against Hitler's tanks, other tanks had to be launched.

Primo Levi evokes this dilemma in the only novel that he devoted to the fate of the Jews in the war, *If Not Now, When?* One of the main characters, a Jewish partisan, asks himself whether it is right to kill to save other individuals from death, in other words, whether it is right to use the enemy's weapons against the enemy. The answer is yes, because it is the only way of stopping evil. Physical courage and the ability to take risks (without, of course, seeking danger for its own sake) are essential qualities in such cases. But they are exceptional qualities, not given to everyone. On the other hand, ordinary virtues are within everybody's reach and we need them as much in normal situations as in moments of crisis.

In Facing the Extreme, *you deliver a rather encouraging message in the end: do not feel guilty for not being a hero or a saint, for other more ordinary deeds are equally worthy of esteem, if not more.*

Do not despair, because much humbler and certainly much easier deeds contribute also, and even more surely, to the happiness of humanity. The heroic act can be misdirected from its purpose — you think you are serving goodness and at the end of the day, you contribute to evil. Think about all those who have fought for the victory of Communism. The act that consists of making somebody happy, or simply less unhappy, cannot be put to improper use, it cannot be made to serve a higher purpose.

What are these ordinary virtues and what method did you use to identify them in the concentration camps?

I did not deduce these ordinary virtues from an abstract principle. I read a great number of accounts by survivors and recorded all the acts that I intuitively attributed to this category. I then grouped them by affinity, and I tried to understand them. The key virtue is, of course, caring for others. Then comes dignity, which is no more than a way of being coherent with oneself, then the life of the mind, then artistic and intellectual production or contemplation which imparts more meaning and beauty to life.

Even facing the extreme, these qualities are essential. In my book, I dwell on the fate of a young girl, an inhabitant of the Warsaw ghetto. Her name was Pola Lifszyc. One day, of her own free will, she got on a train transporting Jews on a one-way journey to Treblinka. She got on because her mother was one of the Jews who had been rounded up. She must have suspected that this trip spelled death, but she went anyway because the idea of leaving her mother alone was unbearable to her. I find this deed admirable even if it did not in any way contribute to Hitler's defeat — even if, on the contrary, it helped him carry out his plan by leading to the death of one more Jew. I find it no less admirable than the struggle taken up by Mordechai Anielewicz, the leader of the ghetto uprising who, for his part, aspired to kill as many Nazis as possible. They were probably acquainted with each other, since Marek Edelman, a surviving leader of the uprising, knew them both well. He's the one who recounts their stories.

I would like to focus a bit on one of the 'virtues' you describe: the life of the mind. In what respect is this a virtue . . . a virtue by delight?

Works of art, to take one example of the life of the mind, need not illustrate a moral. The artist submits to other requirements: he or she aspires to tell the truth about the world, to imbue it—and I am deliberately using this very general expression—with more meaning and beauty. Mozart was not concerned with morality when he wrote his quintets or even his operas, neither was Michelangelo when he sculpted nor Shakespeare when he wrote a scene (and if he was, that is not the reason for its greatness). From this standpoint, we have no need to know whether these artists were pious or impious, virtuous or corrupt.

But everyone is not an artist—I am far from being one myself. Fortunately, the life of the mind is not limited to artistic creation; knowledge and thought constitute a no less essential part of the life of the mind, even when we are not its initiators. Reading, learning, receiving a powerful thought and contemplating a work of art are also experiences that make the world around us a little better. This was true even in the concentration camps. I give numerous examples of this spiritual aspiration and the beneficial effects it produced. Charlotte Delbo, an Auschwitz prisoner, exchanged her precious ration of bread for a copy of *The Misanthrope* and never regretted it. A world in which Molière is read is preferable to one in which he is not. This enrichment of the world is a value and not exactly a moral act, since it is addressed to ourselves, which is why I use the more neutral term 'virtue' to describe it. Aside from the interaction with others, there is also self-fulfilment. Both are necessary.

A common objection immediately comes to mind. Eichmann was an avid chamber music lover and he played the violin; but this did not keep him from organizing the deportation of the Jews to the concentration camps. And there is no need to take such an extreme example: the most remarkable philosophers can be humanly mediocre. Witness Rousseau himself.

Admittedly the conclusion is rather paradoxical: the life of the mind makes the world better, but not the individual who participates in it. It is the works of artists, scholars and philosophers that must be admired, not their lives or who they are as human beings. Bruno Bettelheim, who wrote penetrating pages on extreme experiences, tells the story somewhere of Beethoven's nephew, a poor boy whom the brilliant uncle did his best to torment. Think of all the wives who have suffered agony while their husbands struggled to beget their great masterpiece!

This is, moreover, one of the lessons of Rousseau, which I've already mentioned in passing. Whereas his encyclopaedist friends were advocating education and culture, believing that moral and political progress would automatically follow as a result, Rousseau, in his *Discourse on the Arts and Sciences*, already noted with bitterness and lucidity that, no, men do not become individually better because they go more often to the theatre or read more books. Their horizons become wider, their possibilities increase in number, but their sense of justice and injustice is not necessarily enhanced; nothing guarantees that this new knowledge will serve anything but selfishness and the enjoyment of power. This lesson, though, has a hard time being heard, especially by the artists themselves. Joseph Brodsky, the Russian poet, believed in the redeeming virtues of beauty and asserted that anyone who had read Dickens could not really be a bad man. I am not convinced of that. Mao wrote beautiful classical poetry, it seems, but this did not keep him from killing millions of Chinese.

Having understood this did not make Rousseau stop writing, fortunately for us. For reading his works today helps us understand the world better. And an intelligible world is a better world, in the sense that each individual life, enhanced by these experiences, brings us a little closer to the vocation of humankind: to give shape and meaning to the gestures of one's life.

But what did Eichmann's and Charlotte Delbo's experience of beauty have in common? Molière for one and Schumann for the other — is it through this that both Eichmann and Delbo, no matter how outrageous the parallel might seem, remained human beings?

Never for a second did Eichmann stop being a human being—not when he was dispatching trainloads of Jews nor when he was devoting himself to chamber music. The human includes the inhuman, as Romain Gary liked to recall. And every human has access, if only sporadically, to the life of the mind. But, thereafter, Delbo and Eichmann's experiences part. Eichmann divided his existence into separate parts, disconnecting his love for music from his other experiences: we do not see any sign of it outside of the sessions he dedicates to Schumann. Delbo introduced literary experience into her life in Auschwitz; perhaps she would not have survived without Molière. *The Misanthrope* became her companion, more real than the guards and the kapos. She did not escape into literature; on the contrary, literature became an integral part of her life.

You've presented heroic and ordinary virtues as appropriate in different contexts, and thus as equally worthy in principle. What then explains your inclination—to return to the same question—for values cultivated in everyday life, for dignity, caring and the life of the mind, and your relative reservations vis-à-vis heroism?

Apart from the reasons we have just discussed, particularly its susceptibility to misuse, it is worth noting the proximity of heroic virtues to mental and social habits of the past. They have an affinity with the code of chivalry and with a hierarchical view of humanity. Once again, I am judging based on myself. I am not at all sure that, if ever the circumstances required it of me, I would be able to act like a hero; on the other hand, ordinary values are familiar to me, even if I do not always succeed in putting them into practice. The book of interviews of Marek Edelman by Hanna Krall, one of the starting points of *Facing the Extreme*, gave me food for thought in this regard. Edelman himself, a courageous leader in the ghetto uprising, subscribed to heroic values as did his friend Mordechai Anielewicz.

But when he recalls these events, 40 years later, it is the gesture of Pola Lifszyc, the young women accompanying her mother to Treblinka, that comes most readily to his mind.

But why do we need heroes? Is it a need to admire, a need to identify with someone, a need to believe?

Perhaps we should draw a distinction between heroes and models. I think we do need models, human beings whom we admire and would like to resemble: it is our very humanity that is at stake and our capacity to aspire to what we believe is over and above us. In this respect, the destiny of an individual is much more eloquent than abstract principles. That is why I presented a series of portraits of admirable people in *Hope and Memory*, from Vassily Grossman to Germaine Tillion. These people do not, however, embody heroic virtues. To reformulate Brecht's statement, happy are the people who don't need heroes! Today, in our world, this need makes itself felt only exceptionally.

In praise of rescuers

In your book, you give pride of place to people you call 'rescuers', that is to say, those who, instead of fighting for the victory of their group, set out to save lives.

Indeed, rescuers are not fighters; they do not fight for a cause but content themselves with protecting individuals. Rather than struggle against the enemy, they try to limit the damage; they introduce a touch of humanity into a world that is lacking in it. During the war, the Jews were the particular targets of persecution and so it was a matter of rescuing them. The acts of rescuers are situated midway between ordinary and heroic virtues. Like the former, the beneficiary is an individual, not an abstraction; like the latter, he or she is a stranger and not kin. As in the former case, the acts are simple — offering a place to live, food and clothing; as in the latter case, they are dangerous — whoever hides a Jew risks being deported like a Jew.

During the war, rescuers and members of the Resistance had the same enemy — the German Occupation forces — but they came into conflict from time to time because their interests diverged so. In Chambon-sur-Lignon, a village where the protection of the Jewish refugees was well organized, the priest André Trocmé and his wife Magda did not always appreciate the activities of members of the Resistance because it endangered the lives of their protégés.

Incidentally, I noticed that rescuers often acted as a couple. I don't think this was by accident. The man and the woman, or sometimes two men and two women, would share the responsibilities in a complementary way; it was as a twosome that they formed, in a manner of speaking, a whole moral being.

Does this mean that it is difficult to reconcile the two priorities at the same time? In short, that one cannot simultaneously fight for ideas and take care of human beings, one by one?

Perhaps . . . On the other hand, nothing keeps you from giving priority sometimes to one and sometimes to the other. Germaine Tillion, whose destiny, as I was discovering it, appeared to embody what I value the most, managed to do both. During the Second World War, she immediately engaged in frontal combat, contributing to the founding of one of the very first Resistance networks, the Musée de l'Homme as she would later call it. At that point in time, she was participating in the world of heroic values: she risked her life, she herself was ready to kill and the Germans shot a number of her friends. Fifteen years later, she found herself involved in the Algerian War. And there her attitude was closer to that of a rescuer: she did what she could to prevent torture and capital punishment but also terrorist attacks. The priority, then, was not her country but individual lives.

This shift corresponded at once to a difference in context—the two conflicts did not resemble one another—and to her own personal development. I think that, in 1940, the requirements of justice prevailed over those of compassion; in 2000, but also already by 1955, the opposite is true.

tzvetan todorov

You slightly modified Facing the Extreme *when the second edition was published in 1994. Why?*

The writing of this book was a shattering experience for me; I worked on it in a somewhat feverish state. When I reread it, a year later, I found several points that needed to be clarified or amended. The one that affected the book most fundamentally concerned the thinking and destiny of Etty Hillesum, a wonderful young Dutch Jew who, in the midst of the roundups and deportations, chose to accept all and to love all, to live even the worst misfortune serenely because she had decided once and for all to say yes to life. Etty Hillesum was admirable, but I do not subscribe to her value system and to her lack of resistance to evil. We can respect her as a person, but I would not advise anyone suffering in this world to accept evil rather than resist it and try to eliminate it. Her capacity to convert suffering into a source of joy is too exceptional to serve as an example. I did not state this clearly enough in the first edition of the book and I realized that it could be misinterpreted as a result. I also moved certain passages to make the whole more coherent. Finally, I removed a few hyperbolic expressions that were not necessary and could have prompted a debate, which seemed out of place to me in this context. As for the rest, it is the same book.

Evil: a political approach

In Facing the Extreme *you focus as much attention on 'vices' as on 'virtues'. Taking again the extreme conditions of the camps as a starting point, you attempt to describe how evil comes to pass. You try to explain it. With great precaution, you declare several times that to understand is not to absolve. Were you afraid that you might be criticized for looking for excuses for the murderers?*

If I had followed my own personal inclination I would have kept to the first part of the book, which shows how morality was maintained even in the world of concentration camps. I would rather think about forms of good than modalities of evil. But it seemed to me that the picture would have been too unbalanced. The camps were, after all, a place where the evil done by man to man reached levels seldom seen before. To ignore it would have been odd, to say the least. I therefore tried to confront it.

How can one approach evil through thought? An initial reaction, which is quite widespread, consists in raising an impassable barrier between the self and the individuals responsible for the evil — the murderers and torturers — and in stigmatizing their monstrosity. This is a very understandable reaction, but it seems to me to be of limited use. With regard to the self, it amounts firstly to defending oneself and refusing to recognize ones own aggressive and violent impulses. With regard to the evil-doers, it amounts to seeing them as a species apart, a species that it would suffice to condemn. Yet we need to try to understand evil not in order to absolve it, of course, but in order to prevent it from coming back, at least in the same form. To declare that the crime is incomprehensible (on the grounds that it is inexcusable) is a position whose premises are highly questionable. It means denying the unity of humankind — there would be monsters on one side and normal people on the other. This is precisely what we reproach these same criminals for doing — for having cast out of humanity one of its branches, for having decided it could be eliminated.

In situations of violence, the torturer is the only one to really pose a problem. He has the choice, his will is free, at least to a point, and he choeses to torture and to kill. Why? There is nothing to 'understand', in this sense of the term, about the victim's attitude. Victims are compelled; they are subjected to violence, like raped women. Victims demand compassion, not comprehension. What we must try to understand and explain, on the other hand, is the behaviour of the agent of violence, of the rapist.

It follows that the former victims are not in a good position to undertake this task. And it would be cruel to ask them to. Do we ask the victim of a rape to enquire into the psychology of her rapist? Primo Levi went far in this direction, much too far in my opinion when I think of all the suffering he endured, not in the camps but in the years that followed, when he tried to understand the motivations of his torturers. You can feel it above all in his last book, *The Drowned and the Saved*. He could have spared himself the pain of this immersion into evil but he was too scrupulously honest to hold himself back.

Such immersion is no doubt unbearable for the victims but I wonder whether, for some people, it corresponds to a fascination with evil. You yourself, a peaceful man — at least, on the surface! — have spent a great deal of time scrutinizing violence and piles of corpses — in The Conquest of America *and, even before that, in* The Fantastic. *How do you explain this attraction?*

Any interest in the evil that surrounds us can surely not be explained by a fascination with evil — just think of the work accomplished every day by the police, by judges and by youth workers. And yet this attraction also exists, and probably in me too, since my books bear witness to it. Why are we so impressed by acts that are said to be 'monstrous', be it an item in the news or a major event in the history of a nation? Great misfortunes produce, of course, the most poignant stories, but why? I believe that we see something magnified in them whose presence we ignore in ourselves although we can sense it. These acts are not entirely unfamiliar to us. The fascination would arise from the encounter between these two contradictory feelings. We thus observe with avidity acts committed by others and read with both curiosity and disgust the confessions of great murderers. We cannot peel our eyes away from these suffering bodies and we sense that these situations that come out of the human reveal a secret part of the human.

But I will immediately add that this anthropological perspective on evil — we all are capable of it — must not be conflated with a legal or moral perspective — we all are guilty of it. Some act on the impulse, others don't. The difference is considerable.

tzvetan todorov

So what did you learn, once you had accepted the human nature of inhumanity?

I was immediately led in directions that Tillion explored in *Ravensbrück*, in the chapter entitled 'Ordinary People', and Arendt in *Eichmann in Jerusalem* on the 'banality of evil'. Is it pure coincidence that these are women writing on this subject? Perhaps men have more of a tendency, because of their own traditions, to see conflicts in terms of mutually exclusive forces: here, the good, there, the bad.

I was convinced that Tillion's and Arendt's analyses were the right starting point, although I would not employ the expression 'banality of evil'. Not only because this particular evil had nothing commonplace about it (Arendt knew this was so; what she had in mind was the banality of the evil-doers, but the expression gave rise to confusion), but also because there was nothing banal about Eichmann, Rudolph Hoess, the commandant of Auschwitz, and the other mass murderers at the time when they were committing their crimes. Of course, they were men like anybody else at the start. They managed, however, to suppress all feelings of compassion to an uncommon degree. Even when we do not actively seek to improve the fate of humanity, all of us feel a pang of anguish upon seeing misery and human degeneration—this is what is commonplace. To be detached to such an extent from all feelings of humanity is hardly banal . . . even if the Nazi murderers do not have a monopoly on such detachment.

I tried to develop Arendt's and Tillion's principles to see what fed such evil, both ordinary and extraordinary.

What characterized this inhumanity?

The inhumanity emerged here from the meeting of the ordinary and the extraordinary. On the one hand, a project for the violent transformation of society; on the other, what could be called 'ordinary vices', the kind found in any modern society.

The project promised happiness for everyone except the enemies who were designated the cause of all contemporary ills. Such hope makes people fanatical, capable of sacrificing everything to achieve their ideal. It is in this context that 'ordinary vices', with which we are all familiar, can become dangerous. To identify them, I used the same approach as I had for 'ordinary virtues', reading and comparing accounts of life in the camps. This led me to discuss the concept of 'fragmentation', the capacity we have to divide up our lives, even our consciences, into impermeable compartments, each one governed by its own particular laws. Then there is the concept of 'depersonalization', or the way one can treat human beings as pure instruments, as representatives of a category, without recognizing their status as individual subjects endowed with will. Finally, there is 'enjoyment of power', a position that heightens our sense of existing and something we all need greatly. These attitudes are not at all reserved to the world of concentration camps — all you have to do is approach a bureaucrat in the immigration office in Paris to see the 'enjoyment of power' at work. But in the extreme conditions of the camps, these 'ordinary vices' became the source of tragedy.

In a way, you too practised fragmentation when you were living in Bulgaria. To protect yourself from the totalitarian state, you divided your life into two sides: one public and submissive, the other private and free. Did this fragmentation work efficiently and did this experience help you to understand — all differences notwithstanding — the mental fragmentation of such a zealous servant of Hitler as Eichmann?

In ordinary times, we all have multiple personalities. You remember Montaigne saying he bends his knees, not his reason? He was thinking not only of the constraint coming from the outside. Individuals, in their public lives, are compelled to put on an act, to adopt certain postures, to respond to a certain type of question and to necessarily repeat themselves. We each have several masks. But, normally, these facets of a single personality communicate with one another. They may be distinct but they remain compatible nonetheless. This form of separation, which is conceivable, even legitimate under an ordinary regime, did not work in the case of subjects in a totalitarian state because the latter also has an insidious hold over our reason. Fragmentation, the normal function of which is to defend the individual, was ineffective. Montaigne could not have imagined the totalitarian hold over everyone's life.

On the other hand, the function of the fragmentation practised by Eichmann or Hoess or Stangl, the commandant of Treblinka, was to numb the conscience — its purpose was to enable them to lead their victims to their death by day and turn into good fathers, loving husbands, lovers of beautiful music and great literature by night. There are therefore two forms of fragmentation: the totalitarian state encourages one (for it guarantees the state servants who will not balk at any task) and makes the other impossible (its subjects cannot take refuge in their own private universe). Everything depends on the strategy of the moment.

Hence, 'banality of good' and 'banality of evil' — such is human nature?

This brings us back to the humanist postulate. Human beings are morally indeterminate. Hence, education counts, as do the social and political systems in which they live which can either nurture their humanity or imperil it.

It follows that our greatest enemy should be not so much the individuals, even criminal individuals, but the regime that encourages them to act the way they do. Of course, particular individuals always embody the regime — the German Occupation forces in France, for example — and these individuals must be fought. But once victory is achieved, what matters most is not to punish each individual but to make sure that the criminal regime cannot be revived.

So you agree here again with Tillion when she declares that she is for an official condemnation of the use of torture during the Algerian War, but against the trial of the former torturers?

Tillion was always sensitive to what she described as the 'tragic ease with which "nice people" can become torturers without even realizing it.' She wrote this sentence about Ravensbrück, not Algeria. But it can be applied to the Algerian situation too. In the latter case, the 'becoming-torturer' occurred in a democratic country — France — but in a time of crisis — the Algerian War. This just goes to show us how much harder it is to judge individuals in a totalitarian country where the crisis is, in a way, ongoing. The former beneficiaries of the regime acted badly, of course; they have nothing to be proud of, but it is too easy to play the part of the hero after the fact, to make peremptory judgements and be outraged by the fact that not everybody acted as they should have.

Totalitarian evil

You see totalitarianism as the embodiment of political evil. Could you explain in what respect?

Totalitarianism is a regime that denies the individual as a value. Science, it claims, defines the aims to be reached and the means that are to be used to attain them — a classless society and the elimination of the bourgeoisie; a society without 'inferior races' and the elimination of the Jews. It is the Party that controls society; it is the leader, the Führer, who makes decisions. In all of this, the ordinary subject in a totalitarian country can do nothing but submit. What I call depersonalization is thus embedded in the totalitarian agenda itself. We have already discussed the fragmentation imposed by the system — the fragmentation inflicted upon individuals to stifle all protest, and the fragmentation practised by the latter to protect a corner of their lives.

It was the enjoyment of power that struck me most when I was living in a totalitarian country. My experience of totalitarianism was unrelated, as I have said before, to its moments of paroxysm. I was not living in the Ukrainian villages in 1933 when the whole population was starving to death and parents took to eating their own children. I was not in Auschwitz in 1944 when entire trainloads of Hungarian Jews were emptied and sent to their immediate death. In my personal experience of Bulgaria in the fifties and sixties, it was the reign of the will to power and the enjoyment of power. All the proudly proclaimed goals were nothing but hypocritical facades. Those in power spoke of peace, equality, freedom and justice, and what we saw all around us was exactly the opposite. So it was also the reign of widespread lying. What was behind the hollow words was a passion for power, cynical selfishness and an attitude of 'I'm filling my pockets while making you pretend that you think it's for your own good.' In a totalitarian country, this is all that is left once you've given up on utopia. And political wrongdoing spawns moral wrongdoing; it produces spineless individuals solely bent on their own self-interests. Not everyone, of course, but a great majority.

Do you regard the inhabitants of totalitarian countries as victims, no matter what they have done? In what respect were you yourself a victim?

Totalitarian regimes leave you no freedom of choice. Or rather, freedom of choice still exists, but all choices with the exception of one are declared criminal. You can try to flee the country, but you risk getting caught at the border by police dogs and thrown into jail. You can try to live in internal exile and practise silent resistance, but you will soon be marginalized, if not sent to a labour camp. That is why my condemnation of these regimes is absolute but that of their citizens, only relative. I left before I had the time to be compromised in a deep-seated way. Yet, just knowing that you are capable of cowardly petty acts to safeguard your own comfort, that you are capable of the worst if only the state tells you that it is right, is something that leaves its mark on you. Perhaps my interest in morality comes from there.

I might add that condemning totalitarianism without hesitation does not amount to seeing it as the embodiment of absolute evil. An isolated act can embody evil, not a regime, which is an infinitely more complex entity. Moreover, imagining that there is an evil intention does not help us understand totalitarianism — its agents always believed that they were working towards good, they saw themselves as benefactors of humankind. I do not think that human beings act to please the Devil, with the intention of imposing the rule of evil. It's just that all gods are not equally good for human beings.

Don't you think, then, that there is a book missing from your catalogue, a book that would draw even more closely on your personal experience to examine moral life in the ordinary conditions of totalitarianism?

I find that I have devoted quite enough time already to examining different forms of evil. I would rather devote myself, in the coming years, to understanding what I admire: the vitality of the mind, the creation of beauty.

Is there only totalitarianism that corrupts freedom and morality to this point? What about the way the Church, a religion, a sect, a guru, or even simply a social elite (mediatico-politique, *as we say) defines this much talked-about 'good' to which we are expected to conform?*

Each one of us speaks about what he or she knows best, of course. For example, it is said today that our whole society in France has evolved towards a soft totalitarianism, subjected as it is to advertising, fashion and the clichés spread by the media. In my opinion, only those who have not lived through the totalitarian experience can lump the two together, thereby erasing the difference between social determination and police coercion. Even if we take the more particular case of sects, where the mind does in fact become a prisoner, individuals accept, of their own free will to submit to additional rules. After all, the sect is a unit that exists in a society that obeys other principles and to which you can always return the day you open your eyes. You can hear a different discourse from people who are not members of the sect and you can change your mind. All of which is impossible in a totalitarian society that is coextensive with the entire country, where all authorized discourses tend in the same direction and where the powers-that-be readily make use of physical force, be it the police or the army.

From this point of view, as you suggest in your analysis of the camps, the Nazi and Communist regimes are equally totalitarian. You know to what extent this comparison is considered taboo but you do not hesitate to establish this parallel, even if it means finding yourself accused of being the one to blur distinctions this time. What is your interpretation of this taboo and what do you think of the arguments of those who defend the unique and hence incomparable character of the Nazi crimes against the Jews?

I do not see any reason to respect a taboo concerning this parallel. Or rather, I can see the reasons why but I am not convinced. Since Hitler has come to symbolize absolute evil, the defenders of Communism are shocked by the comparison. But both regimes have similar structural properties they engendered comparable suffering. And there was a period, from 1939 to 1941, when they joined forces to divide Europe between them. Drawing a parallel between the two does not mean conflating them, of course. There are also many differences that are even more clearly visible against the backdrop of the common elements.

The condemnation itself is similar for it is absolute. Certain distinctions, which are justified in their context, are no longer valid on the level of judgement.

For example, we speak of three genocides in the twentieth century: the Armenians in Turkey, the Jews in Europe and the Tutsis in Rwanda. And in so doing we omit the Ukrainian peasants in 1932–33—five to six million deaths—and the Cambodian city-dwellers—more than a million, or a seventh of the population. The argument that excludes these crimes committed by Communist regimes from the category of genocide is based on the fact that these people were exterminated not as an ethnic group but as a class or a social group. This is a valid distinction, but it should have no effect on our condemnation. In both cases, people were killed for belonging to a group and not because of their acts. And being a 'kulak', a 'bourgeois' or an 'intellectual' was considered by these Communist regimes as indelible a defect (and quasi-hereditary) as being Armenian, Jewish or Tutsi—children of kulaks were themselves persecuted as kulaks.

No reasonless evil, no unadulterated good

You have written two books on particular episodes in the history of the twentieth century: The Fragility of Goodness, *on the rescue of the Bulgarian Jews during the Second World War, and* A French Tragedy, *about a little-known episode in what you call the 'civil war' in France, the fighting between the* milice *and the* maquis *in 1944. In both cases, you show the extent to which the course of history can depend on a particular individual's acts and, in both cases, you pursue the tribute to rescuers that you started in* Facing the Extreme. *What are you trying to demonstrate through these stories?*

One can analyse a country's history from different perspectives. Personally, what attracts me are the problems of morality and politics that this history brings into play. To be even more precise, I'm interested in cases when good and evil are not positioned along predictable lines, when you find one in the other or one leading to the other. Clear-cut monolithic situations do not teach me anything. My feeling is that they do not enable me to really penetrate into the secrets of human conduct.

I believe that all evil is done for a reason, and that this reason is not necessarily evil. And vice versa; the idea of an unadulterated good seems to me to belong to the realm of illusion. This good always has a price, and it has unpredictable and undesirable consequences which we cannot allow ourselves to neglect on the pretext that the aim is noble.

Perhaps this refusal of dualistic thinking is the main message that I would like to get across to my readers. This is why I am attracted to ambivalent, indecisive and complex episodes in history. Faced with any assertion, I want to ask myself why its opposite is not entirely false. Including this one. This tendency probably comes from the fact that totalitarian politics is grounded in a dualistic outlook on the world which divides humanity into friends and foes—the former to be defended in all circumstances, the latter to be eliminated at all costs. Seeing evil in good and good in evil does not, however, mean that all values are indistinguishable and that all choices are equivalent. That would be falling into the opposite extreme of nihilism and the refusal to judge. I would like to continue exercising judgement but, at the same time, avoid the ease of pleasing certitudes.

Let us take the case of The Fragility of Goodness. *How did you come to take an interest in this episode in Bulgarian history?*

Like all Bulgarians, I always knew the main outlines of history and I knew that the Bulgarian Jews had not been deported to the concentration camps during the war. But nobody made a big thing of it when I was a child in Bulgaria, probably because the people responsible for saving the Jews were not valiant Communists, who always played the part of the benefactor, but less 'commendable' figures. In other words, this page in history did not fit properly into predominant dualistic categories; so it was mentioned but not discussed any further. I learnt that, a few years after I left for France, the ruling Communist leaders had changed their attitude on the subject. Realizing that they could draw international prestige from this glorious moment in their past, they undertook to take credit for it themselves. Zhivkov, the head of the party and the state, was adorned with a new role, that of having organized the demonstrations that stopped the deportations. The country's Jewish organizations, which were under the party's heel, even proposed Zhivkov's name for the Nobel Peace Prize! Fortunately their proposal did not lead to anything.

This view of the past started to shift with the fall of the Berlin Wall in 1989 and the opening of the archives. An Italian journalist, Gabriele Nissim, went to Bulgaria to investigate these events and discovered in the national archives a manuscript written by one of the main protagonists in the affair, Dimitar Peshev. He wrote a book on the subject. He told me about it when we met on the occasion of a commemoration of Primo Levi's work. I too obtained the text of these memoirs and found in them the material for a moral and political study, along the lines of what I had undertaken on other occasions.

The *Fragility of Goodness* is not really a book by me; it is a collection of documents that I selected and presented, Peshev's memoirs as well as those of other protagonists, and especially documents written at the time when the events occurred: open letters, resolutions, newspaper articles. I like this form of historical work. I used it for *Voices from the Gulag* and also for *Guerre et Paix sous l'Occupation* (*War and Peace under the Occupation*). It gives the readers access to the documents so that they can compare for themselves their impressions with the interpretations of historians.

In what respect does Peshev's act escape dualistic categories?

Firstly, it must be said that all credit does not go solely to Peshev. This is one of the lessons of my investigation and that is why I speak about 'fragility'. The rescue of the Jews required the intervention of many people, on different levels, from King Boris and a number of public figures whose voices could be heard down to anonymous ordinary people. A failure on any one of these levels would surely have led to the failure of the entire operation.

That being said, Peshev was one of the most active figures. The Sofia metropolitan (orthodox bishop) Stefan was another. Peshev was Vice-President of the National Assembly, in a country dominated by a conservative coalition and allied with Nazi Germany in terms of foreign policy. He was a dyed-in-the-wool conservative who had not hesitated to vote in favour of the anti-Jewish laws in 1940. But, in 1943, when the deportation project began taking concrete form, under the direction of the same Theodor Dannecker who had organized the deportation of the Jews in France, Peshev saw the real consequences of the measures: the suffering and death of thousands of people. At that point he had a sudden burst of scruples and he decided to follow his conscience rather than the government's orders. The action he took stopped the deportations—the Jews of Thrace and Macedonia, territories then controlled by Bulgaria but not part of it, died in Treblinka but not the Bulgarian Jews.

At the same time, Peshev seems to have acted with a certain degree of pragmatism by emphasizing the interests of the Bulgarians themselves. Is this to say that indignation without political acumen is worthless?

What I find interesting in this chapter of the story is precisely the way Peshev went about reaching his goal. He was not the only one to express indignation at the time; other public figures did so too but their cries did not have any effect on the situation. He was, indeed, the only one to find a political response. His goal was to save the Jews threatened by deportation. He lucidly analysed the situation, weighed the passions of all involved and found the solution—he wrote a resolution and convinced 42 other deputies to sign it, all of whom belonged to the pro-government majority. Peshev insisted on this to ensure that their gesture would be interpreted not as global opposition to the government but as a protest against one particular measure. He then managed to bring widespread attention to his gesture. Forty-two deputies, a third of the Assembly—that was a lot! And it was this split in the government that convinced King Boris, the highest authority in the country, to stop the deportations.

Peshev succeeded in his task not because he had a stronger moral conscience but because he had a better comprehension of politics. It was his political acumen rather than his generosity of spirit that enabled him to save 9,000 Jews from immediate deportation. This is how good came to pass and it is for me a lesson that deserves to be heard . . . and pondered.

Peshev's methods call to mind the way Aron, at the time of the Algerian War, spoke to the French leaders in terms of their own interest.

If you want to be engaged in the world of political action, you must seek success and not your own moral elevation. I am not sure that Aron's arguments really hastened the end of the Algerian War but, at any rate, he was right to act the way he did. Pious protests, alas, do not change much in the world—they simply give all those who profess them a good conscience.

From milice to maquis

In A French Tragedy *you turn your attention once again to rescuers. One of them, more-over, resembles Peshev: René Sadrin, the Vichyite mayor of Saint-Amand-Montrond, whose memoirs you also published,*[1] *as you had Peshev's.*

I discovered the story I tell in *A French Tragedy* by accident, as the result of a trip (I'm beginning to realize that trips count a lot in my choices of subjects). This time, the destination was closer: I was spending a year with my family in the region of Saint-Amand, in the centre of France. I was working on a project with a friend, Annick Jacquet, interviewing ordinary people about their memories of the war period which later led to *Guerre et Paix sous l'Occupation* (*War and Peace under the Occupation*). During one of these visits, our interlocutor handed us a typed manu-script and said, 'Here, since you're interested in this kind of thing.' They were the memoirs of René Sadrin, former mayor of Saint-Amand, essentially devoted to an

---

[1] These memoirs are included in the French version of the book. [Trans.]

episode that took place in the summer of 1944, between the Normandy landings and the Liberation. Immediately after the landings, Resistance members occupied the town. Forced to leave the following day, they took hostages with them: Militia and members of their family. In retaliation, the *milice* threatened to destroy the whole town and they, in turn, took the families of the *maquisards* as hostages. In the end, hostages were exchanged, but the Militiamen and the Gestapo retaliated by murdering all the Jews whom they managed to round up in the region — they were thrown into wells at Guerry.

This horrifying story struck me considerably. I enquired about it, read the published testimonies, pored over documents in the regional archives and questioned other witnesses. This is indeed another story of rescuers but with a less happy outcome. It was even a full-blown tragedy.

What exactly is the complexity in this case? Frankly, the choice between the milice *and the* maquis *is clear, isn't it?*

Yes, the choice is clear, at least it is for me, at the political level. But political engagement does not exclude all other considerations or else we would have to maintain that the ends justify the means, that once a respectable goal is established we have to admire everything connected to it. If all the resisters had behaved like saints and all the collaborationists like fiends, the story would have only substantiated our noble convictions. And if that had been the case, I would not have written *A French Tragedy*.

For one thing, I wanted to show that one's ideological persuasion does not entirely determine the human quality of an individual. You can be on the right side of the fence and nevertheless behave in an irresponsible or cruel way; likewise, you can march under a questionable banner and be capable of a deed that protects the life and dignity of the persecuted. Take the example of Sadrin. Here was a middle-aged man, a mayor appointed by the Vichy government, hence considered close to the Occupation forces, who was not about to join the Resistance. Yet he got actively involved in protecting the welfare of the residents of his district and he managed to do so in what were sometimes dramatic circumstances. Neither did he refrain from helping people on both sides to obtain documents or ration coupons. He even tried, on this precise occasion, to act as a mediator between the *milice* and the *maquisards* until he sprained his ankle.

Meanwhile, the other mediators continued to travel back and forth across the small roads of the centre of France, in the Creuse, the Indre and the Cher, until they obtained an agreement between the adversaries.

The adversaries, the *maquis* and the *milice*, were threatening to execute their hostages if the others did not release theirs first. This kind of situation, as you can well imagine, lends itself to one-upmanship in terms of bravado and machismo: 'If you don't give in, I'll do something you'll regret!' You will object that one of the causes was just, the other was not, and that liberation is better than collaboration. Of course, hostages killed for a good cause would be dead nonetheless. The mediators interceded in this context, trying to convince each party to make concessions, to be less intransigent, so that the hostages could be spared. There were in particular two intrepid generous oddballs who took messages back and forth in an old jalopy, exposing themselves at any moment to fire from fighters on one side or the other — there was a lot of shooting going on in the French countryside in the summer of 1944! They could have stuck to choosing sides — after all, for a person of sound constitution, it couldn't have been too hard to guess who was going to win. But no, rather than cast themselves in the role of heroic fighters, they preferred to save lives. And they succeeded in doing so for the hostages in question. But other massacres followed in relation to these events.

In this book, more than in any other, you deal with the fate of people who are still alive and close to you, spatially speaking. What was the reaction to the book in the Berry, or more generally among those who felt directly concerned by the story?

The reactions varied quite a bit, depending on the nature of the group concerned. First, a special case was the families of the Jews murdered in the wells in Guerry, in reprisal to the activities of the Resistance members (a typical scapegoat situation). These people remembered the massacre as sheer absurdity, as an utterly arbitrary act. The book, I think, put it in the context of a coherent sequence of events; it made it intelligible. Understanding the rationality behind what had happened — even though the rationality was atrocious and revolting — brought them a certain peace of mind. This is why I feel that we have something of a duty to try to understand and to explain.

I also had positive reactions from a few specialists on the history of Vichy — among them, former members of the Resistance. The great American historian Robert Paxton wrote a laudatory review of the book.

The reaction of the former resisters from Saint-Amand was more nuanced. I had met them and asked them questions and, before publishing the book, I had sent the manuscript to a few of them. They approved it except for some minor corrections which I integrated. It was after the publication, when reviews in the local press said that the Resistance did not come out of the book with enhanced prestige, that they expressed disagreement with its overall thrust. But they took it no farther.

The strongest reaction of rejection came from where I didn't expect it: from a group of former Resistance fighters whom I had not met, in the Creuse, a neighbouring region. They were among the troops of a man called 'François' in the book, who was, admittedly, not portrayed in glowing terms. The leader of this group pushed the family of 'François', himself dead by the time the book was published, to sue me for libel. The trial took place in 1996, two years later. I might add that other former resisters in the Creuse sent me letters congratulating me on my work. Differences of interpretation had already manifested themselves between them.

What exactly did they reproach you for?

For speaking ill of 'François' and, in particular, for comparing his behaviour, in the hostage affair, to that of the Militia leader. They pointed out in the plaintiff's letter that 'François' was a Companion of the Liberation, and that General de Gaulle was surely in a better position to judge such matters than Mr Todorov, who was probably still walking around in short trousers when the events occurred—and in Bulgaria, to boot!

The court ended up issuing a mixed decision. It did not follow the initial request and oblige me to suppress or modify any passages in the book; it also rejected the petition for a large sum of money in compensation. But the publisher and I were ordered to pay nominal damages and a few expenses. The reasoning of the court was purely formal, as is often the case in such matters; what interested the judges was not so much whether what was written was true as whether the rules had been respected. And not only had I spoken ill of 'François' but I had not interviewed his fellow resisters or his family—that was considered an offence.

The plaintiffs did not say my descriptions were wrong either. They did not contest the facts; besides, I had published them in a collection of texts when

'François' was still alive and he himself had not contested them. They denied me the right to speak ill of a Companion of the Liberation. All in all, it was a classic conflict between memory activists and historians. Whereas the former are driven by the desire to keep a cult alive, the latter are doing what they can to find the truth. It is certain, however, that in expressing judgements, I had departed from the traditional role of the historian. I was perfectly aware that these judgements would not please the people close to 'François' but I thought that, because he was a public figure, he could be discussed freely. Neither the Gaullist Party nor de Gaulle's family are going to sue someone for speaking ill of General de Gaulle.

Were you aware when you were writing the book that you were doing something politically incorrect by showing that a member of the Resistance could be something less than a pure hero?

To tell the truth, no, I wasn't. Worse yet, I thought that it was an obvious fact and that nobody was asking me to write a pious story. I understand that at the time of the fighting it was important not to discourage the troops, but 50 years later? It's not because I adhere to the values of the Resistance, generally speaking, as I do, that I am obliged to approve of all acts accomplished in its name or of all the people associated with it. Individual responsibility is maintained; it is by no means abrogated by a general engagement. The war had hardly ended when Romain Gary said all this very clearly in *A European Education* and in *The Company of Men*. Admittedly, he himself was a Companion of the Liberation whereas I did not participate in the Resistance.

The offence to the individual remains. I thought I had protected him enough by using his war name only. Maybe I should have used a pseudonym. I am not sure that I found the right formula. But, as for the gist of the matter, I continue to believe what I wrote: at that time, this particular member of the Resistance did not behave in an admirable way. After the war ended, Romain Gary said that we needed to pray for the victors. The vanquished will be forced to think about their errors, whether or not they like it. The victors risk taking themselves for the embodiment of good, which is a very dangerous belief.

A French Tragedy also, paradoxically, brought me an aesthetic experience. I discovered the work of a sculptor, Georges Jeanclos, the nephew of a couple murdered in Guerry. He made a commemorative monument that stands at the site today and which I greatly admired. I then discovered the rest of his work which is equally remarkable. I managed on two occasions to have a picture of his sculptures on the cover of my books, for the English-language cover of *A French Tragedy* and, more recently, for the original French cover of *Hope and Memory* (*Mémoire du mal*). I felt singularly close to this artist, who is now dead and whom I never met. What particularly affects me in his work is his capacity to show human frailty without ever lapsing into sentimentality. He is the artist of compassion par excellence, which is rather paradoxical since compassion is thought to be a specifically Christian virtue and Jeanclos practised Judaism. But his work transcended any particular affiliations, drawing inspiration from Buddhism as well as from so-called 'primitive' art. Asked to do a monument to the memory of Jean Moulin, he portrayed the suffering instead of the combat. Ordinary virtues were closer to him than heroic ones.

9. Memory and Justice

Strategies of memory

CATHERINE PORTEVIN: *In all your books since* Facing the Extreme, *you have been relentlessly addressing the question of memory and its political implications. Let's start, if you will, with the famous quote by George Santayana, 'Those who cannot remember the past are condemned to repeat it,' and your changing attitude to it. It underpinned your writing of* Facing the Extreme — *you say so in your introduction — but in your other books you reconsider the statement, to the point of challenging it. Why?*

TZVETAN TODOROV: I object to the sense that is usually given to this oft-quoted sentence although I do not ignore the kernel of truth it contains. The statement is insufficient because it could be understood in the positive sense as saying that provided you know the past, you are sure not to repeat it — the implication being not to repeat past errors. And this is not true. The meaning of events is not inherent to them, no more than it is inherent to natural processes. Meaning and value are brought to events by human beings asking questions. Besides, you can know the past and want precisely to repeat it because, from your point of view, it is a positive example, even if others have suffered. Murderers today can look to past murderers for inspiration. We know that Hitler liked to recall the Armenian genocide:

'You see,' he would say to his friends, 'one can exterminate an entire people with impunity. Let's do so with the Jews!'

All kinds of things are to be found in the past. That is why unconditionally praising memory — the preservation and recreation of the past — seems senseless to me. Memory is a neutral instrument in its own right; it can serve noble or ignoble ends. It is like language, in Aesop's tale — both the best and the worst thing in the world. In the name of the past, thus of the memory we retain of it, we can kill as well as save human lives. Consequently, I do not subscribe to the idea of a 'duty to remember'; it implies that the mere fact of holding onto traces of the past guarantees our virtue. I was happy to see that Paul Ricœur criticized it as well in his recent book on memory.

He mentions you as the author of the expression 'the abuses of memory', an expression which has shocked some people as a sacrilege of sorts.

Whereas it is, once again, an obvious fact. It is not memory, not the recollection of the past that is sacred, but the values that can be drawn from it.

How do you explain the multiplication of appeals 'to memory' in the recent past?

By a more long-term movement. Modern society was founded in the Renaissance on a break with traditional society, with a society that venerated traditions. We saw it with the conflict opposing Cortés and Moctezuma. Pitted against this world, in which the past controls the present and the Elders lead the tribe, stands modern society which gives pride of place to new values. Descartes said, 'there will be no need of memory for any sciences,' implying thereby that reason and observation suffice. He was wrong, but the statement is telling and this attitude enabled the break with scholasticism. Consider also the democratic principle: a law is good not because it is old, or because it corresponds to a tradition, but because it is the will of the people, through their representatives. As a result, the modern world has become

tzvetan todorov

forgetful and future-oriented. In reaction to this trend, which is obviously excessive, and which remains ignorant of whole aspects of our existence, comes the cult of the past, the duty to remember and the obsession with commemorations. A similar phenomenon can be seen around us in the identity tensions, a reaction to the way in which modern society is constantly enjoining us to be more flexible, more mobile and to adapt to every new situation, whatever it might be.

I understand this reaction but I cannot altogether approve of it. When I see written on the walls of the city, as I did during the Irish conflict, 'No forgetting, no forgiving', I say to myself that we are moving a few steps back to barbarism. Don't get me wrong, I am not advocating forgiving or forgetting: the former is often undesirable, the latter impossible to command (the will has no control over forgetting). But the meaning of the statement, even though the word is not formulated, is that revenge must be sought. Yet the main movement of our civilization consists precisely, as Aeschylus' *Oresteia* recounts, in substituting justice with vengeance, in putting laws in place of acts directly dictated by memory. It is in this respect that the life of the polis is preferable to that of the tribe—because the injunctions of the law prevail over the injunctions of memory. Violence cannot be entirely eliminated—which is why peace is always fragile—but it can be contained all the same.

Memory does not necessarily lead to vengeance. The past can remain an open wound within me, entirely determining my present conduct. It can also, without disappearing, change status, as happens when we have lost a loved one; we do not forget but the person leaves our present-day life. History, in turn, is neither forgetting nor forgiving but it isn't settling scores either.

The duty to remember does not seem to apply to everything. The latest debates that we have been witnessing concern the shameful past of the French state. Can we say that the duty to remember is always embedded in a relationship between victims and torturers?

The duty to remember is brought up not so much by the former victims as by their representatives, often their descendants. Indeed, the victims themselves, when they were lucky enough to survive, usually try to thrust aside painful memories and tear themselves away from the past, not necessarily to forget it but to push it out of the way so that it does not interfere with the present. On the other hand, for those who symbolically identify with them, this reminder is seen as an imperious necessity — which is understandable. The most acute moral pain comes from the suffering of our loved ones. To think of the humiliation of our parents, when they are the embodiment of protective strength for each of us, is unbearable. In this case, and as paradoxical as it may seem at first sight, identification with the victim is no less desirable than identification with the hero — both are advantageous roles for the subject.

This does not, however, render the attitude of these representatives of the victims irreproachable. First of all, this role is not always beneficial to those who assume it. We all know the problem of African Americans: they have benefited from various forms of 'affirmative action' but have suffered from the negative consequences of assuming the image of victims which does not encourage them to take their destiny into their own hands. This role of victim can become a trap: you benefit from certain immediate advantages and, at the same time, you have difficulty taking control of your own life.

Moreover, former victims are in no way immune to the temptation to become torturers themselves in a new situation, thereby enacting a displaced vengeance of sorts. It is common knowledge that most abusive parents were battered children. I know perfectly well that there is no rigid determinism, and Boris Cyrulnik is right to focus on the cases of 'resilience', when people overcome the weight of the past. But it is precisely a matter of successful resistance; if we let ourselves go, we reproduce the traumatic experience of the past and simply switch roles. Having suffered does not inoculate any one against evil. We can see this also in the case of groups or entire peoples. The French were victims of the Germans during the Second World War which did not keep them from later repressing, persecuting and torturing their 'enemies' in Algeria who were fighting, as they had, for independence. Even today, the victim's memory from the past can serve, in Israel, as a justification for the ill treatment of Palestinians in the present.

The historian Henry Rousso said in a recent interview that 'the only duty to remember is the duty that survivors take upon themselves to testify for those who did not return.' Would you agree?

This is an altogether different, and more respectable, conception than the one that prevails nowadays. It is a duty towards the dead, a duty that people impose upon themselves, not upon others. Many survivors have felt this way about the need to bear witness.

We could go further and speak about a duty of survivors towards the living, who are suffering now, as the survivors did in the past. No, the term 'duty' in this case would be an overstatement. Let's just say that it would be a particularly appreciable virtue. As we have seen, this is what David Rousset, a survivor of Buchenwald, did a few years after his return from the camp. Not everyone followed his lead, far from it. Tillion did so, but the former Communist detainees, Daix and many others, opted for loyalty to the Party and defending their identity over the cause of justice.

The memory of the past leads to two very different reactions: giving testimony, and asking for reparations. The testimony is always legitimate, although it can sometimes be used ill advisedly. The demand for reparations is justified in certain cases and not in others. The demand for reparations for eighteenth-century slavery formulated by certain African heads of state seems groundless to me. I do not see why modern states should be held responsible for the wrongs committed by their remote ancestors, neither do I see why the offspring of slaves or of their neighbours should today benefit from these reparations. It is, all differences notwithstanding, like reproaching the Jewish people for being responsible for the death of Jesus. It is also slipping without any transition from individuals (victims or culprits) to the institutions (states, public organization or companies) that represent them across the centuries; it is confusing the legal guilt of certain people with the historical responsibility of others.

We also have to accept the fact that certain acts are simply irreparable. It is pointless for the parents of murdered children to ask for the death penalty for the murderers — no new death could diminish their pain. Court sentences are not meant to make up for the individual disaster or to act as therapy — the aim is to restore and protect public order. And no present-day reparation will erase past slavery or genocide. History cannot be rewritten according to today's standards.

Finally, according to you, the 'abuses of memory' are anachronisms that deny the passing of time and history.

In a way, yes. In *Hope and Memory*, I identify two opposing dangers, the Scylla and Charybdis of the work of memory which I call 'sacralization' and 'banalization'. Sacralization is the refusal to let the event become part of history, to contextualize it, analyse it, compare and contrast it.

The past is congealed in a way that provokes an almost religious attitude towards it. Banalization, which is probably even more dangerous, consists in tacking the past event onto the present, and acting accordingly.

The most common example of banalization is the use that has been made since the Second World War of the figure of Hitler. As the personification of absolute evil,

tzvetan todorov

any enemy today must be likened to him. The conservatives in Russia accuse the reformers of acting like Hitler in undermining the power of the country. In the Middle East, first Nasser and then Arafat were seen as doubles of Hitler. Now, seeing a new Hitler in Arafat is not only absurd, it is detrimental to the resolution of the current conflict. Not to be outdone, the Palestinians themselves accuse Israeli leaders of following in Hitler's path. By dint of seeing the present through the prism of the past, we end up misreading it. If this present is threatening, the consequences can be serious indeed. Shouting 'CRS-SS'[1] is stupid, but it does not lead to a disaster. Confusing the far Right today with the fascist or Nazi movements from the inter-war period is dangerous. The comparison only confirms the convictions of the people who are making it, and does nothing to convince those who are hesitant or neutral. In addition, it works to whitewash the conscience of supporters of the far Right in elections, since they feel unconcerned by the reproach.

How can one avoid both Charybdis and Scylla?

In order for the past to shed light on the present, we need to draw from it a general rule, a principle of action; we have to universalize the lesson. This principle can then be judged and assessed in a debate, with rational arguments that call upon values common to us all. The fact that my people suffered in the past does not give me the right to treat others unjustly in the present. Memory can be good, provided that what we seek is truth and justice, not intangible rights. Germaine Tillion does not speak of a duty to remember, but of a duty to truth and justice. To attain these noble ends, we can make use of memory — but not only memory.

Speaking of Tillion, she acted differently during the Second World War and during the Algerian War. Would you say she was an example of putting memory to good use?

---

1 Common May 1968 slogan comparing the police, the CRS, to the Nazi SS. [Trans.]

Definitely. Tillion was not the only former member of the Resistance to find her-self involved in the Algerian War—there were many. The upper echelons of the French army in the fifties, at the time of the colonial wars, came from the London Free French Forces and from the ranks of the Resistance. Read the memoirs of General Aussaresses, a master torturer during the 'battle of Algiers': he speaks only of former members of the Resistance, former fighters for the good cause. He was one of them too. The 'François' I wrote about in *A French Tragedy* became the head of a regiment of colonial paratroopers that was in the front line during the battle of Algiers, and which we now know specialized in extorting information, hence in systematic torture. Every one of these anti-German heroes reasoned as follows: their country was threatened, as it had been in 1940, but this time they knew how to defend it better. In this case, the duty to remember counselled them poorly. They erred through what I term banalization: they conflated two situa-tions that were not alike.

From the same experience, Tillion learnt a radically different lesson. I must say being an ethnologist prompted her to observe and understand before acting. She was convinced that the struggle of the Algerians was legitimate, and that Algeria's independence had become inevitable. She was also perfectly aware that the French people of Algeria felt at home in Algeria where they were born, as were their parents and grandparents, and that they had reason to fear for their posses-sions, even for their lives. To be sure, this did not give them the right to humiliate and exploit other Algerians in the framework of a colonial state, but there were not simply good people on one side and bad people on the other, as the '*porteurs de valises*' or 'suitcase carriers'[2] believed.

---

[2] French supporters of the National Liberation Front, the FLN. [Trans.]

tzvetan todorov

At first, Tillion attempted to work towards reform within the existing framework, to promote education and neutralize the negative effects of colonialization. Then, when the conflict became too fierce and any chance of reconciliation seemed impossible, she did her best to fight the violence. As you can see, it was a completely different attitude from that during the Second World War when she threw herself into the struggle against the enemy. In Algeria she acted on the basis of a duty to justice inherited from her first experience, not a duty to remember. She saved many lives although that did not suffice to prevent what Aron called the 'Algerian tragedy'. The latter was due, in part, to that fact that voices like Tillion's were not sufficiently heeded.

I recently attended a gathering in honour of Tillion. In the room were former National Liberation Front (FLN) members, *harki*s, *pied-noirs*,[3] people from Metropolitan France, people from all sides of the political spectrum. I believe that only the name of Germaine Tillion could have brought all these people together: all of Algeria and all of France. This woman had chosen a path that gave pride of place to the life and dignity of people, not to one policy as opposed to another. This is an exemplary use of memory.

How do you explain the fact that, despite the huge number of books, movies and TV programmes about the Second World War, and particularly about the genocide of the Jews, this event remains today both the most sacralized and the most banalized of all, and that we have not made more progress towards putting this memory to good use? How can you give meaning to the past if a whole library does not suffice to do so?

It is true that these events have given rise to a wealth of material: they are probably the most well-known, most commented events of the twentieth century.

---

3 *Harki*s are Algerians who fought alongside the French; *pieds-noirs* were Algerians of European descent. [Trans.]

We do not make more progress because everything that is related to our identity, hence to the past that our memory reconstructs, makes us react with our hearts and not our heads. If I think that your people killed my father and made my mother suffer, I do not feel like thinking in general terms, looking for reasons, and analysing the context. From this point of view, the library does not carry much weight and I will always have a tendency to subject the past to my passions. Our emotional choices are not motivated by logical arguments but by identification processes that we then content ourselves with clothing in a rational language. I chose my side because it is that of the people who speak the same language, or practise the same religion or come from the same lands or have the same physical appearance. There is nothing to be proud of, but that's how it is. Our only chance of getting past this defensive reaction of identity is to substitute argumentation and public debate for conduct dictated by affect alone.

Let's not forget that experience is always and solely individual; it is neither hereditary nor contagious. An individual can be changed by experience — a young German boy who was in the SS at the age of 20 can be transformed inside, bitterly regret his past choices and end up leading a life based on very different values. There are experiences in the life of individuals that mark them for life; they are irreversible. But such experiences, often bitter, are of no use to the next-door neighbours who may think that, the circumstances being different 20 years later, they can act as if nothing has happened. What are we supposed to learn from the past anti-Semitic persecutions, now that anti-Semitism is not one of the serious threats hanging over Europe any more? To protect the persecuted, whatever their origin or religion might be, and whoever their persecutors are.

The misuses of justice

Aren't you concerned that, because you speak so much of right and wrong and of passing judgements on the events of the past, you will be seen as a sermonizer and a lesson-giver, even if the judgements are nuanced?

To my mind, a clear boundary separates morality from moralism. I try not to cross it. Maybe I do not always succeed. There is nothing unusual about taking an interest in the moral life of human beings; might as well say that one is interested in human life itself. It does not prejudge the position we take on moral issues. This was the meaning in the past of the term 'moralist': the moralist as an explorer of moral life, not a lesson-giver. La Rochefoucauld was a moralist, even if his early readers (wrongly) perceived him as immoral.

As far as the exercise of morality is concerned, it has a curious peculiarity: its injunctions can only be formulated in the first person, and addressed to oneself. As soon as we address another, we leave the confines of morality to enter the sphere of moralism. When we say 'be generous' we are not doing a moral deed, we are simply pronouncing a moral injunction. 'I will try to be a little more generous' is the only possible form of moral imperative.

Thus, it is possible to exercise morality without moralism. But in my public life I try to analyse rather than exercise morality. I would like to see the development of an anthropology and an history of moral life.

Moralism is also what you call 'moral correctness'.

My expression is obviously modelled on 'political correctness'. The latter comes, as we know, from the United States. I was well acquainted with it, since it is strongly present in universities. The 'politically correct' (abbreviated 'PC') is to be distinguished from conformism, which is a much more general phenomenon and, to tell the truth, inseparable from the life of modern democracies. The 'PC' is more recent and more particular. In conformism, one imitates the dominant model and, in so doing, one sides with the strong and the victors. The 'PC', on the contrary, emphasizes the value of the former vanquished, by which I mean the groups that were victims of discrimination in the past: ethnic groups such as African Americans or Native Americans, but also social groups, including women, homosexuals or the disabled. Consequently, this attitude stands out also by what we could anachronistically call its 'theologically correct' content, which was rife for centuries (witness the persecutions of heresies). The values in the name of which we now pass moral judgements are secular 'left-wing' values: equality, justice and the right to equal respect.

To repair this injustice from the past, a series of measures are applied: a language code is imposed ('African Americans' instead of blacks, 'differently abled' or 'challenged' instead of disabled), pejorative judgements about these groups are

tzvetan todorov

prohibited and social policies are founded on this basis. This is the case for 'affirmative action' (which favours formerly mistreated groups), hiring quotas or interventions in the couple's private life, justified by the fight against sexual harassment. These actions are all political in form but moralizing in content, unlike their precursor in the McCarthyism of the fifties when the witch-hunt was aimed at Communist sympathizers. This is why I prefer speaking of 'moral correctness'.

And in France?

Its forms are different but they are of no lesser intensity. Here, 'moral correctness' is essentially found not so much in universities or in the public administration as in the press and the media at large where it gives rise to what has been called 'vigilance' or, with less sympathy, 'media lynching'. This is not the Inquisition's stakes, fortunately, but it is not innocent either—a moral accusation regularly repeated in public becomes a condemnation. The content is also somewhat different: the social groups (women, homosexuals, etc.) in France weigh less, the ethnic groups more. The worst accusation is that of racism or anti-Semitism. This is the hard core from which the rest is extrapolated by contiguity or by resemblance.

You say morality is not moralism. In your opinion, is morality bound up with justice? Don't you get the impression that judges are being asked these days to play a role that was reserved for priests in the past?

Indeed, I think we are entrusting all sorts of tasks to the legal system that do not belong to it and for which it is ill-equipped. The task of education, for a start. I am not sure that the recent trials in France for crimes against humanity did a good job at playing this role—supposing that this is the role of the courts. For such education to be effective, we must feel concerned by the trial. This means that we must identify not only with the accuser but with the accused as well, and that we continue to

352

ask a lot of ourselves, not only of others. It is too easy to say that evil is the other, someone who does not resemble me in the least. How could the French public identify with Klaus Barbie, a German policeman during the war? His trial could eventually have had educational effects if it had taken place in Germany; in France, it only reinforced the French sentiment of having been either heroes or victims during the war. Touvier and Papon were French, but their trials did not permit identification either—too much time had gone by and young people could no longer see themselves in them. The fact that polls showed that a majority of the population approved of the trials is a telltale sign that people were not really feeling targeted, that it was, rather, a means for them of procuring a good conscience at little cost.

I would say the same for the current trials of the political and military leaders from the wars in Bosnia and Kosovo. If the aim had been to educate the peoples themselves, Serbs, Croatians, Bosniaks or Kosovars, these trials and investigations should have been held at home and among their compatriots. How can anyone expect Serbs to become more moral when the court paid millions of dollars for their former head of government to be extradited for the trial? It is more akin to a Far West give-and-take version of justice. It is also more akin, in another way, to divine justice, meted out with no concern for circumstances or for the effect of the judgement, than to human justice which is always relative, as Rousseau would have said, in the sense that it is always related to a context and to a human group.

There were other aspects of the French trials that did not strike me as particularly uplifting. Each time, the notion of 'crimes against humanity' was redefined to suit the defendant. The government and the media intervened extensively prior to the judgement; it would have been nearly impossible for the jurors not to be influenced by this. And the fact that these defendants were the only ones to be judged when others like them had done likewise, brought with it the idea of punishing the individual because the group was guilty, an idea that we found so hateful when the Nazis shot hostages. 'Acquitting Papon would amount to exonerating Vichy!' people said the day before the verdict. Thus, the entire regime was being judged in the trial of a single man.

Actually, it is the very principle of educational, not to say uplifting, trials that seems questionable to me. It calls to mind the trials of deserters in wartime, executed by a firing squad to set an example and not because they were guilty. The legal system must try to establish the factual truth and then apply the laws—that's all. If priority is given to the educational aspect, we may find ourselves in the position of fiddling with facts and bypassing laws so as not to demoralize people.

The thing about crimes against humanity is that they are the only ones to be imprescriptible. As a result, people who are responsible for certain particularly heinous crimes cannot evade justice. This, at least, is a positive achievement, don't you think?

I'm not so sure. Firstly, I'm not convinced by the very idea of imprescriptibility. It implies that the person who is being judged has remained unchanged for 50 years, and this runs counter to everything we know from biology and psychology. More seriously, it contradicts humanist principles. Men are perfectible, they can change. Nothing proves in advance that the person who committed a crime at age 20 is the same as the person who is standing trial at age 70. Here again, this notion corresponds better to God's justice than to human justice. Should we go to the other extreme and declare that all judgement is impossible, since we can never judge human beings at the moment of their crime? No, for there is, of course, a certain continuity between my past and my present self. Therefore, a line has to be drawn somewhere on this continuum. Obviously, setting prescription at 20 or 30 years is arbitrary: why so many years, and not more or less? It is nonetheless necessary for all that. Time must go by and children become parents.

I am equally unconvinced by this way of establishing a gulf between impre-scriptible crimes against humanity, and all the other crimes, including war crimes for example, which are prescribed after a certain time. If we want to give ourselves the greatest chance of understanding how a crime against humanity is commit-ted—with the hope of also finding a way to prevent it in the future—all ties between this crime and other crimes, collective or even individual, should not be severed. Claiming that certain human beings act this way simply because 'that's who they are' amounts to believing that a part of humanity acts according to the Devil's will, which doesn't get us anywhere.

So the court should not be confused with school or any other place of education. Would you be more indulgent of the tendency today to produce a definitive, finally tangible, version of history, or even to rectify the past?

Not really. Obviously, the legal system has investigators and police detectives at its disposal, which enables it to establish factual truth. When I worked on *A French Tragedy*, I had access to the file of the trial of a French collaborator who had worked for the Gestapo. The interrogations and the testimonies of witnesses were a great help to me. But this was not what happened at all during the recent trials for crimes against humanity. The aim was not to establish factual truth. Too much time had gone by; many of the witnesses were dead and as for the others—their memories could play tricks on them. What was sought was the meaning of the events—a task for which judges are not especially well qualified—and this meaning was immedi-ately exploited for the needs of the prosecution or of the defence. It was thus much less impartial than the meaning to which historians aspire. At the time of the Papon trial, we saw simplistic versions of recent French history resurfacing, variously presenting Pétain as a shield or Pétain as a collaborator when research work by specialists has rendered such versions obsolete for quite some time.

At a more general level, the court only knows two colours: black and white, yes or no, guilty or innocent. The human world possesses more—Primo Levi's vast 'grey area'—and historians are in a better position to recreate this complexity.

You are not, therefore, in favour of laws that define historical truth, like the French Gayssot Act penalizing the denial of the Jewish genocide?

Even if it comes from unquestionably good intentions, this law seems out of place to me. We are stepping outside the strict confines of the legal system here, since it is Parliament—that is, the representative political body—that voted in favour of this law. However, these deputies are no more qualified than the judges to write history. The idea itself of fixing the meaning of events in a law, of prohibiting any reappraisal of an interpretation, is contrary to the spirit of historians. And just imagine the number of laws that would have to be passed in order to encompass all of the events that stir passions! The French Parliament has already voted to recognize the Armenian genocide. Is this really its role? How many deputies are expert enough both in Turkish history and in legal definitions to be able to give a competent opinion and distinguish big massacres from genocides? If their intent was a political gesture, to demand a change in the attitude of Turkey before it joins the European Union, fine. But to write historical conclusions into a law? Will there soon be a law prohibiting the assertion or the negation of the existence of torture in Algeria, and another penalizing the criticism of a member of the Resistance? Totalitarian countries bring the quest for truth in line with reasons of state; such an adjustment is totally incompatible with the spirit of liberal democracy.

Would you go so far as to say that the legal system today has taken the place not only of school and history but even of politics?

Public discourse, the image society produces of itself, is being undermined by the rise of individualism with its predilection for the private world. Producing this representation is still one of the roles of politicians. It is because they do not play this role any more that we increasingly turn to the legal institutions, as if the court had become the last refuge of public discourse and of our common world. Professing common values, expressing blame or regret and penalizing can all be necessary to the life of a community, but one does not need courts for this. This is the role of schools, the media, respected public figures and, at another level, committees of experts. Heads of state can occasionally play this role, in so far as they are not only political figures but also embody moral authority. Witness Willy Brandt kneeling in front of the former ghetto in Warsaw — that was a gesture befitting a politician. The role of these political figures and institutions is not to produce knowledge but to show appreciation to those who deserve it.

We transfer to the legal system requests for reparations and the desire for confession, repentance and forgiveness. What do you think of the way in which such very Christian terms have become omnipresent in the legal system and society at large?

I am not competent enough to judge the expression of repentance recently formulated by the Catholic Church; I would have liked it to come with the opening of the Vatican archives. Forgiveness also has a meaning in the Christian framework that remains alien to me. For me, forgiveness is a private affair; it concerns the person who suffered the offence. In this sense, for the dead, no forgiveness is possible — they are no longer here to grant it. The only thing we can do is hope that the loved ones of the victims will know how to deal with the feelings of resentment that poison their lives, but this kind of thing cannot be decided by decree. If someone killed my mother or my son, I do not think I would be able to forgive him or her.

The political and public acts I'm thinking of do not need this Christian framework; they are assumed by democratically elected people, not by servants of God. It is important to see, firstly, that every society needs common values, hence a public morality and, secondly, that this moral need not be formulated by representatives of the Church. Not accepting this conclusion amounts to regarding all secular people as immoral beings, which is obviously not true. If we refuse to admit the first part of the affirmation, we open a door to the 'moral correctness' we were discussing earlier, a presumed consensus of sorts on what should or should not be said. The place left empty by the politicians is occupied in a surreptitious way by the usual lesson-givers and by short-sighted prosecutors eager to denounce evil in others and indicate the right path for everyone. This tendency to rectify the wrongs of others and to require everybody to conform to what is right is a characteristic feature of modern democracies to which we must be attentive. That is what I call the 'temptation to goodness'.

Historical justice, international justice

What do you think of an eventual trial, for crimes against humanity or others concerning the torture practised by the French army in Algeria? There was talk of it when General Aussaresses put out the book you mentioned earlier, Services spéciaux (Special Services),[4] *in which he relates in great detail, and without the slightest regret, what could hardly be called services.*

First of all, as far as this war is concerned, a general amnesty was declared, and I would be quite disturbed to see the French state go back on its own decisions. All the more in that the amnesty was justified by the circumstances. In France, we have the precedent of the Edict of Nantes which prohibits putting someone on trial for acts committed in the context of the religious wars. It is the same for civil

---

4 Translated into English as *The Battle of the Casbah: Terrorism and Counter-terrorism in Algeria, 1955–57.* [Trans.]

wars—there are too many culprits on either side, and every one of them is convinced that the political and moral legitimacy is on their side. Since it is impossible—and unjust—to punish them all, it is better to grant amnesty.

If we give up on the idea of removing amnesty, the possibility remains to bring Aussaresses to trial for the writing of the book itself rather than for the events he recounts in it. This is the avenue chosen by the complainants. I find this choice regrettable. Today, we are more in need of truth than of justice. By this I mean that instead of condemning one person or another, who will necessarily appear to be a scapegoat—a victim tried for the sake of example—France needs to look its past in the face without concealing anything from itself. We are all aware that present-day tensions around the Maghrebi immigrant population are due in part to resentment for the colonial period. It is important to understand that one cannot search for truth and justice in the same breath. We cannot expect former officers, soldiers or the simple inhabitants of the country to tell the truth, to reveal the buried past, if there is a threat of trial hanging over their heads for what they did in the past. You cannot ask people to speak up and to question their own acts if one of the possible consequences is imprisonment. Aussaresses was a torturer among others; what distinguishes him in the first place is that he spoke up whereas the others have remained silent. He would therefore be penalized for the sole deed that deserves to be encouraged.[5]

The virtuous indignation triggered by his comments also serves to evade the question that he nevertheless manages to ask: can a state refuse to use certain means when it comes to safeguarding the lives of its citizens? If Paris were threat-

---

[5] Aussaresses was eventually brought to trial and condemned for 'apology for war crimes' in January 2002.

ened by terrorist attacks, would we be willing not to use every means possible, including torture, to stop them? And we are speaking here of a context of war, when killing the enemy is considered not only lawful but praiseworthy. At the very least, the question is worth asking. My conclusion from reading Aussaresses' book is that torture must be prohibited. He believes the opposite.

How do you judge the position he takes?

I would draw a distinction between past and present. Torture, during the Algerian War, was decided in high places, by Prime Ministers, Ministers of Justice and of the Defence and Interior Ministers who asked the army to win the war 'by any means'. Their responsibility is much greater than that of the rank-and-file torturers who did what they were ordered to do. Of course the most courageous officers, those with strong convictions, refused to torture; today, however, we cannot bring the others to trial because they submitted to laws and orders. Soldiers have neither the time nor the vocation to analyse a situation in depth and distinguish by themselves right from wrong. They were sent to Algeria to kill the *fellaghas*, as we used to call them, so they killed as many as possible. Politicians had the time to think, they were the ones responsible for morally debasing France during those years. If somebody is to be condemned then it is the politicians, not the soldiers for obeying orders.

But Aussaresses reveals in his book that he was doing much more than executing orders.

And how! For him, the state of war suspended all rules of justice, everywhere. This is an act of sedition comparable to the subsequent insurrection of the French Generals in Algiers. He was willing to execute prisoners inside French prisons, along with all public figures who interceded in France on behalf of the FLN or even those who took a stand against violence. If Germaine Tillion had fallen into his hands, he would not have hesitated for a second to eliminate her. This is criminal behaviour (even if it is now covered by the amnesty).

tzvetan todorov

Personally, I do not disapprove of the fact that Aussaresses tells what he did, that he contributes to establishing the truth. But I am impressed by his lack of comprehension of the world and of himself—I think he is a mental and moral invalid. He writes today as if he were still hoping to win the Algerian War— ah, if only certain sentimental politicians had not gotten involved, and then there were those nasty American anti-colonialists. He reminds me of the Japanese soldiers found on an island, 40 years after the end of the Second World War, who thought that the war was still on. His total lack of compassion or regret, even 40 years later, speaks of someone who can hardly be held to be a commonplace example. But we cannot regret the existence of his book; it is rare to see torturers and murderers opening up with such frankness.

When it comes to torture in Algeria, we've seen the entire range of possibilities: those who admit and don't regret it (Aussaresses), those who admit and regret it (Massu) and those who do not admit and do not regret it (Bigeard).

So you think that the legal system should not get involved, that it should leave the matter to historians alone?

To historians, of course, by making their research easier, by encouraging the creation of chairs in colonial history, by opening the archives, by removing all taboos, those of patriotism poorly understood as of moral correctness. But also to politicians. I wouldn't mind seeing the deputies in the Assembly give up concocting new laws codifying historical truth, and engaging instead in a great public debate on this recent, painful page in French history. Not to produce an official version of history but so that the different reactions to these dramatic events can be publicly stated and argued, so that experiences can be expressed and recognized. This would ease the task of assuming this past for the rest of the population. And we would be able to ask about what should be done in the future if anything really bad happens.

Do you think that international justice is also threatened by 'moral correctness'?

Whereas laws govern life inside a country, at least in principle, relations between countries are governed by force. There is no 'general society' englobing all countries; what prevails between them is the 'state of nature', to speak in the terms of seventeenth- and eighteenth-century philosophers. Of course, groups of countries exist, like the European Union, for which this statement is no longer true, and there certain rules are respected by all. As for the rest, it's simply gang war (I'm hardly overstating the issue). What can international courts do in such a context?

It's a trade-off. Either they sacrifice efficiency to equity and stay in the realm of absolute, general justice, without being able to apply it. This is already the case for the crimes committed by super powers — they are intangible, and with good reason. Where would the force or army capable of arresting Russian, American or Chinese heads of state come from? Might as well say from the outset that we want to start the Third World War. As a result, we let the Russian army kill in Chechnya or the American police overthrow governments in Latin America. Or, they sacrifice equity to efficiency and, for decisions to be followed by consequences, we enlist on the side of the powerful. It was the selective justice of the International Criminal Tribunal, the ICT, that brought it to accuse Milosevic of crimes against humanity at the exact moment that NATO was dropping bombs on his country. Western armies could not have dreamt of a better gift than this legitimation of their action.

It would be better, to my mind, not to cover up with legal veneer what is in reality a straightforward power struggle. By doing so, we are compromising the very idea of justice.

tzvetan todorov

We could also imagine, in a utopian spirit, another situation—the Tribunal would have its own army, more powerful than the others. Aside from seeming unlikely to me, this solution would have the drawback of leading us to a total universal state where the same people would decide the destinies of the whole of humanity. I remain attached, for my part, to a pluralistic world.

For a moralist, you seem to be actually quite realistic and pragmatic.

I refuse to separate the two positions. Blind idealism, ignorant of the world, serves only to flatter the good conscience of those who profess it. Realism limited to itself does not see the difference between torture and interrogation, between war and justice. This opposition between realists who get their hands dirty and noble spirits who defend morality will not get us far. It reminds me of the idle debates between economic experts and generous souls, with the former saying how things are and the latter how things should be. It's a dialogue of the deaf. We must start with the world as it is to try to make it as we want it to be.

Dreaming of a system of absolute justice is, I think, not only vain but harmful: human existence, as we have seen, is an imperfect garden. Misguided moralists are dangerous. But a life deprived of the very idea of justice is not a human life any more. We should not be ashamed to steer a middle course.

10. The Contiguity of Opposites

Extreme moderation — Overcoming oppositions — The calling of a go-between —
The others in me — Leaving the twentieth century

Extreme moderation

CATHERINE PORTEVIN: *We can read your work as an attempt to reconcile opposites, even —*
and this is perhaps your only militant side — to fight against impermeable separations
(iron curtains), against divides, against the irreconcilable between academic disciplines,
but also between ideas and acts, the spiritual and the material, good and evil, us and them
and so on. Is this stance related to your experience of totalitarianism?

TZVETAN TODOROV: Every life is a confrontation with differences. Political, religious
and philosophical doctrines propose conceptions of these differences that are
themselves different. Totalitarianism's conception is one of the most extreme that
exist. In this case, every difference is immediately interpreted as an opposition,
every opposition as a combat and every combat must end with a slaying.
Totalitarianism favours binary thinking; everything is reduced to a choice
between two terms, one of which is venerated, the other loathed, until the ultimate reign of unity comes into being. No place here for what we call 'otherness'
or difference without value judgement.

Democracy, on the other hand, grants another status to differences since it starts from the recognition of pluralism—what Montesquieu, as you recall, termed 'moderation'. Because democracy recognizes that society is heterogeneous, that several points of view are legitimate, forms are invented that promote the coexistence of differences. We favour mediation, compromises, concessions and contractual relations with reciprocal obligations; we praise the virtues of dialogue. So there is nothing surprising about me opting for this side.

But aren't you becoming somewhat totalitarian yourself, in pitting totalitarianism against democracy in such exclusive terms? Is this difference something you approach in a democratic or in a totalitarian manner?

My categorical condemnation of totalitarian regimes does not keep me from noting that they belong to the same hypernym as democracy—what we call 'modernity'—or from criticizing what goes wrong in democracies or, lastly, from seeing that totalitarian society is not bad through and through. Let's return to an example we mentioned during our first interview: Communist Bulgaria gave artists and other creative people means to which they no longer have access in post-Communist Bulgaria. It was, of course, a way to vassalize culture to the will of the regime, but the result was no less tangible: there were many subsidized theatres, actors earning yearly salaries, orchestras in every large city, operas, a good number of films produced every year, sizeable print runs of books and, consequently, substantial royalties.

We can thus pit totalitarianism against democracy without putting all the good on one side. Bulgakov and Grossman had tragic, broken lives, to be sure, even if they were not sent to the camps. And when they died, they did not have the slightest guarantee that their work would be published. What can be more heartbreaking for a writer? But if, under Communism, writers could go to jail for their writings, it was precisely because these writings had the capacity to change society and why the leaders of the day feared them. When Suslov, Secretary of the Party, received Grossman, he told him, 'Your *Life and Fate* would cause more damage than an atomic bomb. Publishing it is out of the question.' What a compliment! Solzhenitsyn's books were one of the greatest blows to the Soviet regime. In France, you can publish anything and everything—nothing is of consequence, it does not count. Here, a manifestation of boldness amounts to recounting your sexual life, preferably if it's scandalous. A little pointless, isn't it?

That the artists were able to take advantage at times of the Communist conception of culture may be true, but what about the rest of the population? It is often claimed—as partisans of Castro's Communist regime in Cuba still do today—that the cultural level of Communist countries is globally higher. Was this the case in Bulgaria and, if so, how can you explain it?

We could speak of an education *en creux* or by default, which is not a quality intrinsic to Communist regimes but rather its paradoxical consequence. You see, public distractions did not exist; or, if they did, they were really awful. You could not spend your day singing patriotic songs, viewing conformist paintings or reading soporific newspapers. As a result, a certain amount of spiritual energy was released to be channelled elsewhere. No television, no clubs and no rock music, but the avenue to classical culture was wide open; books were inexpensive, concerts too. After all, you could see Chekhov's plays in theatres—they were canonized by Soviet orthodoxy which was not such a bad thing!

I remember I had wanted to go to an organ concert (a non-existent instrument in Bulgaria) during my visit to Moscow in 1959. The concert was sold out, but I was able to buy a ticket at the entrance to the concert hall. I found myself seated next to the person who had sold it to me because his wife was sick. We talked for a long time during the intermission. He was a technician in a factory on the outskirts of Moscow. He knew all about classical music, had read all the great writers and been to the museums in Moscow to see the art collections. I am not sure I would have been able to find many people like him at a concert in Paris.

I also remember when Kafka's letters to Felice were translated into Bulgarian. People—and I'm talking about all sorts of people, not only intellectuals—queued up all night in front of bookstores to purchase a copy, just as I had waited in line to see Yves Montand. The same would happen when a new edition of Dostoyevsky's works was published. Can you imagine that in a Western city? And don't tell me that if there are no lines in front of bookstores here it's because French booksellers are better at their business.

Do you know whether Bulgarian artists and writers regret what, from a certain point of view, was a golden age for them?

Blaga Dimitrova—the great Bulgarian poet who had become a figure of dissidence before the fall of the regime—told me on my last visit to Sofia that her books used to sell 'only' 20,000 copies under Communism—so few because the Writers Union saw her as a non-conformist and imposed a smaller print run on her books. Now that she can say anything she wants, her books barely sell 500 copies. She was somewhat perplexed. 'Tell me, Tzvetan, is that what I fought 40 years for?' she asked. 'Before, people read my poetry instead of newspapers; now, they read the newspaper instead of my poetry.' Newspapers—or horror novels or pornography. It's a hard question to answer.

What are we to conclude? Are we to take a stand in favour of oppression because it produces, as an indirect consequence, a thriving artistic life and an appetite for culture?

That would be quite a paradoxical conclusion. Why not sing the praises of slavery for contributing to the production of more beautiful works of art? I don't think we need to go quite so far. I would tend rather to agree, once more, with Constant who said that even if slavery contributed to the prosperity of Greek culture, we ourselves would rather have fewer masterpieces and live freely. Under Communism, the life of the mind could be intense but not long-lasting: individuals were corrupted or broken, demolished by the wearing effects of time, submerged by discouragement and alcohol. Without a space of freedom, creativity dies. Let us not conclude, for all that, that freedom alone suffices to beget masterpieces. It is an understatement to say that the logic of immediate profit is not propitious to spiritual development. It leads, for example, to the explosion of pornography—the downside of freedom of expression—which has become in democracy the freedom to cultivate misogyny and to make an easy buck. I thus conclude that there is a potential antagonism between culture and democracy, and, to come back to our starting point, that even the opposition between totalitarianism and democracy is not absolute.

Overcoming oppositions

There is never a radical opposition with you between two absolutely mutually exclusive camps. You are always working on intersections, on meeting points, on nuances, and 'grey areas' when you are not looking for a third way that will reduce the conflict. Do you recognize yourself in this description of your work, and which schools of thought, among those you've studied, does such an approach draw upon?

I am incapable of outlining the history of the question, but several names readily spring to mind. Aristotle praised the middle ground, at an equal distance to both extremes. For example, courage is opposed both to cowardice and to a reckless, daredevil attitude.

What is perhaps more interesting was the controversy established over the centuries in the Christian doctrine. The very idea of a human God, of incarnation, implies that the opposition between the two terms human and divine, while being maintained, could eventually be transcended. The consequence of this implication did not easily gain ground — it was fought against by a major heretical movement called Arianism, which drew inspiration from Origen, one of the early fathers of the Christian Church and who denied the divine nature of Christ. This doctrine wanted to hold onto the impermeability of the separation between gods and men. At the other extreme, we find a Christian thinker like Nicolas of Cues, a fifteenth-century German theologian, one of the immediate precursors of humanism in the Renaissance, with his idea of the 'coincidence of opposites'. Unlike Origen, he believed that we rise from human to God without a break in continuity. The absolute does not merge with the relative, but we go from one to the other.

Where do you situate yourself within this diversity?

Let us start by putting aside the totalitarian attitude, this, if I may say so, 'heterocide' choice that is also the attitude of all Manicheans — good is on one side, evil is on the other, so it is possible to eliminate the bearers of evil. Let us also put aside the opposite option, that of a generalized deconstruction of all oppositions, in which nothing has greater value than anything else. In the remaining options, we can identify several forms of thinking that acknowledge difference without making it into an absolute. For a start, there is the refusal of extremes in the manner of Aristotle or 'moderation' in the common sense of the word. In the political arena, it comes down to a preference for the centre.

You wouldn't by any chance be praising the soft centre, would you? Isn't being in the centre a way of always being right?

The centre is always soft, I know. For someone like me, whose view of the political world was structured by the totalitarian experience, the important term is 'democracy'. Being a left-wing or a right-wing democrat is secondary — the choice depends on circumstance. I also find that, in a country where there are changes in government,[1] institutionally belonging to neither the Left nor the Right adds to your freedom. You do not automatically vote according to a long tradition or the directives of your party; you choose, each time, according to the situation. This does not, of course, prevent you from making a mistake and subsequently regretting your choice.

However, political centrism also has a drawback—it eliminates the alternation within the democratic choice since it represents the common denominator of the Left and the Right. As a result, the only remaining opposition is anti-democratic extremism which comes out reinforced. French cohabitation suffers from the same drawback: with the Left and the Right joined together in the government, the opposition is embodied in non-governmental, extra-parliamentary movements. The possibility of a democratic alternation between Left and Right is preferable. A healthy democracy must possess a Left and Right that are clearly identifiable and also clearly part of the republican arena. This opposition is possible because the different democratic values, without being, strictly speaking, incompatible, do not all tend in the same direction. For example, liberty and equality are both necessary to democracy but they cannot be furthered simultaneously. The same holds true of the need for continuity and the need for change, or of the emphasis on unity and the emphasis on plurality. Each one of these terms is necessary to moderate the excessiveness of the other and the alternation between left-wing and right-wing governments could serve this purpose.

This then is the first form of gentle opposition: a preference for the middle way, for moderation and temperance—in short, for consensual centrism! And the second?

---

1 The French call this electoral mechanism *l'alternance*, literally alternation. [Trans.]

tzvetan todorov

I know that consensus is not well thought of but I remind you that the extremes are, for their part, always tough. The second form is the inevitable presence of good in evil and vice versa. This acknowledgement — I insist — does not annihilate the opposition between good and evil; it denies its exclusive distribution and, in so doing, makes us sensitive to the perverse consequences of good intentions as much as to traits of humanity in those whose overall project we condemn. On this basis, in *A French Tragedy*, once I had approved of the Resistance and condemned the collaboration, I was able to question the virtues of particular members of the Resistance or of the Militia. Elsewhere, this enabled me to ponder the negative consequences of an attitude as generous as that of Las Casas, since he founds the need for equality on the affirmation of sameness and practically encourages colonization and assimilation.

Primo Levi often illustrated this second form of non-exclusive opposition. Even if there is only one counter-example, he said, we must recall it in order to break the stereotype. I abide by this precept, and if I were to analyse my own style to reveal the thinking through the very forms of expression that I use — as I have endeavoured to do for others in painting — I would note the high incidence in my writings of the conjunction 'even though'.

In this type of opposition, choosing 'even though' means that something remains that cannot be reconciled between the two positions. But aren't you sometimes led to eliminate the contradiction, to bring the opposites together and try to make them coexist by refusing to choose?

This is the most interesting case. I would speak here not of a 'coincidence of opposites', like Nicolas of Cues but, rather, of a contiguity of opposites. The opposition remains, but there is no positive and negative any more, no good and evil; now they are two complementary terms, equally necessary. Like the masculine and the feminine (even if I have a soft spot for 'feminine values' — in terms of social not sexual characteristics, of course), like light and darkness, like night and day or, more prosaically, like the city and the country or like culture and nature. I refuse — and I certainly am not alone in this — to have to choose between the two. I love both passionately and I grow tired of both as well. Hence, I practise alternation when I can. I am happy in Italian churches and in the 'cathedral of trees' in American natural parks; I like the bustle of the city and the silence of the country-side. And let us not forget, in this regard, the opposition between the spiritual and the material evoked earlier. The two terms sustain one another and are sometimes inextricably linked. The relationship between parents and young children often illustrates this inextricable intertwining.

And where would you place another notion that is dear to you, that of the ordinary, which you sometimes oppose to the heroic and sometimes to the life of the mind? Is it a case of 'coincidence of opposites' or of 'contiguity of opposites'? To put it otherwise, do you opt for the value of the ordinary, of material life, 'even though' you admit that there is also value in spiritual life, or do you advocate taking them together, on an equal footing, to the point of denying what opposes them?

I will leave aside the moral sense of the opposition that we have already discussed. In so far as its aesthetic sense is concerned, this is once more a contiguity of opposites but with a particularity. Poetry does not coincide with ordinary language, yet it is not opposed to it either since it is also composed of words and sentences. It emerges from language's potentialities, magnified by the agency of the poet. Rhythm, figures, tropes, thought — all of this is in ordinary language. Therefore it isn't a matter of denying the value of the latter but, rather, of going from a diluted to a concentrated state, from weak to strong density.

tzvetan todorov

Western tradition maintains an impermeable separation between art and non-art when it is not putting the very idea of art into question, as in the contemporary period. I find more fertile the conception that existed in the East for centuries, according to which every gesture can be magnified to the point of becoming art: the art of arranging flowers, of closing a package, of drinking tea, of arranging patches of moss in a garden, even of watching cherry trees blossom. Art is not eliminated, nor is it opposed to the ordinary gesture—it is this gesture in its perfection—a movement accessible to all. Such a conception delegitimizes professional artists in their contempt for ordinary people who don't know how to produce artworks. I believe that artists and thinkers—contrary to what Julien Benda argues in his famous pamphlet *The Betrayal of the Intellectuals*—enrich their works by staying in touch with ordinary life.

You have defended what you call 'feminine' virtues, which correspond to values in the private sphere: love, friendship, the caring for your loved ones, the attention brought to ordinary gestures and to material life. Aren't you concerned that the century to come will agree with you too much, that we will be entirely invaded by the private sphere and that the public arena will find itself empty?

Here is another 'contiguity of opposites'. Feminine values, aside from motherhood, have been neglected, disregarded for centuries. Putting a little emphasis in the opposite direction would do no harm. But the point is not to replace one by another—we need both. Remember, the 'rescuers' were more efficient when they acted as a twosome, joining masculine and feminine values. If the trend in this century is to develop the private sphere alone, we must resist it.

At bottom, you are continually praising the virtues of moderation, in all matters. But, for you, does moderation have its downside, its perverse effects or its limits?

Montesquieu, who also praised moderation, evoked an initial drawback. Because you are in a central position, you receive blows from the left and from the right. He compared the destiny of moderate people to that of people 'living on the second floor of a building and bothered by the noise from upstairs and the smoke from downstairs'. Such was the fate of other humanists as well: Rousseau was considered too religious by the 'philosophers', too atheistic by the devout Catholics; and Constant was not revolutionary enough for some and not conservative enough for others. It is not necessarily a comfortable position.

I am thinking of other kinds of drawbacks. I wonder whether moderation is not condemned to remain a petitio principii, *whether it may lead to an excess of caution, to an incapacity to choose.*

Moderation is not to be confused with indecisiveness, neither is it synonymous with risk evasion, with taking excessive precautions to protect ourselves against dangers. Political moderation comes down to defending pluralism and freedom of choice; this defence must be firm, and it must use force against extremism. The defence of moderation, in this sense of the term, would have required us to resist Hitler more forcefully, both before and after he rose to power. Extremists must not benefit from the protection we give to dissident opinions in the framework of pluralism. Moderation therefore corresponds to a choice; it corresponds to an avenue. It does not lead to abstention, and is absolutely not cowardly.

If any of us, myself and other 'moderates', can be criticized for not being active enough, the fault does not come from our political choice but from our selfishness, our attachment to comfort or our laziness. Moderate people—like others—do not always live up to their own standards.

tzvetan todorov

But isn't there a danger that moderation could lead to a single way of thinking, or to eclecticism or to compromise agreements — anything, as long as it's not conflict?

The danger is real. Maybe I don't always avoid this pitfall, using as many 'even thoughs' as I do. But isn't it more excusable to lose ones way on this path than to stubbornly persist in always seeing the world in terms of a merciless war between classes, between races, between nations, between genders and, we could add today, between civilizations?

If moderation is reasonable and noble, what makes it so hard to get enthusiastic about it?

Unquestionably, the dullness of it. You have a choice between trying to find the attraction in the dullness, like certain Eastern civilizations have done, or making moderation itself extreme (the only acceptable extremism), giving it intensity, pushing it to the pitch of ecstasy. It's up to you to decide.

The calling of a go-between

We have arrived at the end of our course, from Bulgaria to your 'years of journeying' in human and social sciences. Do you have the feeling that the journey is over? In other words, do you think that now that the Wanderer has travelled far and wide to gather knowledge, he is ready to put down his suitcases? What is he carrying in his suitcases and what does he want to do with it?

To look at your life when you are 62, like I am, has something frightening about it — you know that most of your life is in the past. The future and the conditional are driven away by the past indicative. It's irreversible. I could have lived in countless places; I will only have lived at a certain number of addresses. My three children are the children I will have had; I already know the names of the people who will have counted during most of my life and the names of the books I will have written and the deeds I will have accomplished.

tzvetan todorov

But the journey is not over, for all that — at least I hope not! In discussing my intellectual biography with you, I noticed that the critical changes have always been sparked by my amazement at the enigmas of human behaviour and by my admiration for certain people. I do not think that these reactions have become foreign to me. I still want to further my understanding of how people live, think and create, to learn how to decipher the human signature better and to make sense of an experience of humankind. And it always seems to me that it is in the forthcoming book, the one I am currently working on, that I will best succeed in doing so. And as far as people are concerned, I continue — fortunately — to discover new things. In my private life, of course, but also in my professional world, encounters continue to influence the direction and content of my work.

You often gave me the impression that you were more influenced by people than by their work. This is the feeling I got when you talked about Benveniste, Jakobson and Barthes, for instance.

The human being and the work have only an intersection in common and one cannot tell beforehand where the better portion lies. Writers — myself included — put what is dearest to them in their books — their highest aspirations and their most intense moments of thought. Often, the rest does not measure up; with their meanness and ordinary mediocrity, they do not improve on close acquaintance. Yet the opposite is true too. In another sense, individuals are always so very much more than the books they write. The person bears a face, an array of gestures and intonations, his or her presence arouses in you the memory of your shared experiences — that is why electronic exchanges will never be able to replace physical contact. It goes without saying that this is true for my friends who write books, like François Flahault, André Comte-Sponville and Charlie Williams, but it is also true for people a little more distant from me, like the elders you mentioned and whom I admired. I have spoken to you, in the same spirit, of Isaiah Berlin and Paul Bénichou. Such encounters still happen, and they change me inside. This was the case with Germaine Tillion, whom I only met in 2000. She was someone I admired not only because she devoted her life to 'the search for truth and justice' as the title of her last book states, but also because she never took herself for a per-sonification of good. She did not set herself up as a lesson-giver because, if you prefer, she never lost her mischievous eye and her *joie de vivre*. To see my ideal embodied like that has influenced my way of thinking about the world.

Each individual life constitutes a figure that solidifies without becoming definitively fossilized, since it can always be put into question. This is why, as the Greek sages said, human beings cannot know whether they have had a happy life until the day of their death—until then, everything can be transformed, redistrib-uted, rethought and events can assume a different value from when they occurred.

Therefore, that journey is not over. But it is true that I used the expression 'years of journeying' in a more restricted sense, to refer to my years of exploration in the human and social sciences following my years of apprenticeship as a philol-ogist, linguist and literary man. To better practise my profession, I felt the need to know more about the disciplines that take up the human being and human society. I thus successively immersed myself in the history of ideas and mentalities, in cultural anthropology and psychological theory, in political sciences and moral philosophy, each time searching for the appropriate conceptual tool, the one that would enable me to better understand the subject I was examining. In retrospect, I see that, without planning to, I spent about 20 years roaming about like that.

Those were my *Wanderjahre*. They were made possible by the Centre for which I work, the CNRS, which gave me the freedom to do so. Better still, they encourage their researchers in this direction by ensuring them ample leaves of absences. It may very well be that that journey is over.

You have extensively criticized the human sciences in the course of our interviews but don't you think that, of all possible labels, researcher in human sciences or, rather, in humanity(ies), is the one that suits you best?

I criticize what strikes me as the pseudo-scientific drift in human and social sciences today, which is due to the administrative situation in Western countries. To justify the funding they receive, but also to reinforce their prestige among those who practise them, these sciences strive as much as possible to resemble the 'hard' sciences or the natural sciences.

Yet I remain keenly aware of the difference between them. My desire is to bring human sciences closer to literature and not to physics, to see its proximity not only with literary studies and criticism or linguistic analyses but also with the works themselves, poetry or novels. There is thinking evinced in literature, and the knowledge of the world it conveys is every bit as revealing as sociology. And literature gets across what it has to say better than scientific discourse. Even though the message is universal, here there is an individual speaking to another individual. If people want to know what Soviet Russia was like, I tell them to read Bulgakov's *The Master and Margarita* or Grossman's *Life and Fate*. In *Life in Common* I recall the famous scene from *La Recherche du temps perdu* in which the narrator spies on Vinteuil's daughter and her woman friend, to show that Proust had a richer understanding of the individual's psychology than any psychoanalyst. And the same goes for figurative painting—it too is thought and knowledge.

So I recognize myself in your description provided that the course of human sciences is deflected in this direction.

Aren't you, to use a vocabulary with which you are familiar, closer to the seventeenth-century moralist and to the eighteenth-century encyclopaedist than to twentieth-century intellectuals?

Am I that anachronistic? Even though I often suspect novelty to be nothing but a pretension to novelty, I still think that I was shaped by the twentieth century. We've already seen the sense in which I am a 'moralist'—and I do not deny this lineage. As for encyclopaedism, I recognize myself in it in so far as I reject the divisions between the human sciences. Their mutual ignorance does not seem justified to me; it even has harmful effects. To understand a human gesture, you must simultaneously call upon anthropology, psychology, history, politics, ethics and law. So why isolate them? Ideally, encyclopaedism is the approach that would suit every researcher in human sciences. It should be the rule, not the exception.

But in today's reign of experts, isn't there a risk that encyclopaedism will be charged with superficiality, and encyclopaedic curiosity be suspected of versatility?

I understand that, seen from the outside, some people may find the changes in direction in my work surprising, even displeasing. This is a reproach that can be made, but it loses its force if the focus of attention is shifted from my methods of research to the purpose. At bottom, my area of studies is modern Western history starting at the Renaissance; the subject is vast, to be sure, but identifiable nonetheless. From this area, I take segments that I attempt to closely analyse but all the radii of the circle converge at the same centre. This centre, the subject of my research and my reflection, is humanity—comprehended through its past. I like the ancient meaning of the word 'humanist' from this perspective; it implies both knowledge of history (our 'humanities', as a branch of learning) and a philosophical stance.

That being said, there is no doubt, some truth to the reproach. Once I get the impression that I have 'understood' what I'm studying, my interest fades and I move on to a related subject or, at any rate, to a different facet of the same one. Other people take their need to understand much further—they are less easily satisfied and manage to maintain a healthy perplexity about what they are studying much longer than I do. This allows them to delve more deeply into their subject of research than I know how to. I hope that, from this point of view, our approaches are complementary.

In your own way, you have been fighting for the decompartmentalization of disciplines or, at any rate, for establishing bridges between them. Do you recognize yourself in this role of a go-between?

Since I want human sciences to communicate with one another better, I will have to assume this role. Besides, I already played the part during my 'years of apprenticeship'. Before endeavouring to convert one discourse into another, as I've done with psychoanalysis, psychology, philosophy and literature in *Life in Common*, or with classical knowledge in *Theories of the Symbol*, I played the go-between for languages. During my first years in Paris, my feeling was that my entire contribution consisted in introducing my French colleagues to everything I had learned in my readings in German, Russian and English. Generally speaking, I would say that, yes, I do recognize myself in this role of a go-between.

You yourself, as a journalist 'covering' essays in a magazine for the general public, are condemned to this role as well.

Yes, I have to have a 'cross-sectional' approach, to use a fashionable term in managerial jargon. I speak of the sociologist Pierre Bourdieu, the philosopher Paul Ricœur, the anthropologist René Girard, the jurist and psychoanalyst Pierre Legendre, the historian Alain Corbin, the physicist Étienne Klein and the psychiatrist and ethnologist Boris Cyrulnik, to name a few, and yet their works do not communicate to each other and sometimes the men ignore or detest one another. Places (and people) with no academic legitimacy enjoy such cross-disciplinary freedom. The existence of these parallel networks of consecration often poses a problem to academia, sometimes quite rightly. The press does not always promote the works that are most valuable in the eyes of the discipline (all the more so in that the media possess their own laws, most often profit-based, that only accentuate the defects in their criteria of selection). At the same time, in the media, one can voluntarily (and sometimes involuntarily) ignore the divisions (between people, schools and disciplines) that render the human sciences impenetrable to one another, especially to the public at large. I must say that I am often struck by the ambivalent attitude of the great majority of our intellectuals towards the dissemination of their work to a wide public – rare are those who are concerned enough to actually do anything about it (writing clearly and making their research accessible would amount to treason). On the other hand, almost all of them dream of earning extensive 'media coverage'. Whence the resentment that some of them demonstrate towards journalists!

Often, the specialized vocabulary, the incomprehensible jargon and the complex constructions are there to mark the boundaries of their territory, a little like dogs urinating to mark theirs. Psychoanalysts devise an idiom that allows them to be recognized amongst initiates; sociologists devise another one, not to mention linguists or economists. Émile Benveniste was, in this regard, a good counterexample — he managed to be precise without ever seeming to lapse into needless jargon. As far as possible, he used the language of everyday life; he did not have this terrorist use of specialization.

This problem of clarity—which I know is a real concern for you—is very tricky and emi-nently subjective. It's important not to jump from one extreme to another. Intellectuals are often right in resisting media demands for simplification. We want it simple because we want it short; we want it short because short catches the audience-consumer better (which is what interests advertisers, above all), and, in the end, we (the journalists) eschew the com-plexity of the world and of thought which leads to the atrophy of intellectual curiosity—the fundament, in my opinion, of our profession. These imposed canons of communication exert strong pressure on intellectuals. This is the critical analysis made by Bourdieu.

That being said, I have to admit that certain intellectuals take obscurity to extremes, in a play for power, no doubt, but also because they may simply not have a gift for clarity (it is a quality not equally shared by all and there are priggish or confused journalists too). In my work, I juggle with two opposing pitfalls: on the one hand, the fascination with dif-ficult works and the belief that the harder it is to get into a work, the more interesting it is and, on the other, the tendency to think that, since it is so difficult it must not be so impor-tant for 'us', 'us' being the people, 'normal people'. The same pitfalls are reversed in the case of essays written for the 'general public' – the simplicity can serve both trivial ideas and brilliant analyses. Between the two comes all the explanatory work that needs to be done—and which can be very long, and sometimes very tricky, diplomatically—in the hopes of producing from a book that is unreadable, except to specialists, an article that is interesting for everyone to read. And all this without sacrificing the richness of content. It's easier when the intellectuals care about this themselves but, ultimately, it is my job.

Most of the time, however, it is true that the most powerful thoughts are also the clearest ones—unless, that is, they appear clear to me because they are so powerful. And when there is, in addition, the elegance of the author's language, as is often the case for historians (Braudel and Duby, to cite only dead authors), it is a real joy!

I perfectly understand the resistance of intellectuals to seeing their thinking reduced, not to say altered, by media practices. It is a legitimate concern. However, in a variety of other circumstances, scholars and philosophers express their thoughts in an impenetrable writing style which could find some justification in a hierarchical elitist conception of the world (keeping our secrets among intellectual insiders), but not in one based on the principles of democratic humanism. If my doctrine tells me that we should treat the other as a subject, comparable to the subject who I am, then nothing justifies my reserving a privileged position for myself throughout my discourse by my use of a hyper-specialized vocabulary or a convoluted syntax. This was already the reason, as you remember, for my reservations about Lacan—this way of manipulating one's interlocutor is not worthy of respect. Writing as clearly as possible is one of my rules of hygiene.

The others in me

Notwithstanding the great diversity of your work, in terms of its themes and its modes, your interest in otherness, in studying our relationship with others has never ceased. In what way does this central theme personally concern you? Where are you in all this?

When I was a teenager, I was worried that I did not have my own identity. It was a question that often tormented me. I was annoyed with myself for being too easily influenced by the people I spoke to, for always sharing the opinions of the last person who spoke to me with conviction. I found that I only existed in relation to others — alone, I was nobody. I didn't really have any ideas of my own; I was too impressionable, too changeable, as if I was absolutely set on pleasing everyone. I found this, well, not very manly. Maybe it was because I strongly doubted my capacity to please — I was small and sickly, wore glasses (they broke every time I played soccer or basketball and my mother would heave another resigned sigh). I probably wanted to compensate for what I thought was my lack of appeal. Being nobody enables you to be accepted by everybody.

Subsequently, this feeling diminished without disappearing altogether. And I think it was responsible for my early professional choices, notably to devote myself to literary criticism and textual commentary. The interpreter of a text is a go-between in his own way—he tries to ease communication between writers and readers. By devoting myself to the interpretation of others, I was turning my weakness into an advantage: I was going to hear them, to slip inside them and then speak with their voice. I was bespeaking them and, at the same time, they were bespeaking me; they were expressing my convictions better than I knew how.

Then came my emigration to France, which led me to play the interpreter in another way—to juggle with the equivalences between two cultures. It is still the case. I live and vote in France, I think, speak and write in French, yet an important part of me remains Bulgarian, Slav and Oriental. For example, Russian poetry touches me more deeply than the poetry of French authors; it must come from the fact that I learnt Russian when I was a child and French only as an adult. It seems to me that there is an ineluctable order to the sequence of Russian words which I rarely perceive in French. How could even a syllable be moved when Pasternak says:

> *Ja odin, vsë tonet v farisejstve.*
> *Zhizn' prozhit' – ne pole perrejti*

Or again:

> *Sil' nej na svete tjaga proch'*
> *I manit strast' k razryvam.*

The power of these words does not come from a particularly deep thought, which is why I will not give you the translation. It comes from a sense of the absolute necessity of this exact word, excluding all other possibilities. Thus, when Tsvetaeva writes

> *Ty menja ne ljubish' bol'she:*
> *Istina v pjati slovakh*

it is like a bas-relief in bronze.

The effect of my origins can also be felt in my relationship with others, I believe. To give you just one example: I have a tendency to touch people, to grab them by the arm or take them by the shoulder. The French don't act like that and they are always a bit taken aback with me when I do.

Yet, by undertaking an in-depth exploration of French thought like no French intellectual would have thought of doing, in such a complete, almost systematic manner, aren't you more French than the French? Moreover, I'm sure that a lot of people find you 'too Cartesian' even though you were not born in the Loire valley!

Yes, people forget that I am a peasant from the Danube when they criticize me for the overly rational nature of my analyses.

All of this to say that, for a long time, I took the phrase *'je est un autre'* as if it had been written for me.

And today, do you still think you don't exist?

Phew! No need to worry about that one any more. My intuition as a teenager was not absurd, but it corresponded to a stage in my life. Individuals are not fully formed already-existing people who then come into contact with others; these relations with others are precisely what constitutes them. But time passes, and a person's identity progressively takes shape. I could have developed in thousands of directions; as it happens, I took one of them and I have become this person and not another. It's almost an alchemical process—and every human being possesses the philosopher's stone, the one that transmutes a chance encounter into a life necessity. If that day, at that time, I hadn't been in that place, I would never have met my wife—whereas today I cannot imagine or understand my life without her. Alone, I feel as though I'm incomplete, not to say disabled. I live in dependency and seek no cure from it. Isn't it marvellous to have the ability to create the absolute from the relative, the eternal from the transient, the infinite from the finite? Descartes said: 'There is no person so imperfect that we could not have for him a very perfect friendship.' Herein reside both the miracle and the mystery of the human species.

We do not always reach this miracle. We sometimes have the impression that we are wasting our lives in trivial activities. But when we do succeed, we have, on the contrary, a feeling of completeness. It is not a career that is the measure of a successful life but, rather, this miraculous ability.

Little by little, I thus became myself, the person who is talking to you in these interviews and who does not try to please everybody any more—a unique human being and yet one who resembles so many others, of this I am sure. Who today is not brought to live their life as a go-between, as an intermediary, as a being in transition?

Here you are describing your personal experience, but why take the relationship to others as an object of study? When you are talking about others, aren't you talking about yourself and looking at the same time for what speaks to everyone? This would be an approach very similar to that of the novelist saying, 'Madame Bovary is me.'

I would say something along the opposite lines. I do not hide behind my characters, it's the others whom I find in me. My unique being is shaped by my emotional and intellectual encounters with others. It is because I am aware of the impossibility of isolating a self prior to and exterior to contact with others that I try to gain a better understanding of what we call otherness. We are constitutively social beings — the multiplicity of cultures and the contacts between them are the first characteristic traits of humanity.

This is the agenda you announce in the opening line of The Conquest of America*: 'I will be discussing the discovery that the self makes of the other. The subject is enormous.' It includes the distant other, different from us, and the close other, my neighbour, my friend, my brother.*

I devoted several books to the subject. *The Conquest of America* and *On Human Diversity* to the distant other, and *Life in Common* to the close other — or, rather, to the making of the self through one's relationships with others. At the heart of the latter book, which took François Flahault's reflection as its starting point, lies 'recognition', the recognition that is granted (or not) by the gaze of the other. We are never sure of existing without the consciousness of this gaze; and yet we all need to be confirmed in our existence. It begins very early, in the first weeks of the infant's life, when they are no longer content with looking at the world and gradually distinguishing familiar faces, when they want to capture the other's eye and watch that gaze. When they want not only to see but to be seen. This demand is universal. It is not to be reduced to a matter of official recognition, the kind that translates into fame and honours. And it never ends. We look for the gaze of the other until the day we die.

It is through this internalized relationship to others that we gain access to something of a definition of the human. This is what allows human beings, in a manner of speaking, to break away from themselves, to gain an awareness of themselves, to see themselves from the outside. We are humans in the sense that our energy is not totally wrapped up in the pursuit of our immediate interests, in eating and finding shelter to survive and reproduce. It also gives rise to our inner aspirations towards something we are not and brings us to question ourselves, and hence never to fully coincide with ourselves. It is thanks to our consciousness that our finite being comes into contact with the infinite, that it becomes capable of spanning the entire past and the entire future, even eternity, that it can situate itself in the immensity of the universe. This consciousness comes from the internalization of the other who is by my side. I am seen, therefore I exist; something within me becomes aware of myself.

My projection onto others has also facilitated joint projects on books or reviews. Working with others on projects has gone rather well—for more than 10 years with Gérard Genette and, more recently, with Oswald Ducrot and Georges Baudot, Serge Doubrovsky and Marc Fumaroli, Annick Jacquet. And, today, with you. The others are also all the books that have nurtured me and with which I think. If I do not say it more often, it is to avoid sounding too pedantic and because I prefer taking responsibility for what I assert rather than hiding behind prestigious references. But never do I forget what I owe to others.

Leaving the twentieth century

In Hope and Memory *you talk about totalitarianism as the 'central event', the 'great political innovation of the century'. Do you think that is the main thing to retain from the twentieth century and would you say that it is also the central event in your life?*

I would like to say a few words of caution before I formulate this assertion, because I am aware of its arbitrary aspect. Firstly, we are talking about the political world, secondly about the European continent and, lastly, the person who is talking to you is someone whose life has been divided between Eastern and Western Europe. Once this perspective is adopted, the answer is yes. Communism, Nazism, the Second World War and the cold war are events that have influenced the destiny of all Europeans during the twentieth century, mine in particular. I was born in 1939, the year the war started, and also the year that the German–Soviet Pact was signed between Hitler and Stalin which evidenced the complicity of totalitarianisms.

My earliest memories date back to wartime. The inhabitants of Sofia were evacuated because of the Anglo-American bombings, and our family took refuge in our country home in a village near Sofia (which is today part of the city). All of my uncles, aunts and cousins lived there permanently — more than 20 people in a house built for four. The house had stone columns which lent it a certain solidity. Hence, when the siren announced the coming of the bombers at night, the rest of the village would turn up for shelter. They would settle in front of the house, as if the stone columns were going to extend their already quite illusory protection to them.

Besides, the 'evacuation' was only theoretical; in practice, my parents went to Sofia to work every day. They took the tramway and walked for a long time with their backpacks on their shoulders, full of supplies. That is when my mother caught tuberculosis. And the bombings were not always at night, after my parents came home; sometimes they started when my father and mother were still in town. I remember my brother and I holding hands and looking at the city below, where my parents were — we could see and hear the bombs exploding like small displays of fireworks. It was in 1944.

In the fall, we moved back to Sofia. The Soviet army went right through Bulgaria without a rifle shot. When we went back to our country home for the first time after that, we found the doors knocked down, the furniture stolen or broken and excrement in the middle of the room. Russian soldiers had been there. Protesting was out of the question.

The outcome of the war for the Bulgarians was the 45-year slip into the Soviet orbit. If there hadn't been the Communist regime in Bulgaria, I would not have stayed in France after a few years of 'specialization'. There is nothing I can do about it—my destiny is intimately bound up with the great events of war and totalitarianism.

Yet, today, the East-West conflict has come to an end, and the conflict between North and South has returned to centre stage, as if the twentieth century had been but a long inter-lude.

Today, the East is midway, if I may say so, between North and South. It shares the culture of the North, that is to say, Western Europe and North America, and the misery of the South. There is every chance that the East will catch up to the North within a few decades. The South, on the other hand, is lagging increasingly behind. So there is nothing surprising to see poor people going where the rich people are to earn more money or asking for a redistribution of wealth.

I recognize myself in many of the aspirations of those who come from the Third World, but not in all of them. I recently read my friend Edward Said's auto-biographical book, *Out of Place* (How could we translate this title into French? '*Une personne déplacée*' or '*Un homme dépaysé*?[2]) and I was struck both by the many similarities and by a few important differences between us. He was born a Palestinian in Jerusalem and grew up in Cairo in a wealthy family. Living in New York today, he is 'out of place' ('*homme dépaysé*') like I am. We have also written quite similar books on the subject of the plurality of cultures. The major difference is that Communism was never a problem for him, nor as a result was the tension between East and West. From his point of view, it must seem like a quarrel inter-nal to Northerners.

---

2 The book was published in France in March 2002, shortly after these interviews, under the title *À contre-voie* by Serpent à plumes. '*Une personne déplacée*' means a displaced person and '*un homme dépaysé*', an estranged man, as we have already seen. [Trans.]

Taking into account what you know about past centuries, would you say that the twenti-eth century was particularly dark?

The consequences of the totalitarian experience (with the two great wars from which it cannot be dissociated, since it was an experience that was partly caused by the First World War and was itself a cause of the Second) were worse than what past centuries had brought, even though they were, in their own right, generous with disasters. The amount of suffering, humiliation and frustration inflicted, especially on the people of Europe and Asia is incalculable, and the after-effects are still present among us. The number of dead was greater too, but it is not simply a matter of numbers—the new exterminations resulted from seemingly rational projects. As a result, our political and moral certitudes have been pro-foundly shaken. How can anyone in the future trust in reason, science and the dream of happiness for everyone? All of this has invalidated the theories of ongo-ing progress that thrived beforehand. Totalitarianism is an innovation and it is worse than what preceded it.

However, if I compare 1939 and 2001, I can only heave a sigh of relief. The gloomy predictions of the world's continual, inexorable decline have also been contradicted by history. I think sometimes with fright about the year 1940 when Hitler was already happily ruling over most of Europe, Stalin was controlling the rest and the two dictators were thick as thieves! Only England escaped their hold. If they had contented themselves with this division, the regimes could have lasted indefinitely. England would have resigned itself to the situation, the United States would not have gone to war and Europe today would still be dominated by their heirs. But their thieving mentality could not be satisfied with such a pact; it was inevitable that they would try and stab each other in the back. Should we say to ourselves that it is fortunate that Hitler attacked the Soviet Union, thus provoking his own downfall? But how can we say 'fortunate' when we know that 25 million Soviets perished in that war?

Compared to 1940, the year 2000 is almost paradise! There has been no war in Europe for more than half a century. For someone like me, born during the war, that is reason enough to see life through rose-coloured glasses. There has been a phenomenal development of wealth, and I'm not only talking about individuals — just think of what we call infrastructures, and all forms of social insurance, against diseases, accidents, unemployment — and no potentially murderous ideology has a hold over the minds of our compatriots. Believe me, I feel no nostalgia for the year 1940. I greet with joy our awakening from the totalitarian nightmare.

The twentieth century was marked, in Europe at least, by the totalitarian phenomenon. But today, at the start of the twenty-first century, more than 50 years after the fall of Nazism, and more than 10 years after the dismantling of the Wall and the collapse of the Communist regimes, do you think that your experience of totalitarianism can still be useful? If we stick to this conceptual framework, isn't there a risk of 'banalization' that will keep us from correctly reading the present?

The past can be used to educate our mind, but we must refrain from tacking it onto the present. In itself, the past explains nothing. The current malaise in Western democracies is not grounded in a new totalitarian temptation — the great war of the twentieth century is really over. Rather, it seems to me to derive from a break between two unequal groups. On one side is the majority which feels that it takes an active part in current developments. This majority comprises individuals living in relative material comfort, more educated than in the past and open to the outside, to Europe and the world beyond. These individuals sometimes identify with the Left, sometimes with the Right but, seen from the outside, one is mainly struck by what they have in common.

On the other side is a big minority of those who have been left on the sidelines. They are generally less educated, with either poorly paying jobs or unemployed. They are frightened by the thought of exposure to the outside, fearing the competition that may come as a result, and dream of going back in time to the security brought by insularity. They do not recognize themselves in the ruling elite—unable to decipher the discourses of mainstream politicians, they feel closer to extremist and protest movements, left-wing and, nowadays especially, right-wing. We could speak of an opposition between elitist movements on the one hand and populist on the other, except that in this case the 'elite' counts for more people than the 'people'. The leaders, for their part, oppose each other like realists versus demagogues.

Contemporary populism does not resemble the populism that allowed Lenin and Hitler to take power, notably because it does not carry with it a utopian project. Yet both populisms share the same contempt for reality—they promise to solve all our problems without caring that the remedies they propose are either inapplicable or, as was the case for past totalitarianisms, worse than the ills they are meant to cure.

Between the spring and summer of 2001 when these interviews took place, and today, the beginning of October of the same year, now that we are putting the finishing touches on the manuscript, an event of the utmost importance occurred which has left its mark on the minds of all: the destruction of the Twin Towers by terrorists in New York on September 11. By the time the book is published, there will have been new consequences that we cannot predict. Let's focus for a moment on the attack itself. Do you see in it the emergence of

tzvetan todorov

other murderous ideologies which may perhaps lack the rational project that characterized totalitarianism and in which dualism is raging?

The attacks by Islamic extremists were not devoid of rationality and, like the totalitarian projects, they proceeded from dualistic thinking. The connection between totalitarianism and theocracy is not new — in the past, the generic term employed to refer to it was 'ideocracy'. But these attacks were on a much smaller scale, at least so far — one cannot equate dozens of millions of victims of totalitarianism with a couple of thousand in New York and Washington, or established regimes with isolated acts.

The rationality in question is probably not the same depending on whether we are speaking about the instigators, the executors or the sympathizers.

I do not think there is anything original about the instigators' intentions. Like other violent acts of this kind — those of the FLN during the Algerian War or of the UCK before the bombing of Yugoslavia — the aim is to exacerbate the opposition between the two forces involved, to provoke an even more violent response that would reinforce the solidarity within their camp and eliminate those with a neutral or moderate stance. They thus fit into a familiar pattern — the search for an extension of one's own power (knowing whether the means were well chosen is another question).

As to the executors who offered themselves up in sacrifice — the religious component seems fundamental. People accept death much more readily if they are convinced that God has asked it of them and that it will send them directly to paradise. Unlike the instigators, whom I perceive as calculating, the executors appear to me to be fanatics. This attitude may seem enigmatic to us but it is not really foreign to any tradition, not even outside the confines of official religions —

human beings have always been willing to sacrifice themselves for an ideal, to make something good happen. We have a tendency to forget that, to borrow the language of eighteenth-century authors, passions easily overcome interests.

Lastly, there are the sympathizers, a great many of them in the Third World, who have in no way participated in the attacks or undertaken terrorist attacks themselves but who, more or less secretly, approve of them. They have different motivations, I believe. They are shocked by what appear to them, often quite rightly, as the biased, arrogant policies of the West, more specifically of the United States (especially in the Israeli-Palestinian conflict or in the retaliatory measures against Iraq—inefficient against its leaders but the cause of many casualties among the Iraqi population).

These three levels of rationality do not coincide. It is not certain, for example, that the attacks were meant to serve the Palestinian cause.

Several themes in our discussions seem to be strangely echoed in this event. There is, to begin with, the most obvious one: the temptation to goodness. The Islamic fighters want to destroy the Great Satan and President Bush launches the operation originally called 'Infinite Justice' as a crusade of Good against Evil. Between Bush's terminology and Bin Laden's sermons, we seem to have reached the pitch of paroxysm that you were denouncing.

According to another interpretation, we have entered the 'clash of civilizations' that Samuel Huntington described at the end of the Gulf War. What do you think of this analysis and of the way that it is brought up today?

The temptation to goodness can cause great damage—of this we have proof once again today—and one dualist outlook feeds another. I do not believe, moreover, that this is the struggle of freedom against slavery, of civilization against barbarism or of truth against lies—these are formulae employed in times of crisis, but they are not to be taken literally. The very term 'terrorism' is not as clear-cut as it seems. The Algerian FLN was terrorist until the day it took power, and former terrorists became respected heads of the state. That does not alter in any way, of course, my absolute condemnation of the September 11 attacks.

I have never really understood Huntington's conception of 'civilizations'. If he is referring to religions, then his explanation seems far from sufficient to me. Firstly, the great majority of Muslims are horrified by terrorism and Islam can obviously not be reduced to this suicidal fanaticism. In addition, these acts clearly have causes other than religious—political and economic. Religion provides a convenient veneer and ensures the determination of the suicide commandos.

For someone like you who knows American society well, who loves New York and who feels, as you've told us, closer to the American destiny than to the Bulgarian—how did you react to the destruction of a part of Manhattan? And can you imagine what the impact will be on the American mentality?

New York, the most cosmopolitan city in the world, is very dear to me and I have several friends there (who, very fortunately, were not among the victims), therefore it's impossible for me not to feel concerned, if only indirectly. Even though I am ready to criticize United States' policies, I choose without hesitation liberal democracy over a theocratic ideal. Solidarity must not be a vain word, and the United States is our ally. If France, my country, were attacked tomorrow, help would come from the United States, definitely not from Afghanistan. But solidarity does not mean justice. At the same time I say to myself that many cities throughout the world have suffered from American bombings in the twentieth century, and that the greatest novelty of these terrorist attacks is that they struck American territory and not that they killed 'innocent civilians' (which is, incidentally, a puzzling expression: does it mean that the fact of putting on an army uniform makes these same individuals guilty?). The inhabitants of Belgrade, Baghdad, Hanoi or Hiroshima felt as innocent vis-à-vis their government's policies as the inhabitants of New York; they all experienced the violence that struck them as a profound injustice.

The consequences of these acts on the American (or European) mentality are unpredictable. They can range from enhancing receptiveness and comprehension of the other to increasing insularity, reinforcing the conviction of being the incarnation of good (since the enemies are so evil), and restricting individual liberties. The United States was the victim of an attack and, by and large, neither the consciousness of victimhood nor the triumph of the hero fosters a critical outlook on oneself.

There is a unanimous sense that 11 September 2001 marks the end or the beginning of a world? Where does this come from? Is it only a lyrical illusion, a matter of historical shortsightedness or is there, in your opinion, a symbolic impact to this event?

What I find new and worrisome in our world is not the desire to ensure ones supremacy over others, or the divergences between civilizations — these are familiar traits that have always existed throughout human history — but that we are witnessing a new kind of vulnerability that results from the material advances of our society. Technological advances have made it easier and easier to gain access to weapons of mass destruction. Earlier, only a state — and only the most powerful among them — could make such weapons (chemical, biological and, why not, nuclear). Today, progress in technology brings their manufacture (technically but also financially) within reach of private groups. Miniaturization makes it easier to transport them. The malefactors are not states any more and individuals do not have territories, so they can hide and escape a military riposte without too much difficulty. Henceforth, private individuals or organizations can have at their disposal means of destruction as great if not greater than those of a classic state. Economic globalization teaches us the same lesson — nowadays, there are individuals capable of imposing their decisions on states. That is the danger of this new phenomenon — private interests prevailing over common interest, not the multiplication of contacts.

Just as attacking has become easier, so has defending become more and more difficult. For we cannot give up certain — good — habits that we have acquired: free movement across borders, the international circulation of information (scientific information, in particular) and, more generally, our ever-growing material comfort which makes us less economically independent at the same time. The caveman did not have anything to lose but what will become of us without our medicine, our electricity, our gas and our computers?

My worry comes from the fact that our civilization itself engenders the deadly dangers that threaten it. We have become aware of some of the dangers produced by technology: nuclear contamination, pollution, the greenhouse effect, etc. We knew that modern human beings, unlike their predecessors, are capable of destroying the planet on which they live. Now it is our ways of living themselves that lead to new dangers: open borders, information circulation, the accumulation of wealth and the need for comfort.

Let's turn back to our ordinary lives, outside periods of crisis. As a moderate, reasonable man, do you have any motives for revolt vis-à-vis our societies? Regarding what would you sound the alarm today?

One of the striking things, when you read the account of the attack's preparation or of the reactions that followed on the side of those we call terrorists, is the mixture of two ingredients that seem incompatible to us. On the one hand, a remarkable mastery of technology when it comes to piloting airplanes, gathering and exchanging data on the Internet and getting around and communicating without leaving a trace. And on the other, a naive faith in omens, coincidences and the rewards awaiting you in the Heavenly Kingdom—what we perceive as superstitions. We have here an (literally) explosive mix between technological mastery and magic thought. In French society too, even outside the dramatic moments of attacks, what both impresses and worries me is a combination of modernity and archaism. Or, to avoid heaping reproaches on the past, perhaps I should say of technology and barbarism.

When I speak of technology, I am thinking above all of the devices invading our day-to-day lives that do more than facilitate our activities; they actually shape them in turn. I will not dwell too much on a subject that is common knowledge. The television—which immediately transports us thousands of miles from home, acquaints us with forms of existence that we would never have the chance of knowing and which blurs the boundaries between the real and the virtual. The computer, more particularly the interconnection between computers, with the resulting possibilities offered by e-mail and the Internet, the facility of contact with the four corners of the planet and the inexhaustible information at our disposal. The cell phone—which enables us to stay 'connected' at all hours of the day and night.

As to barbarism, I understand it in the sense of the destruction of the social bond. We have discussed this in relation to individualism. Human beings are not born in a vacuum; they are born into a family and a community, a language and a culture, which shape them as people even though they always have the possibility of breaking away from these determinations. Today, we can observe a progressive erosion of the social bond in our ordinary, everyday lives. Not everywhere, not all of the time, but more and more often. What is striking in what are called the 'difficult' quarters in France, for example, is that the acts of aggression are no longer aimed only at the police (as symbols of repression), but also at the few sad symbols of the social bond: at common areas such as elevators or building entrance halls, at sport facilities or theatres and at public-utility workers like firemen or bus drivers. What has taken the place of the many different well-established forms of recognition is the demand for 'respect' and prestige, and these are earned by those who have the most threatening look, the meanest dog, the most fashionable shoes the latest model of cell phone.

This weakening of the social bond, within the family as within society, has several causes, but the technological explosion undoubtedly contributes to it. The omnipresence of the technological 'connection' hides the absence of a true bond. When desirable consumer goods are splashed all over your TV screen all day long, you feel a mounting resentment at being deprived of them as well as the urge to obtain them by any means possible. The blur between the real and the virtual facilitates the passage from thought to act. This new barbarism obviously becomes particularly dangerous when it gets hold of new technologies as we have seen in the recent attacks.

This is what worries me about our society today. I could also describe this situation, to pick up the terms we've been discussing in our interviews, as humanism losing ground to both scientism and individualism. What can we do? We can take advantage of the fact that we are living in an open society, a pluralistic world, which leaves us the choice, as Rousseau said, to acquiesce or to resist.

How is it that, despite your interest in political ideas, you have kept a relatively low pro-
file concerning current political events? Is this a hangover from your Bulgarian heritage?
In the same way, you are enthusiastic about knowledge but are not really active in the aca-
demic world and have taught very little. In short, you are a rather marginal centrist!

Without trying to explain this through historical circumstances, I'd say that my
personal life, my relationships with the members of my family and with my
friends matter a great deal to me. I would not sacrifice them at any price. Proust
put art above love—I think exactly the opposite. The most intense experience I
know is the wonderment in the presence of someone I love. Besides, I came to realize that my preferred vehicle of communication is writing, rather than oral teaching or public debate. I am not defending the choice—it is a matter of temperament. Stendhal said somewhere that an ideal life to him was to live in Paris, on the
fourth floor, writing his books. My thinking runs along similar lines, and so I live
according to this description.

If you consider these two passions—my passion for personal relationships
and my passion for this solitary work that is writing—and add to them my taste
for material life, you will understand why I do not find any time for a public life.
But there is no reason to exaggerate. I am not an eccentric or a recluse—just a 'marginal centrist'.

But we could say then that you would rather devote yourself to your own happiness than
to the happiness of humankind!

My books are addressed to everyone, even if I cannot expect the whole world to
stand up and take notice. While trying to help others, my readers, I am also concerned with helping myself lead a better life, richer in meaning and in beauty,
more open to the absolute, and a happier life too. And this is a contribution, as tiny

as it may be, to the happiness of humankind, since we are all part of it. Caring for oneself is not being selfish when one knows that the self does not exist without others, separated from others. And it is beautiful to love humanity, but, to start with, let us care for human beings taken one by one.

In response to Catherine Portevin's suggestion, I embarked without too much thought on this adventure: being questioned in detail about my intellectual biography. It was not always easy or necessarily pleasant, to scrutinize my identity in this way and to look for my internal coherence. Now the pages are here, transcribed and rewritten. What exactly have we done?

I could more readily say what we have not done. We have not written an history of the last 60 years of the twentieth century, neither political nor even intellectual. We have not produced a real biography or autobiography; I only evoked my personal life in passing. We have not written the perfect summary of my last 25 books. If you want to know what they contain and what they maintain about the subject that is examined in them, you will have to go back to the source.

tzvetan todorov

What we have tried to do is, firstly, to situate the books, the research and the passions in relation to one another. Our interviews enabled me to see each project in the context of the others, to discern the structuring connections and to grasp certain architectonic aspects. Moreover, we ventured in a seldom-explored direction in the field of humanities by questioning the existential context of these studies. Sciences like to present themselves as pure knowledge, free of subjectivity; to bring up the researcher's life is considered unseemly, evidence of poor taste. Here, on the contrary, we did not hesitate to examine the personal motivations behind impersonal reasoning.

As we moved forward in our discussions, our project took a turn that we ignored when we were starting out: breadth turned into depth. The content of my successive engagements, important in its own right and in its original context, came to matter less than the way the engagements were undertaken. I realized that I had lived in more ways than one as a 'go-between.'[1] After having crossed borders myself, I have tried to ease the way across borders for others: firstly, borders between countries, languages and cultures, then between fields of study and scientific disciplines in the humanities, but also borders between the commonplace and the essential, the routine and the sublime, material life and spiritual life. In debates, I aspire to the position of mediator. Dualism and iron curtains are what I like least. And it is interpenetration, once again, that this book illustrates, this time between life and work.

We did not, however, try to explain the work by the man on the model of ancient literary history. No matter how much information you accumulate and how many circumstances you bring together, it does not suffice to mechanically

---

[1] *Passeur*: a ferryman, a conveyer, but also a smuggler. [Trans.]

produce an individual and his or her thought. As far as I am concerned, it is clear that many characteristics of my life and work are directly related to the establishment of a totalitarian regime in Bulgaria, immediately after the Second World War. This was, after all, the cause of my move to France, and hence of my life as a *'homme dépaysé'*; it was the source of my interest in political philosophy, democracy and humanism; it was also, perhaps, the source of my preference for private life and my attachment to relationships between human beings. Similarly, the family in which I was raised, the values my parents embodied, the piles of books in the midst of which I grew up, were all no doubt factors in my development. And yet this does not explain a thing. My brother, who lived in the same family and in the same country, is very different: he is a scientist and not a man of letters; he stayed in Bulgaria instead of emigrating; and his life is organized in a different way. We can thus grasp a context, analyse a situation and highlight the conditions that led to a change of direction and still not penetrate the mystery of personal destiny, even less deduce the thinking of a person from these conditions. Rather than as cause and effect, life and work are here presented as two forms of a single intention. Whence the result: neither a biography nor an exposé of theses but a dialogue between them.

In the present book, I have a dual role: I am both the object and one of its subjects. How has this duality determined my gaze? Have I produced a description of my work, or rather a defence or an apology? You must have a certain readiness to comply when you accept to talk about yourself in public (or in private). The only possible form of modesty is silence. The great Russian poet Marina Tsvetaeva, whose work I hope I'll have the opportunity to study one day, says somewhere: 'Who could talk about their suffering without getting enthusiastic, that is to say happy?' As soon as you talk about yourself, you split yourself in two. The object has

tzvetan todorov

suffered but the subject is happy, because it is engaged in an act of creation. Pointing out my weaknesses, I am nevertheless showing myself off to advantage—the person as object is diminished, but the person as subject comes out enhanced. Even though I find that bragging about yourself is childish, my description of myself could never be truly critical and it is important to be aware of this from the outset. Another danger, another optical illusion, is that chance be misrepresented as necessity. Like everyone else, when I tell the story of my life, I impose a form on it, I look for a reason for everything and I forget what will disrupt my narrative. In reality, there is surely more chaos in it than I have mentioned, and everything cannot be explained. The reader, I hope, will take this into account too.

My feeling is that I have always been looking for the answer to a single question: how to live. This search has taken the path of human sciences, history, anthropology and textual studies. But knowledge to me is not a goal in itself; it is the means of acquiring just a little bit more wisdom.

TZVETAN TODOROV